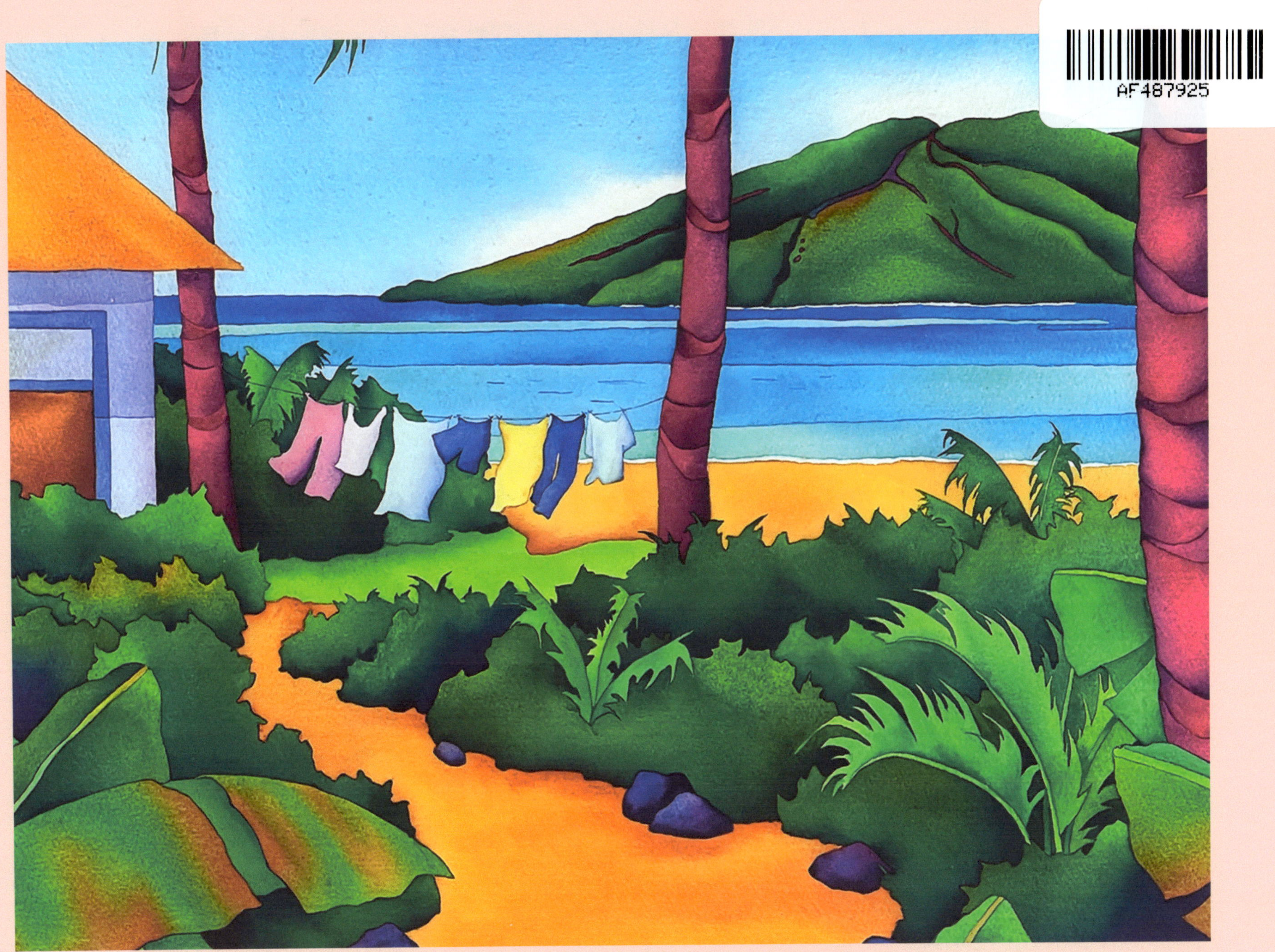

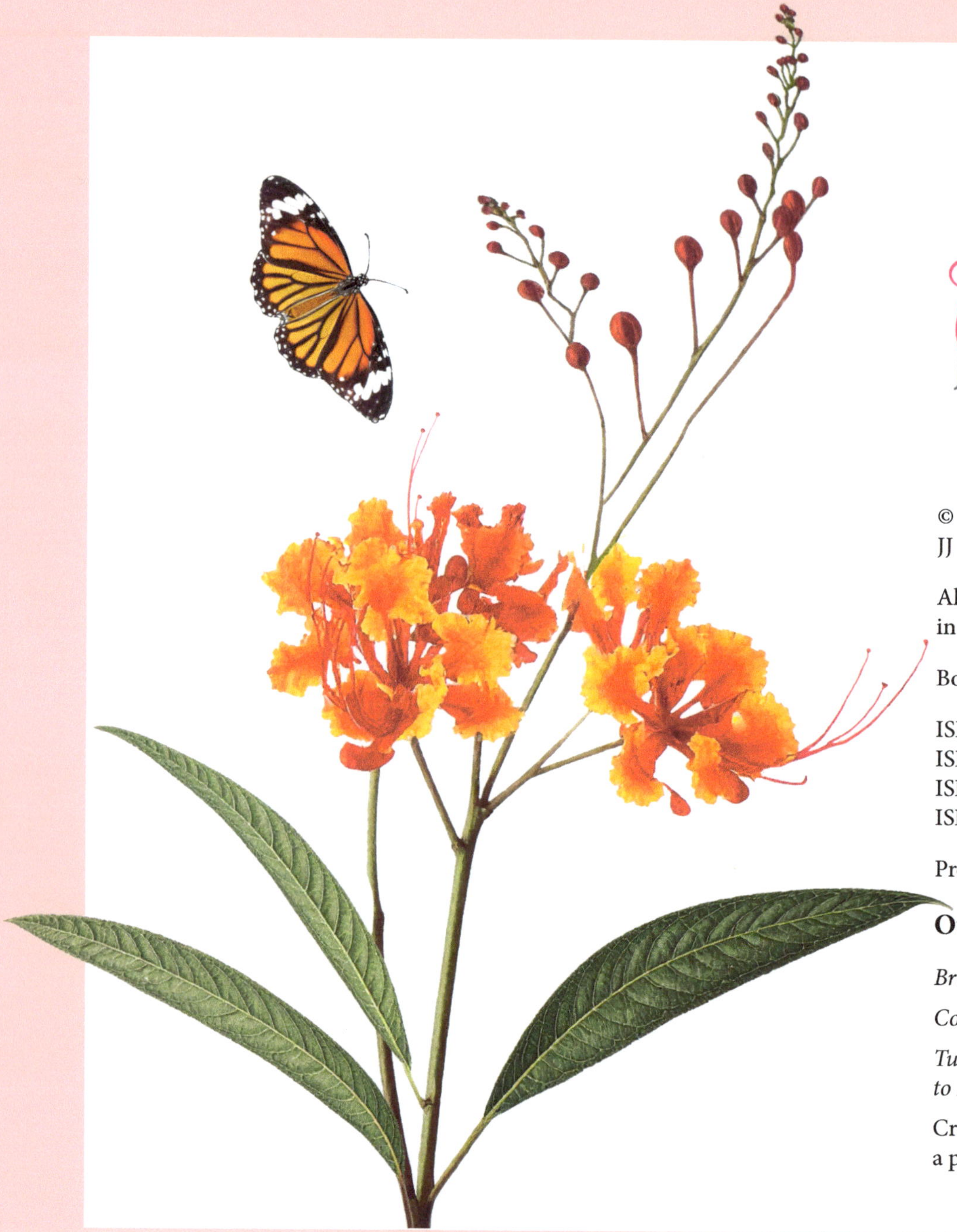

© 2025 JJ Jordan
JJ Poodles Press

Book Design by Jeannie Winston

ISBN: 9798986531373 (pbk)
ISBN: 9798986531328 (hc)
ISBN: 9798986531311 (ePub)
ISBN: 9798986531366 (pocketbook)

Previous Page: Artwork by Susan Szabo, "Maui Homestead."

Other Books by JJ Jordan

Bruno the Poodle's Coloring Book & Creative Pages:

Color, Write, Draw, and Play with Bruno and his Friends, 2019

Turn Your Chaos Into Calm: Bruno the Poodle's Quotes and Prompts to Reveal New Paths to Balance, 2021

Creative journals with inspirational quotes, available in a large and a pocket travel size.

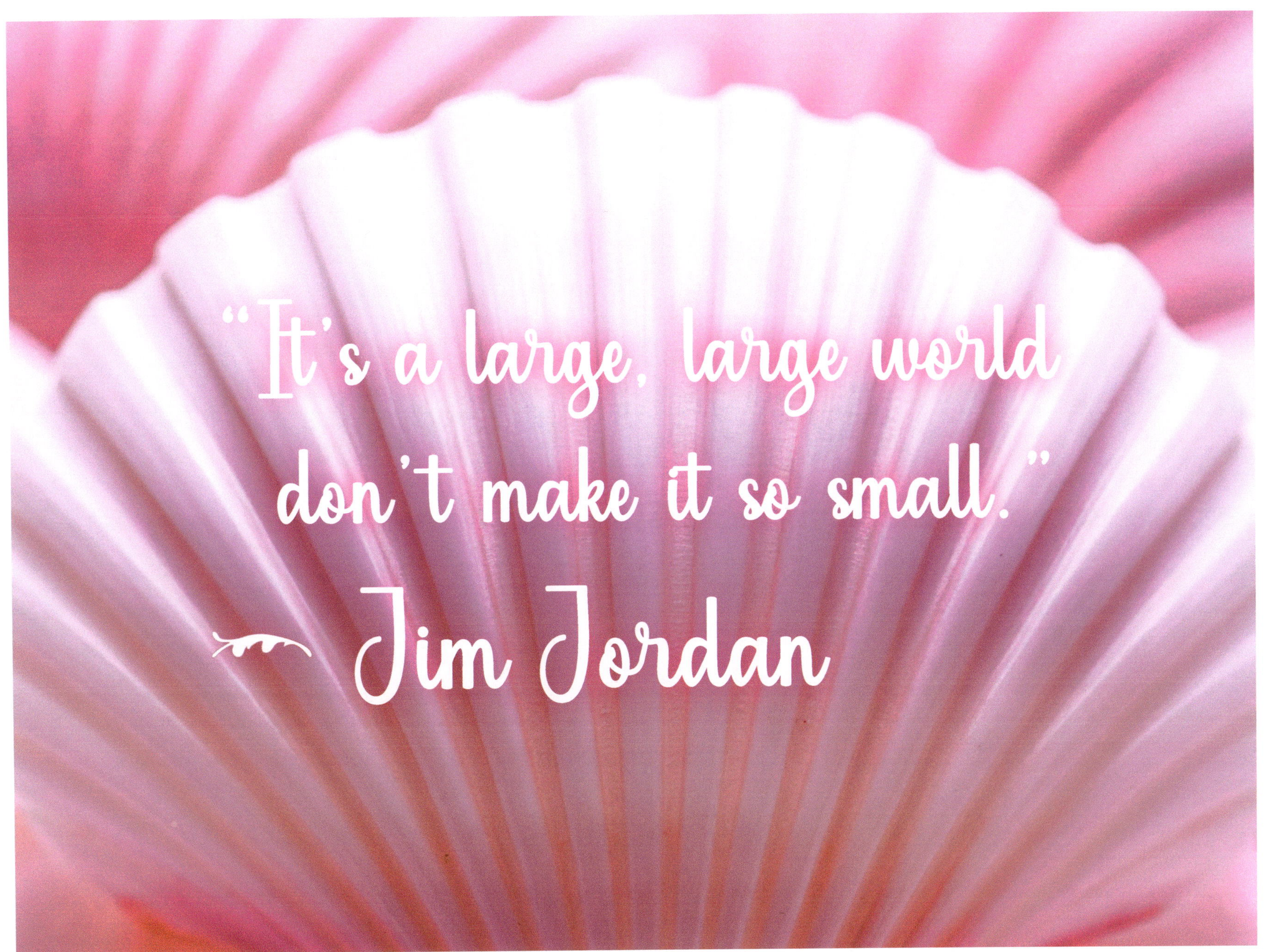

"It's a large, large world
don't make it so small."
Jim Jordan

To my sons, James Wierzba and Will "Rush" Wierzba, and my husband, Charles Pfund —Thank you for your unwavering love and support.

And of course, to my loving Toy Poodle Bruno, my constant companion who filled my days with unconditional love and endless tail wags.

LET'S MOVE TO HAWAI'I !
Bruno's Big Adventure

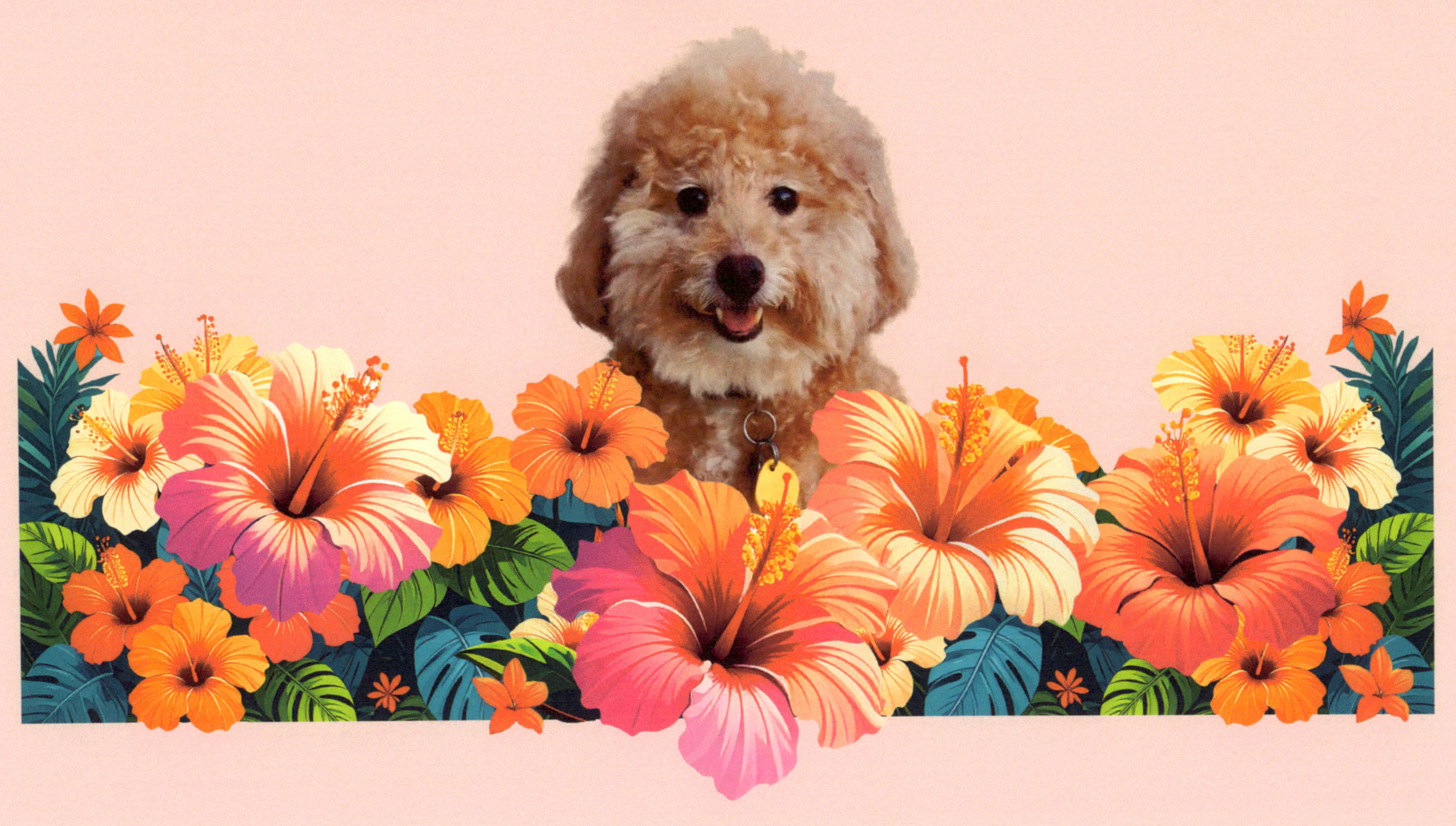

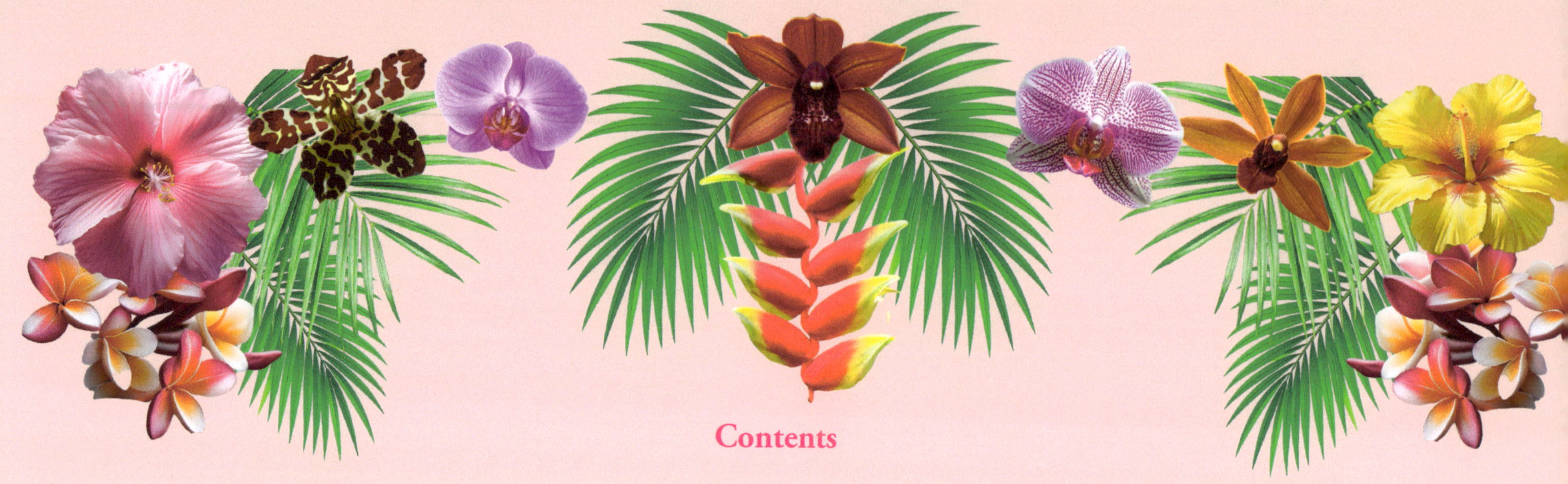

Contents

Watching the captivating movie South Pacific (which came out March 19th, 1958), it became one of my favorite movies of all time. Especially the scene where the island's matriarch, Bloody Mary, meets Lieutenant Joseph Cable, and she sings her lovely song, "Bali Ha'i." With its enchanting melody, the song seemed to float through the air, almost like a spell, calling him to her island. It was as if Bloody Mary's song echoed the very essence of the islands—inviting, enigmatic, and full of hidden wonders. When we moved from Wisconsin to Hawai'i, I found that living in Hawai'i was just that. A magical dream came true! A dream that I never thought would happen in a million years.

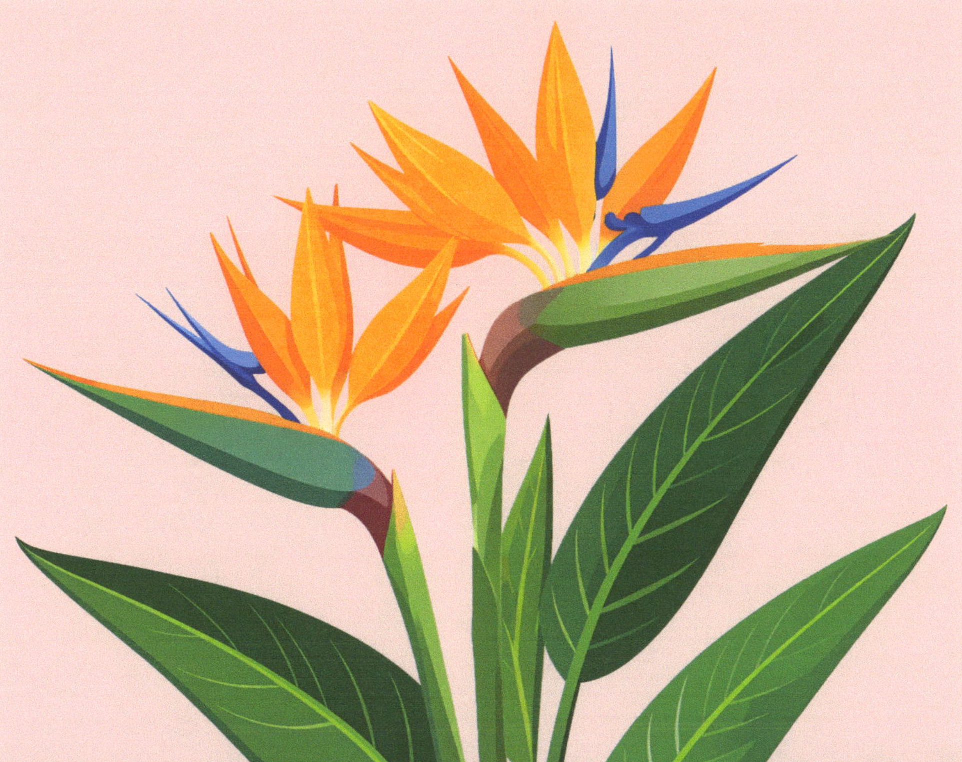

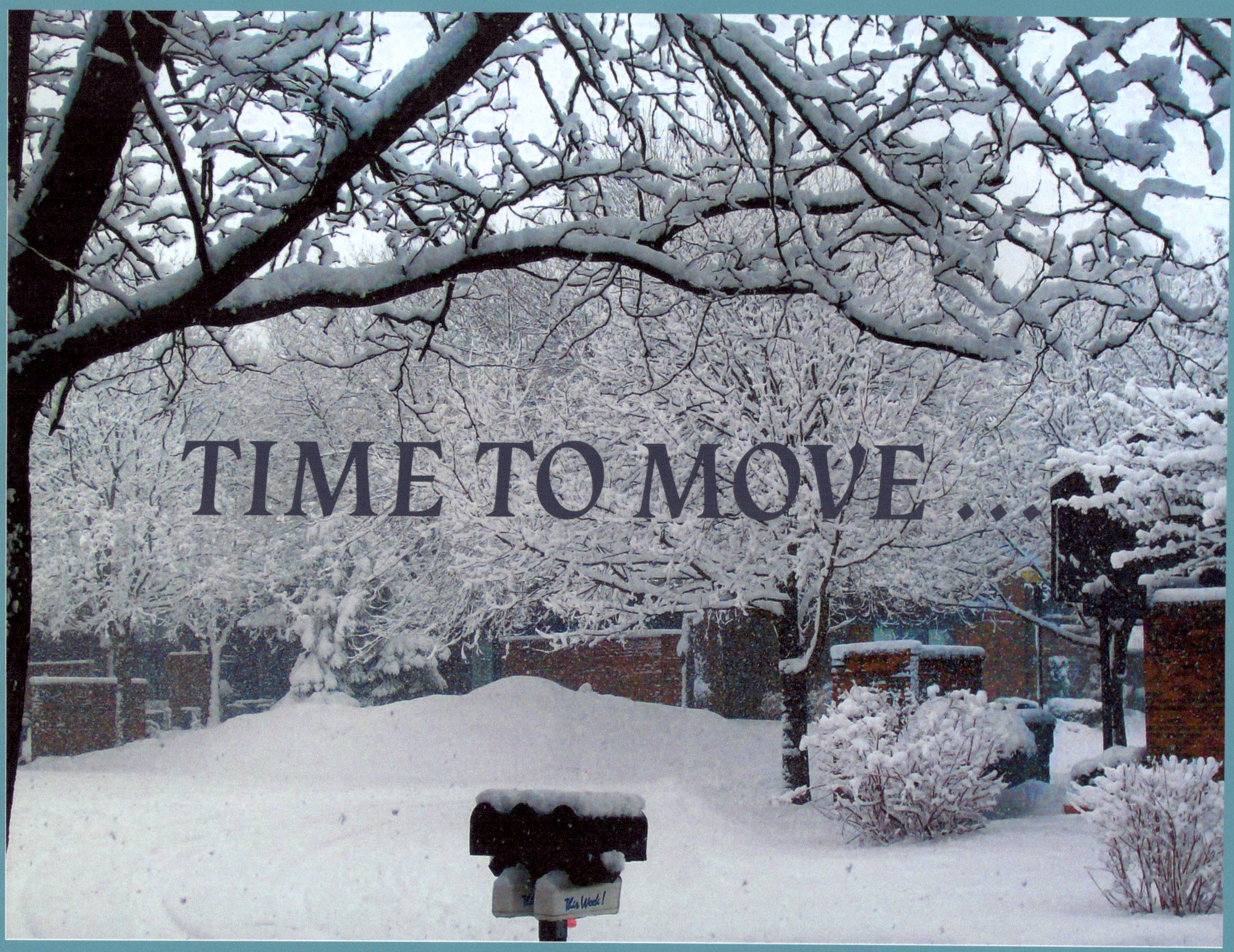

TIME TO MOVE ...

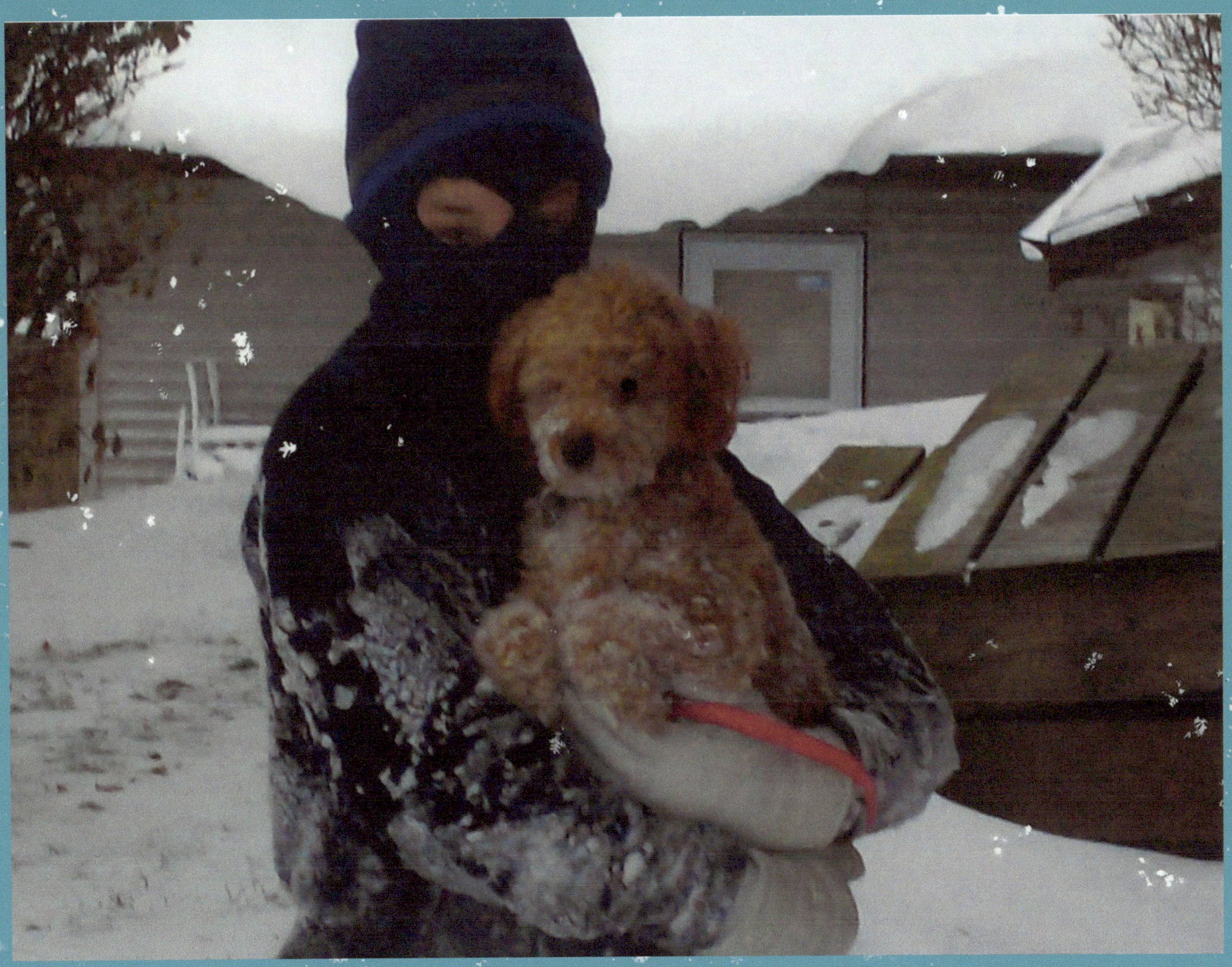

Willie Wierzba, my son with Bruno in February 2006, in a Wisconsin deep freeze.

The

day my family decided to move from Wisconsin to Hawai'i, it was an exceptionally hard Arctic Freeze, it was 20 degrees below zero! I was five years old, and I remember listening to my parents discuss moving, and when they finally decided, I was so happy! I began to run in excited circles around the living room. I did not really know what to expect or what that meant, but I knew we would be leaving the harsh cold behind. How lucky we all were to be able to make that happen.

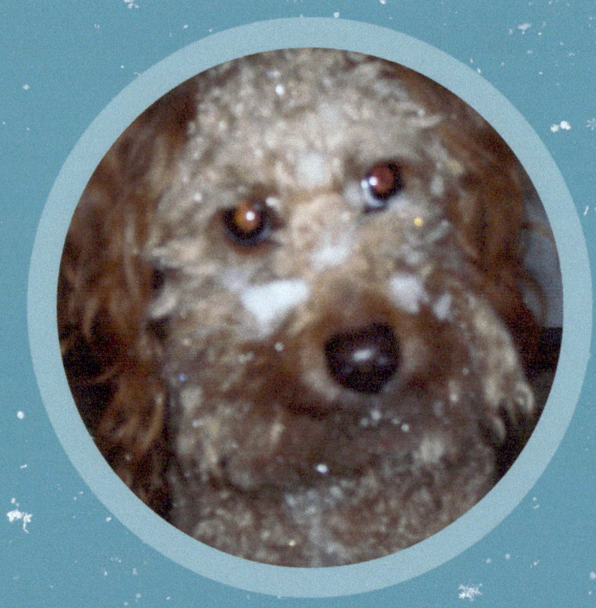

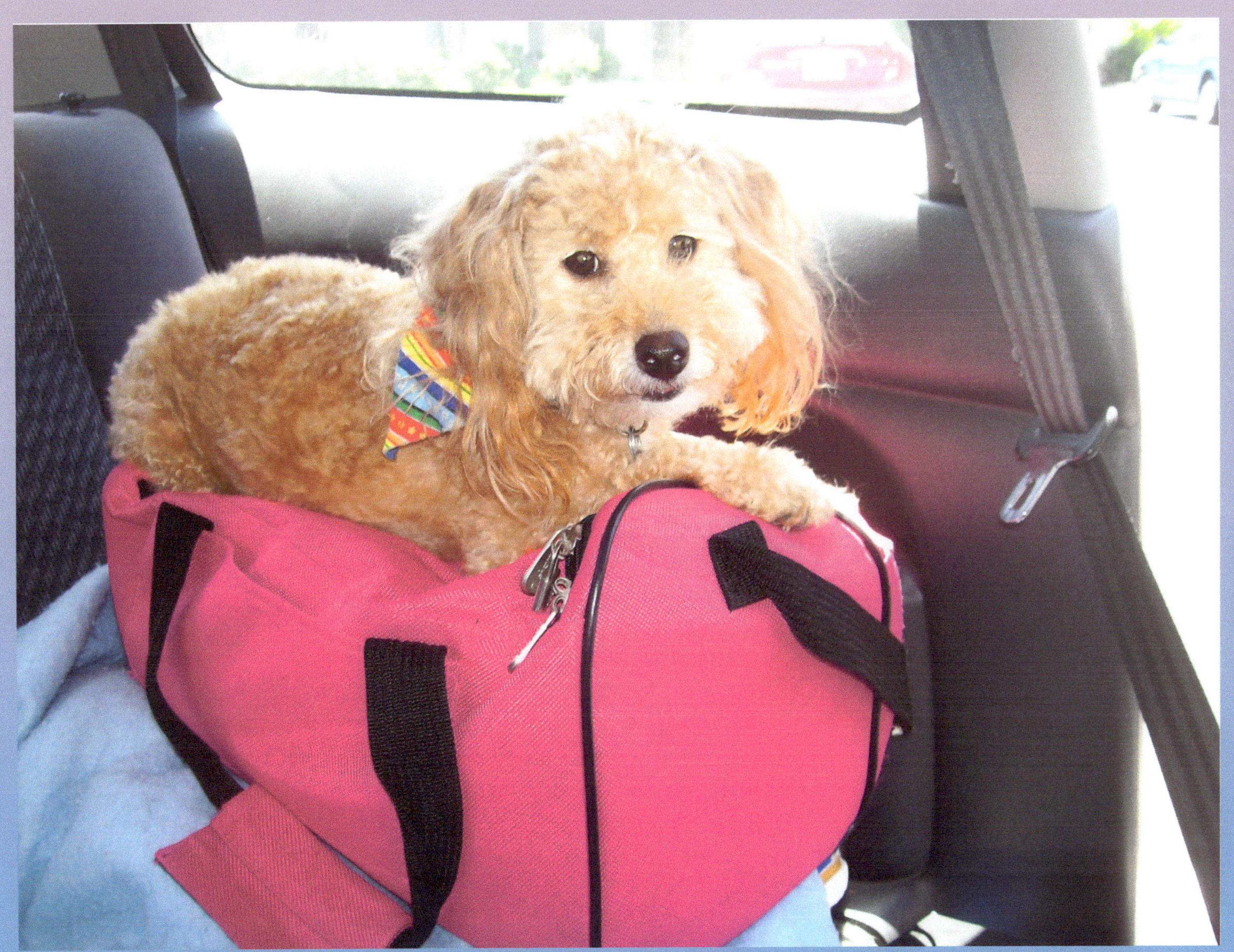

On our way to the airport!

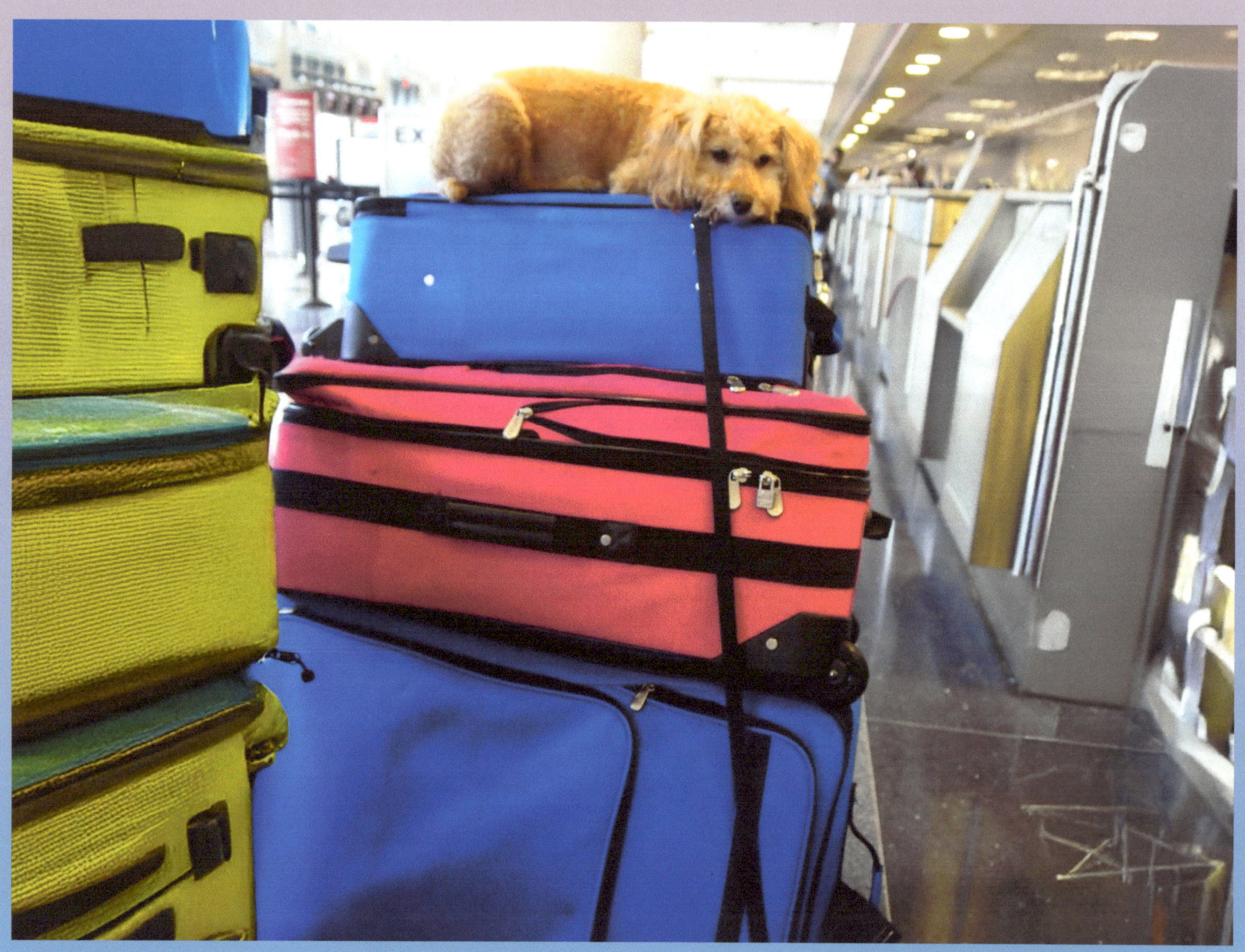

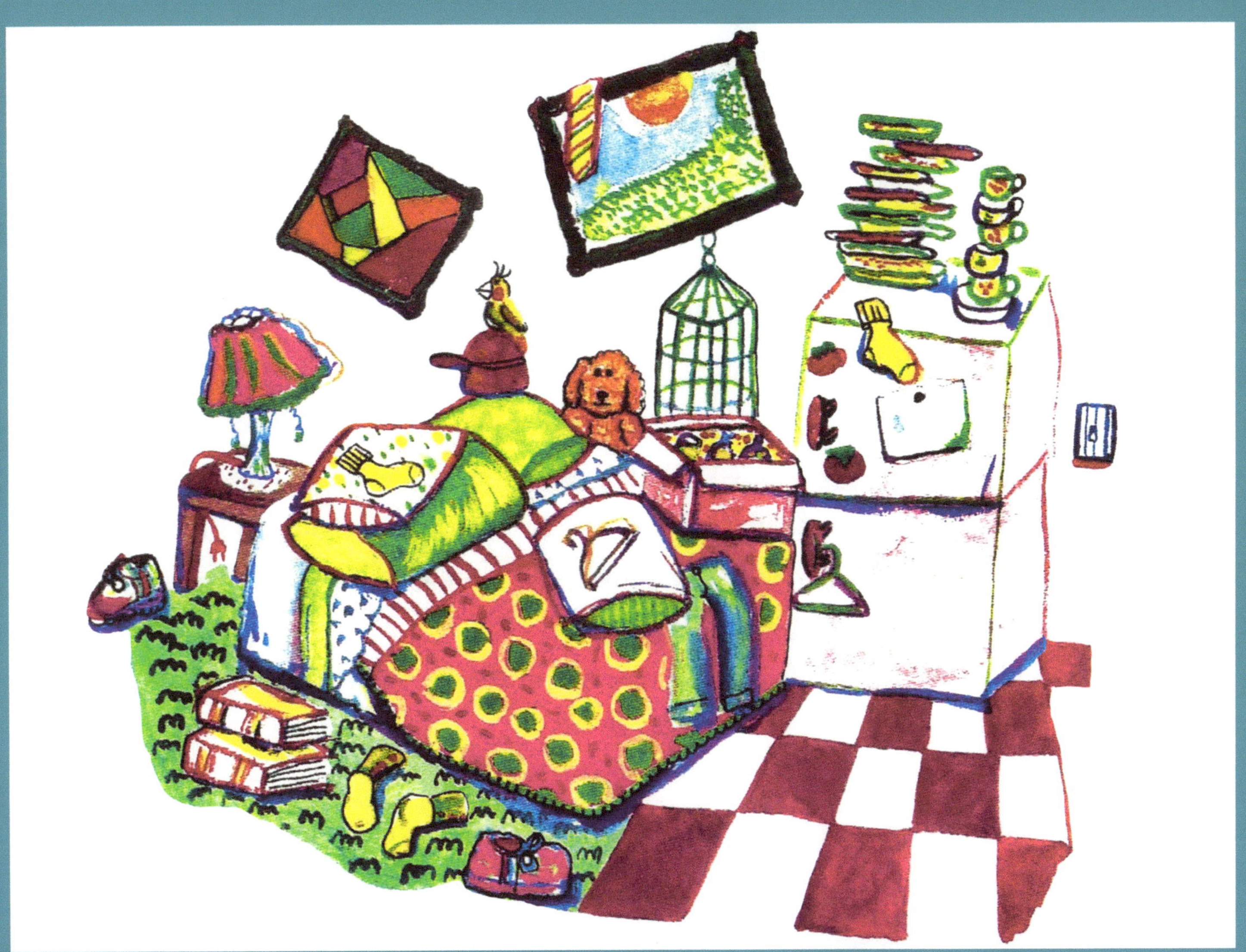

Bruno trying to decide what to pack!

Packing Tips what to pack, or not to pack, that is the question!

1. Rent a storage space for one month in Hawai'i. Usually the first month is free.

2. Use flat rate boxes from the USPS to ship and send it to the rental storage address.

3. Buy your furniture in Hawai'i.

4. Ship your car or buy one because rental cars are expensive Monmoth-car shipping is great shipping service for your car.

5. Buy an air mattress or buy your bed in Hawai'i or find a place already furnished.

6. Try to find a place that has pest control.

7. Find a good long distance mover.

8. No need for heavy clothes, choose fabrics such as cotton linen viscose rayon, and only bring a heavy jacket if you are planning to go skiing or hiking on the Big Island.

9. Take photos of all your belongings you are shipping as well as a photo of your suit-cases, purse, I.D. and, essential papers.

10. If possible keep your furniture etc with a family member friend or rent a storage locker on the mainland so you can travel very lightly.

11. Bring a great camera as well as a waterproof camera.

12. When in doubt, leave it out. You can always purchase items when you get to Hawai'i.

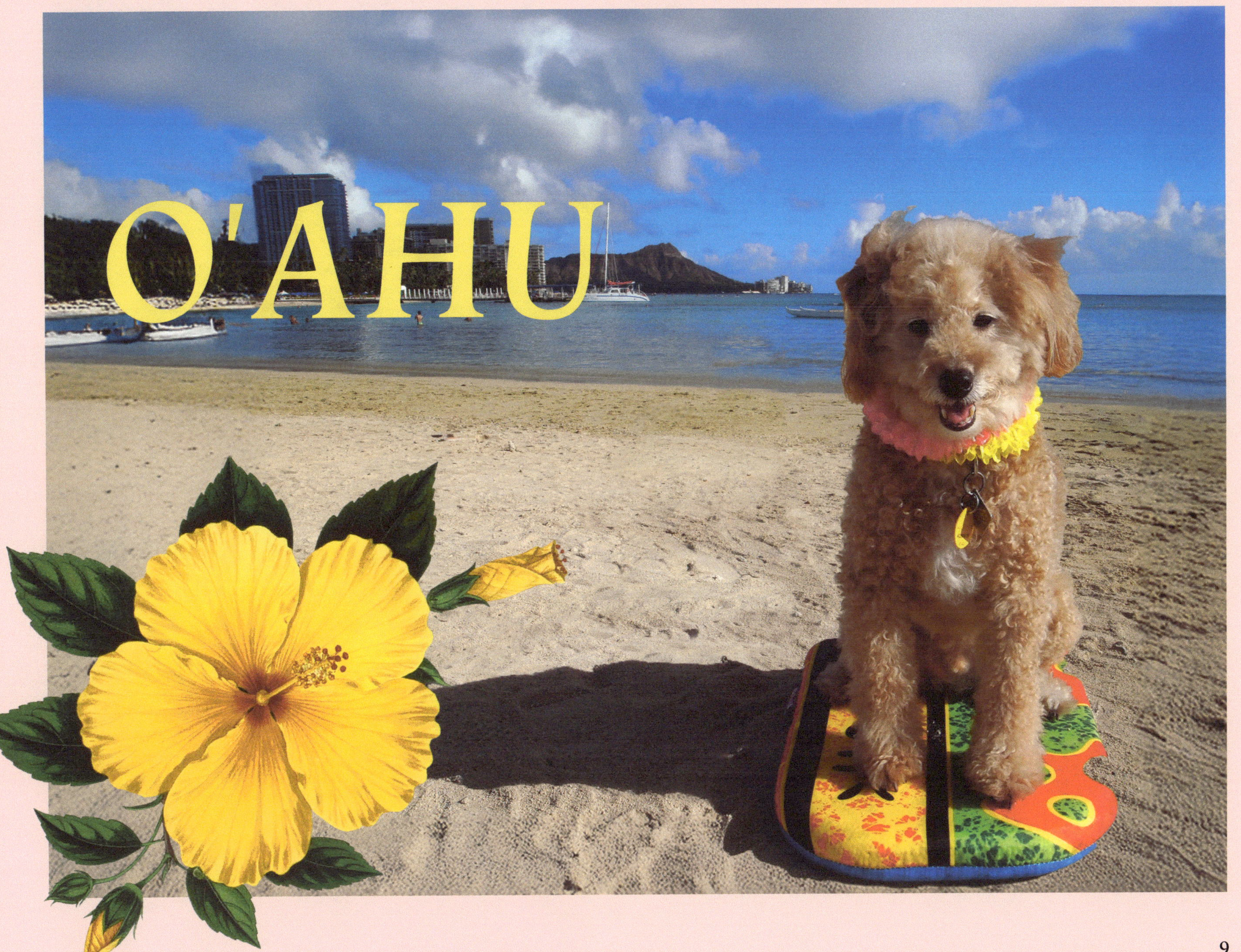

O'AHU

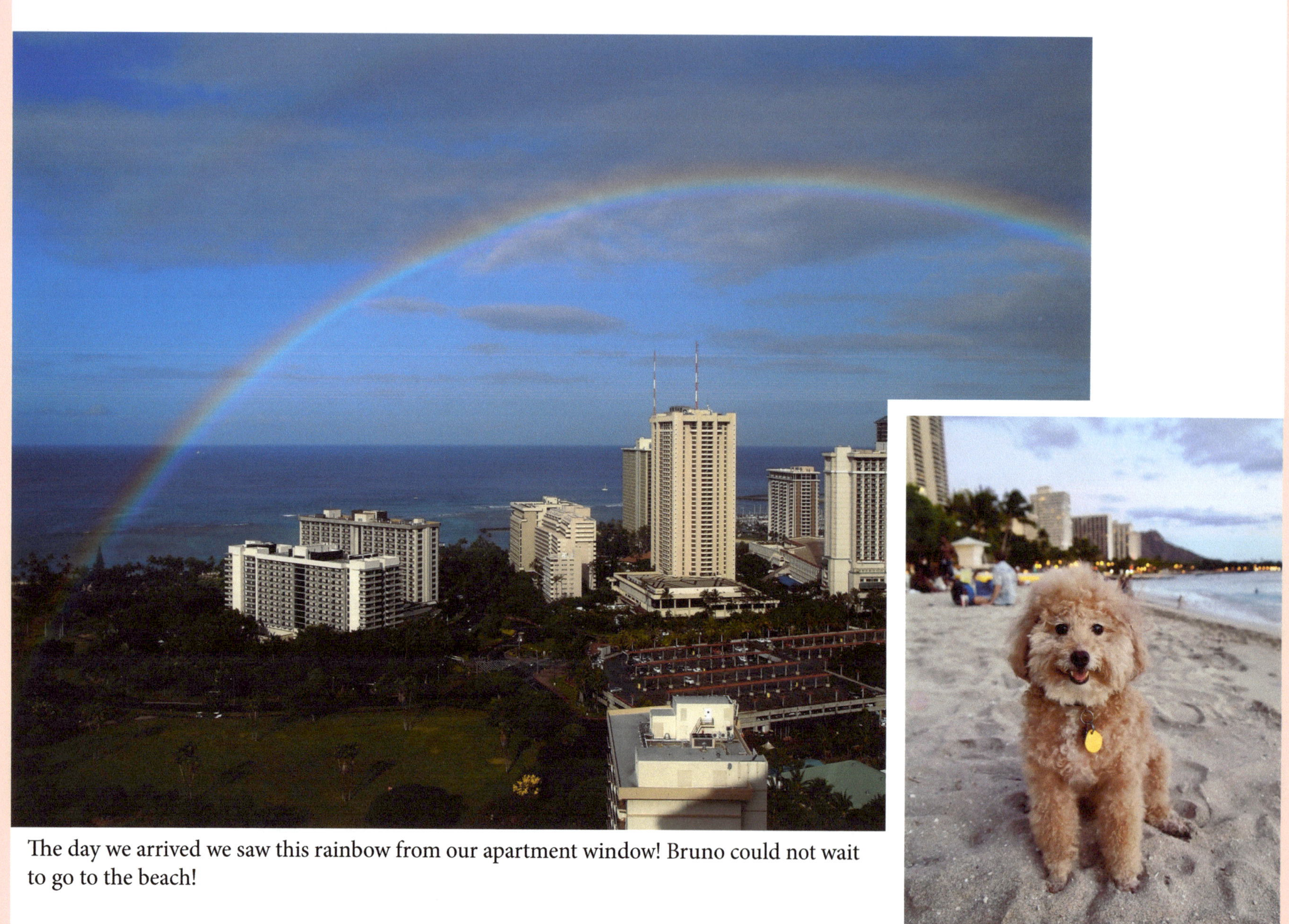

The day we arrived we saw this rainbow from our apartment window! Bruno could not wait to go to the beach!

O'ahu

O'ahu is the most populous and third-largest island in Hawai'i. Located in the central Pacific Ocean, O'ahu is home to approximately 70% of the state's population, with Honolulu, the capital and largest city, situated on its southeastern coast. The island is famous for its mix of vibrant urban culture and stunning natural beauty.

The name O'ahu is often translated as "The Gathering Place," a term popularized by Hawaiian Almanac author Thomas Thrum in 1922. The Hawaiian word "O'ahu" can also be interpreted as "gathering of objects," although the exact meaning is still debated.

O'ahu has a rich cultural history, with evidence of human settlement dating back at least to the 3rd century A.D. It was once the seat of the Kingdom of O'ahu, ruled by powerful Hawaiian monarchs. Ma'ilikūkahi, one of the first great kings of O'ahu, was known for his contributions to the island's governance and laws. By the 18th century, O'ahu was caught up in the struggles of Hawaiian inter-island warfare, eventually falling under the control of King Kamehameha I after the Battle of Nu'uanu in 1795. O'ahu then became a key part of the unified Kingdom of Hawai'i.

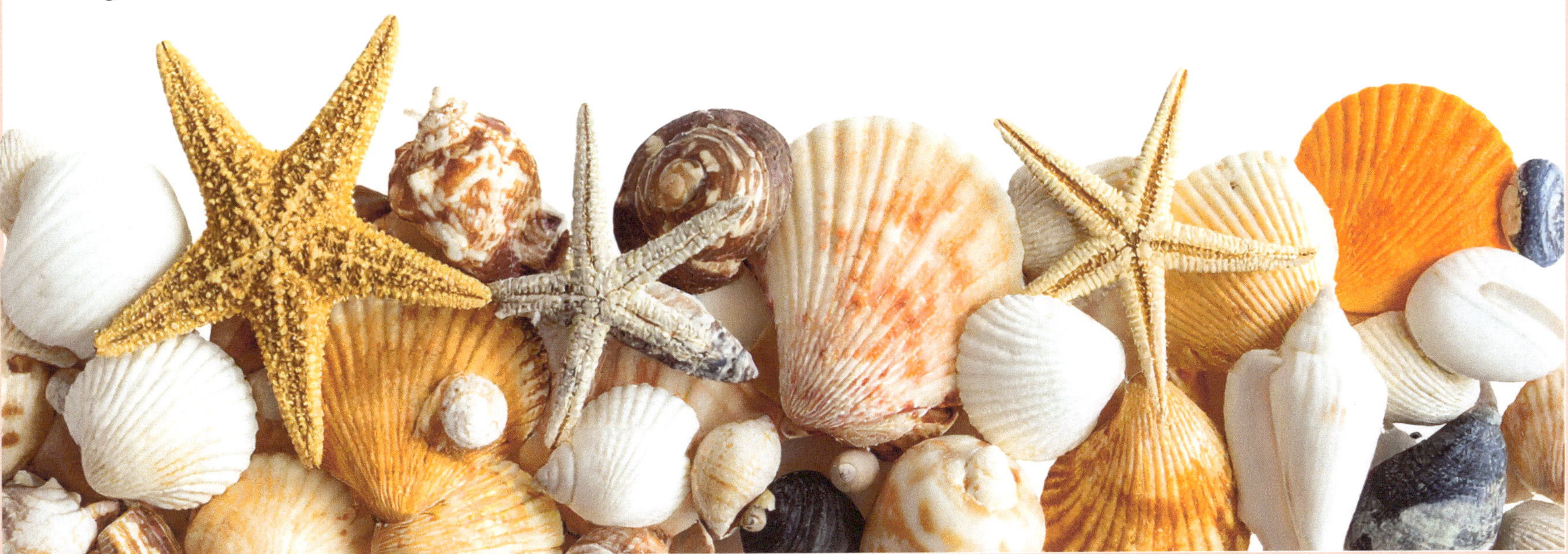

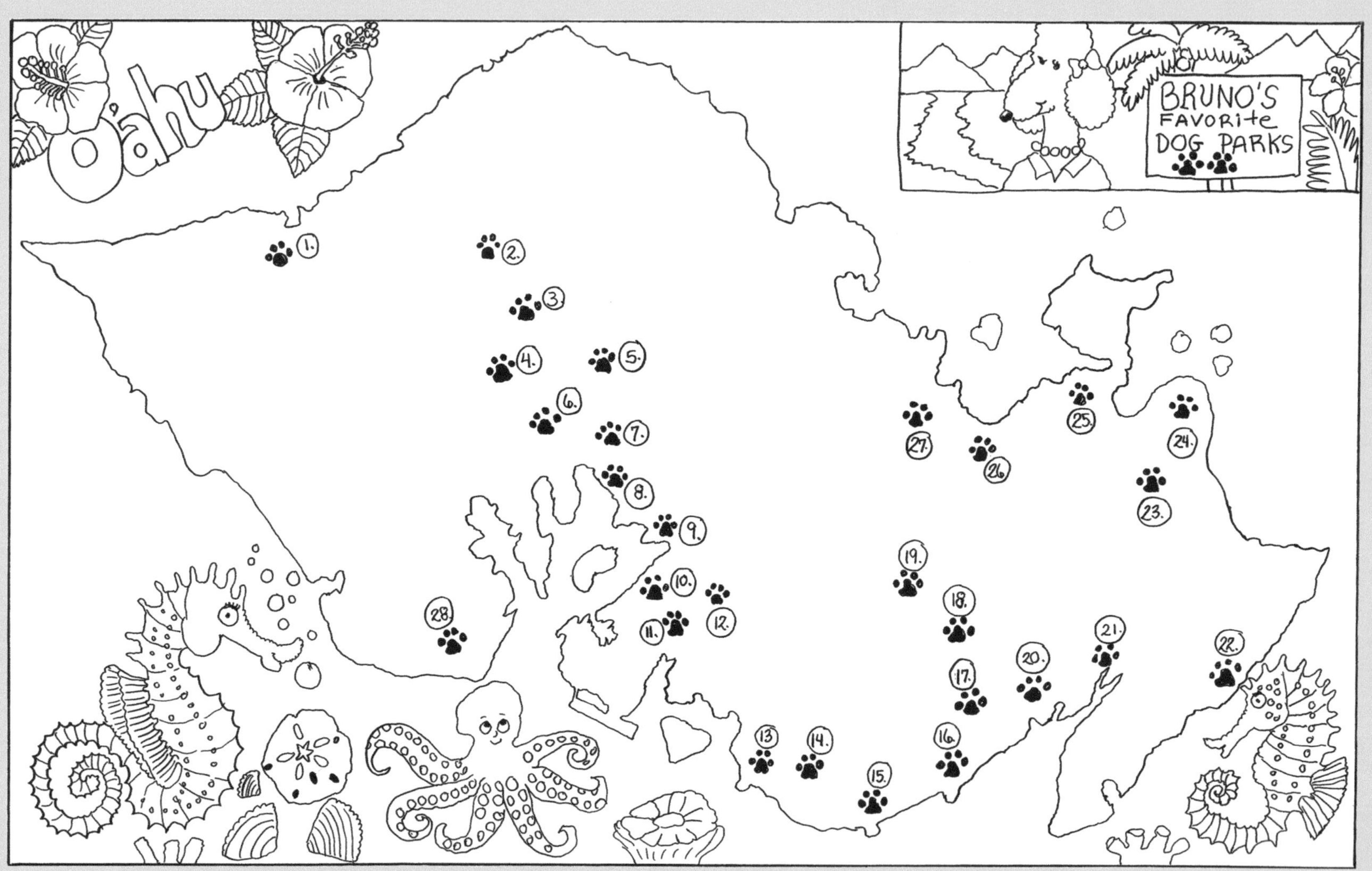

Bruno's Favorite Dog Parks on O'ahu.

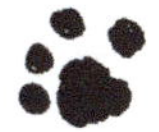

1. Iliahi On-leash Dog Park
2. Mililani Off-leash Dog Park
3. Mililani Waena On-leash Dog Park
4. Iliahi On-leash Dog Park
5. Mililani Waena On-leash Dog Park
6. Newtown On-leash Dog Park
7. Neal S. Blaisdell On-leash Dog Park
8. ʻAiea On-leash Dog Park
9. Makalapa On-leash Dog Park
10. Hoa Aloha Off-leash Dog Park

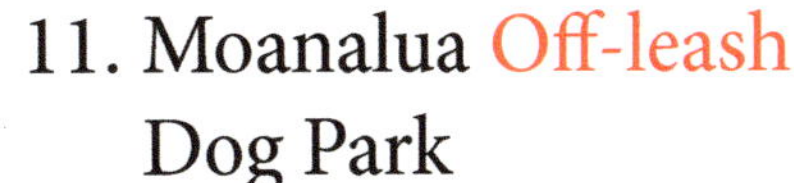
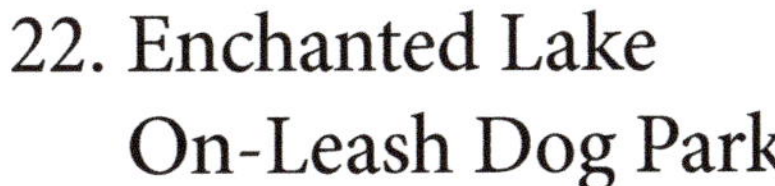
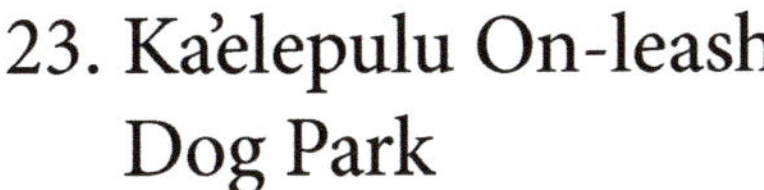

11. Moanalua Off-leash Dog Park
12. Kakaʻako Waterfront On-leash Dog Park
13. Kolowalu Off-leash Dog Park (HCDA)
14. Kapiʻolani Park Median Strip On-leash Dog Park
15. Diamond Head Bark Park Off-leash Park
16. Puʻu O Kaimuki On-leash Dog Park
17. Mauumae On-leash Dog Park
18. Pūkele On-leash Dog Park
19. Kamole On-leash Dog Park
20. Elaine Dobashi Hawaiʻi Kai Off-leash Dog Park

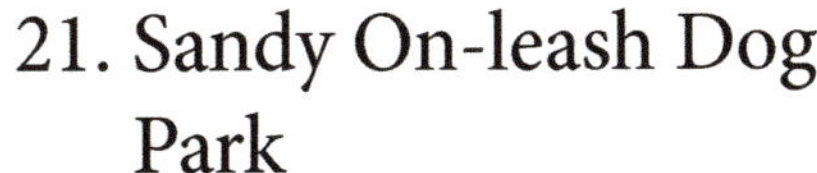

21. Sandy On-leash Dog Park
22. Enchanted Lake On-Leash Dog Park
23. Kaʻelepulu On-leash Dog Park
24. Pōhākupu On-leash Dog Park
25. Kahua O Waikalua Off-leash Dog Park
26. Heʻeia On-leash Dog Park
27. Ewa Beach On-leash Dog Park

Important Consideration Beach Rules:

Dogs must be *leashed on sand*; some may allow off-leash *in the water.*

Dog Park Etiquette: Follow park-specific rules and *supervise dog interactions.*

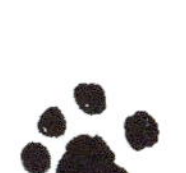

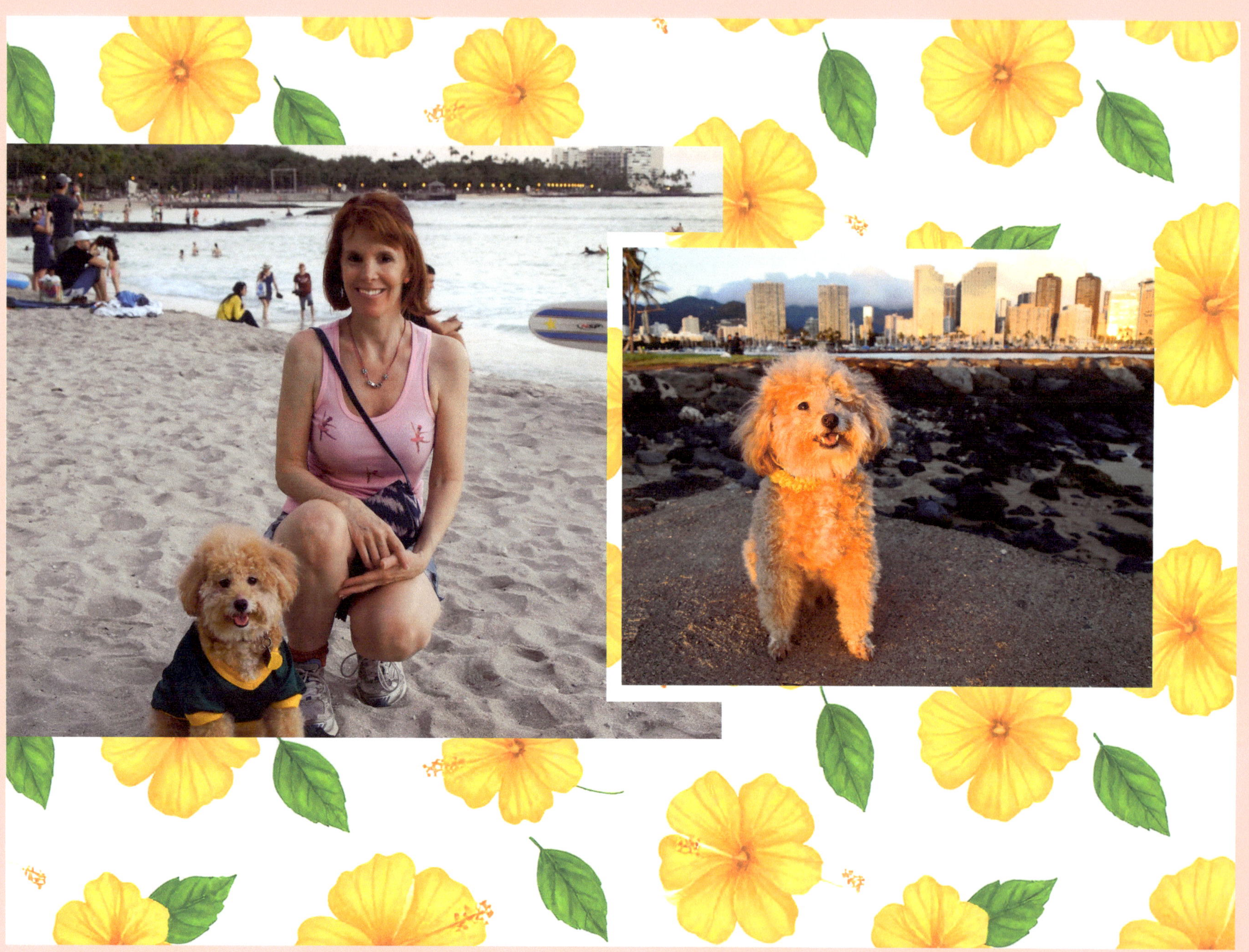

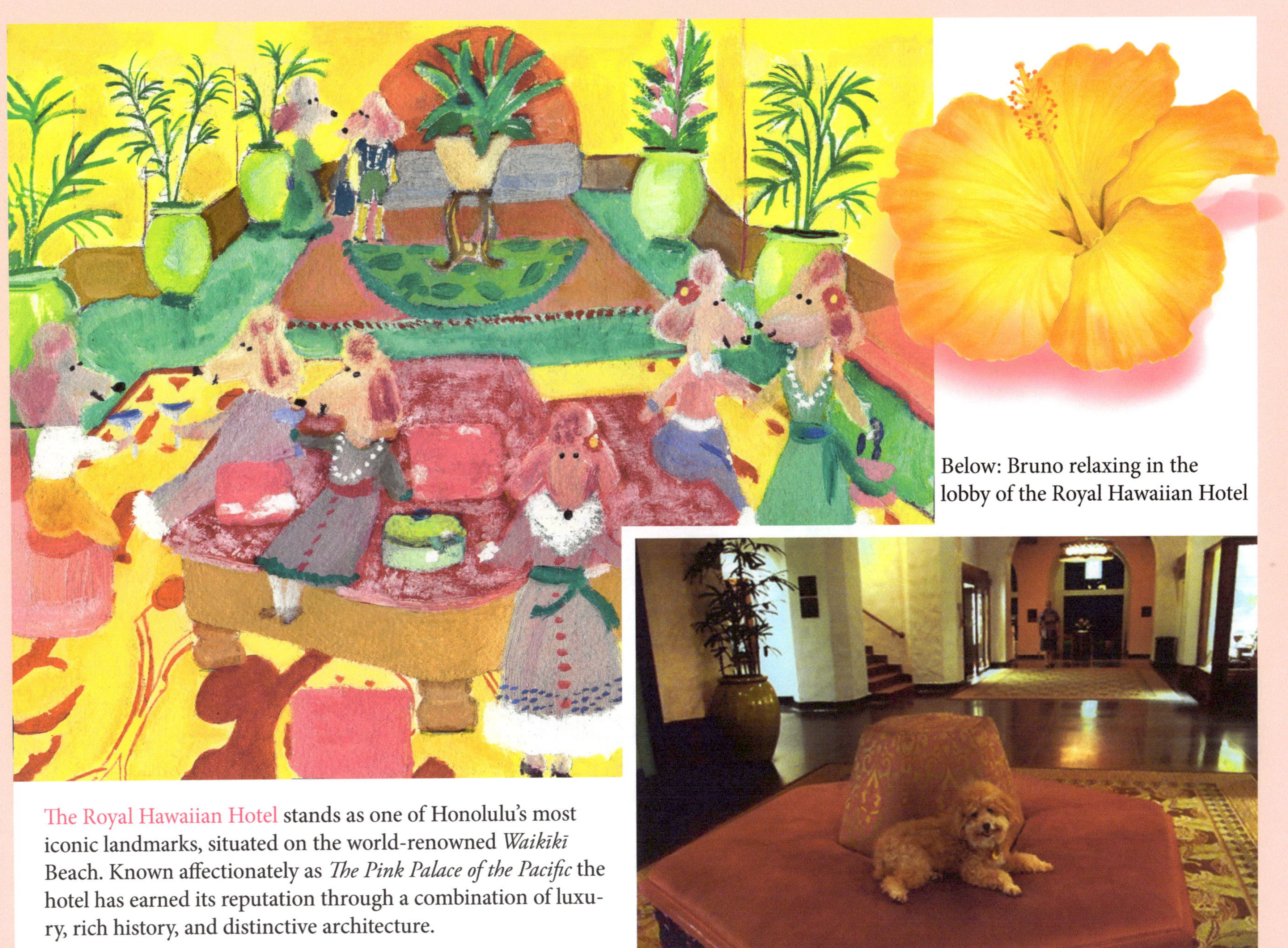

Below: Bruno relaxing in the lobby of the Royal Hawaiian Hotel

The Royal Hawaiian Hotel stands as one of Honolulu's most iconic landmarks, situated on the world-renowned *Waikīkī* Beach. Known affectionately as *The Pink Palace of the Pacific* the hotel has earned its reputation through a combination of luxury, rich history, and distinctive architecture.

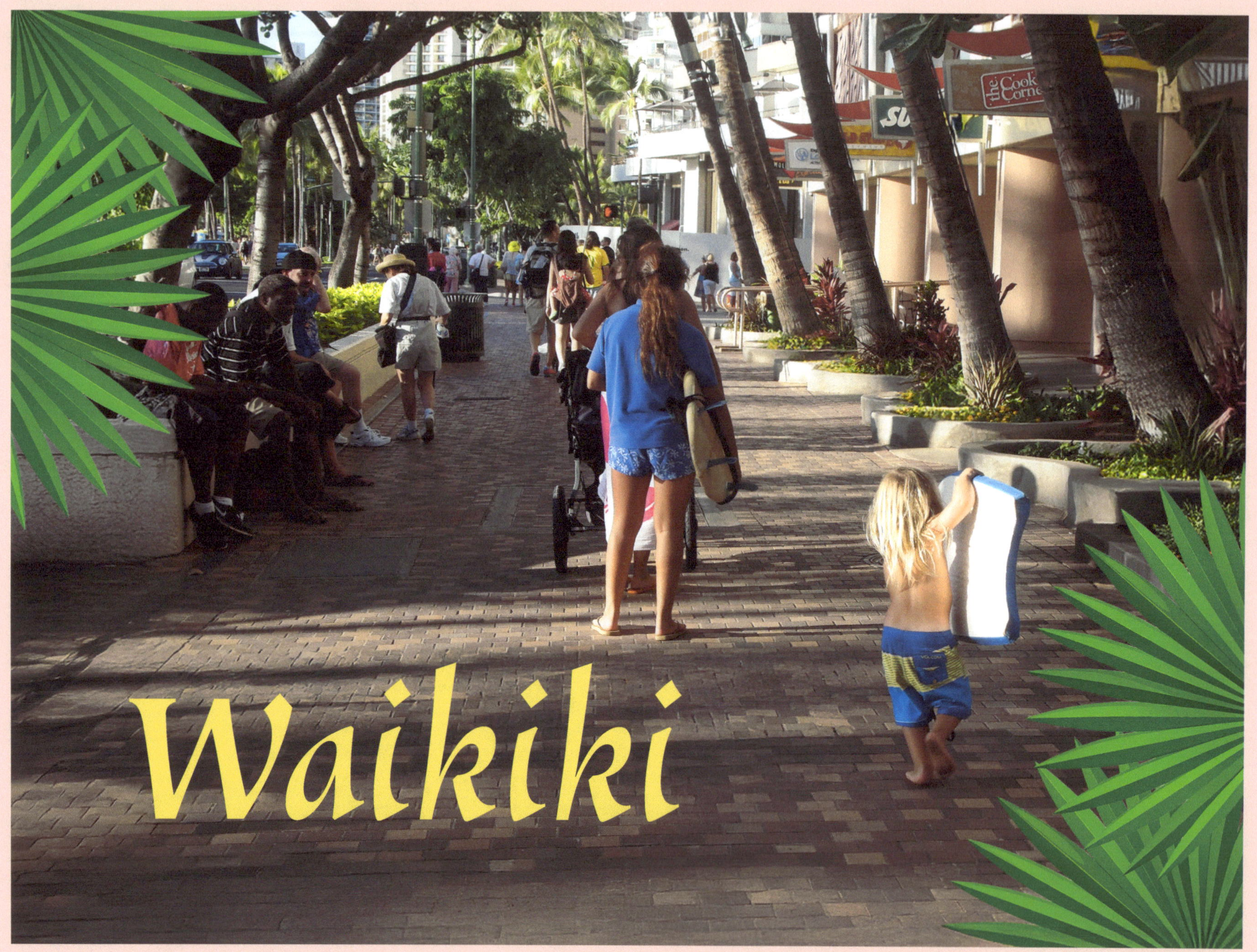
Waikiki

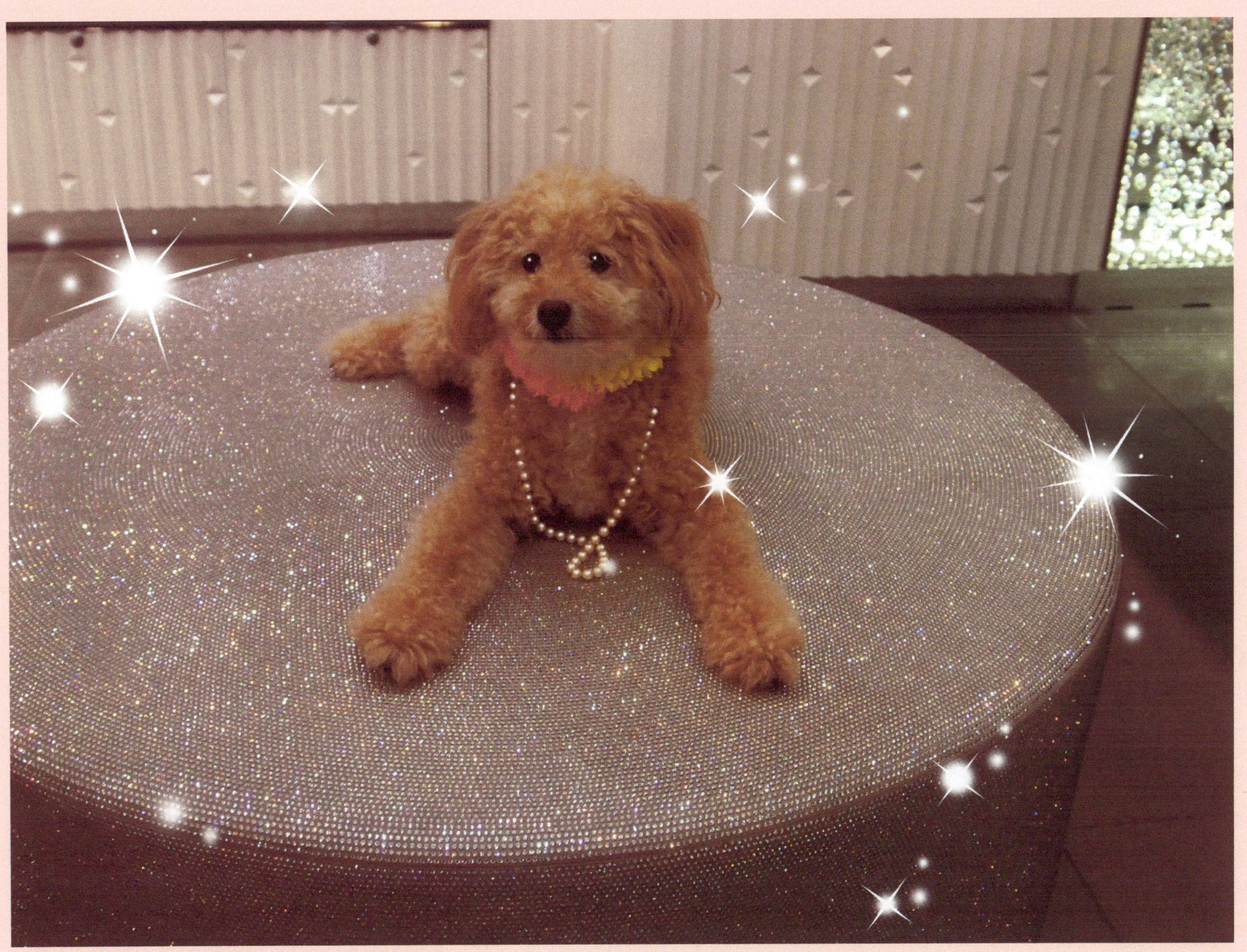

Bruno at the Swarovski Store in Honolulu.

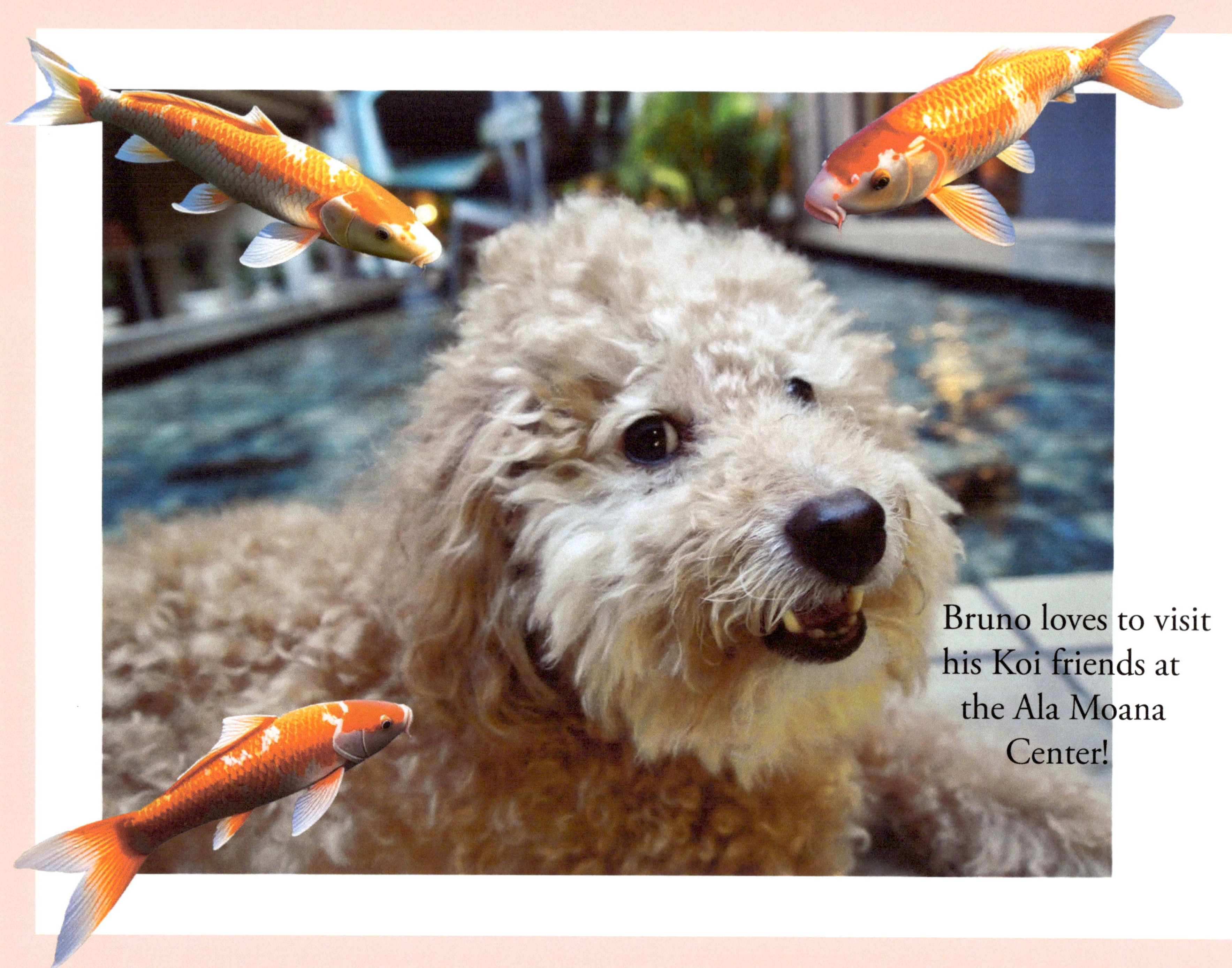

Bruno loves to visit his Koi friends at the Ala Moana Center!

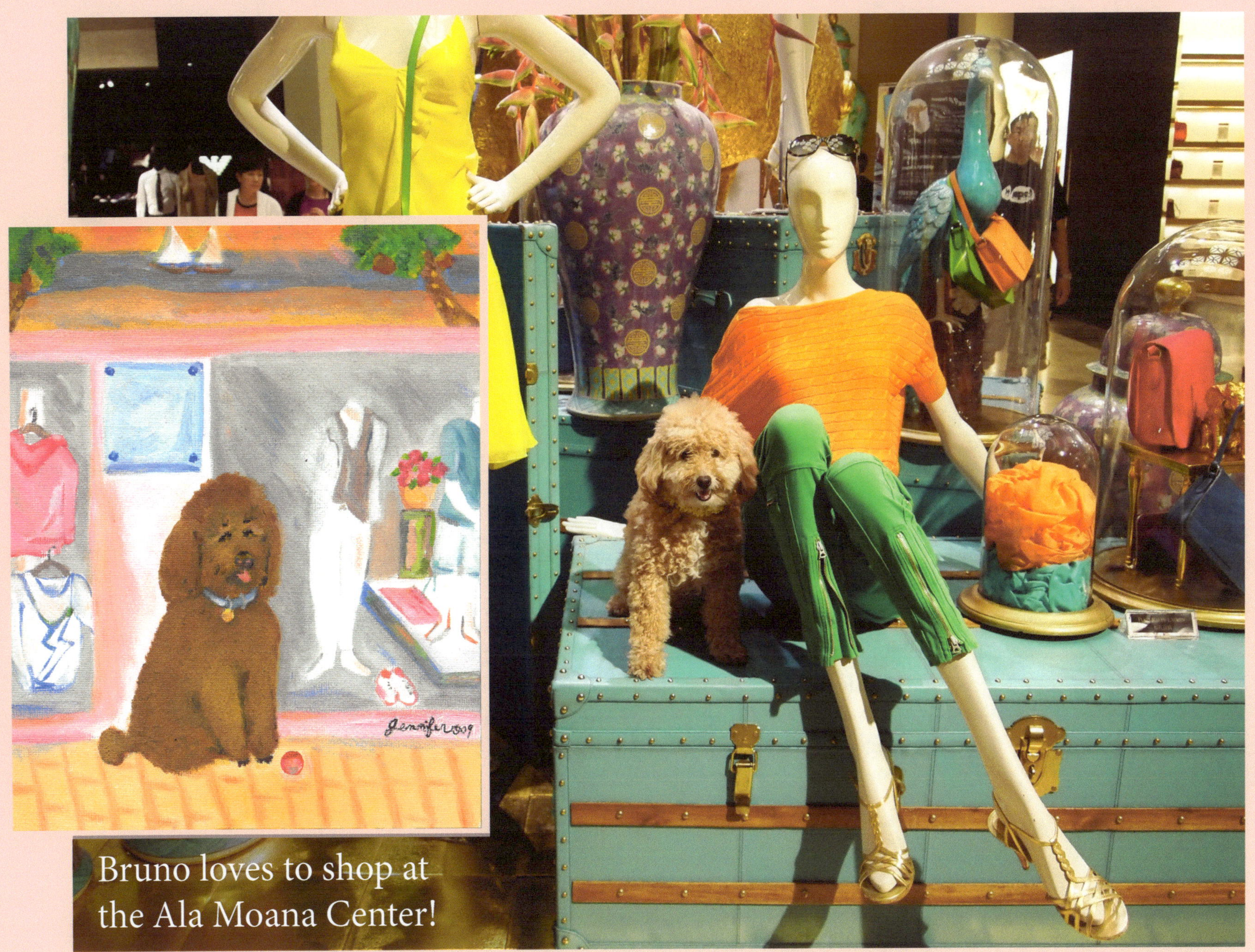

Bruno loves to shop at
the Ala Moana Center!

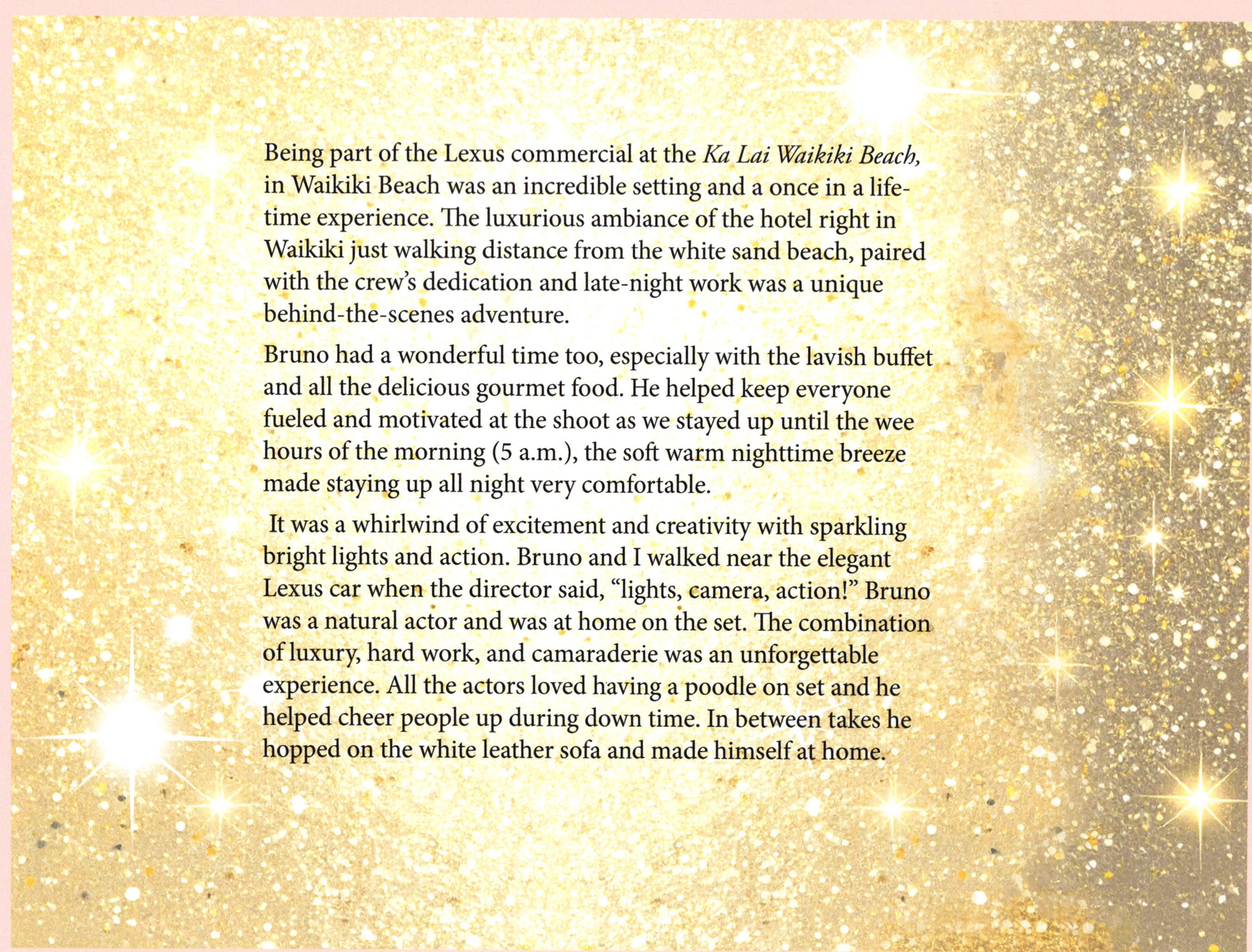

Being part of the Lexus commercial at the *Ka Lai Waikiki Beach,* in Waikiki Beach was an incredible setting and a once in a lifetime experience. The luxurious ambiance of the hotel right in Waikiki just walking distance from the white sand beach, paired with the crew's dedication and late-night work was a unique behind-the-scenes adventure.

Bruno had a wonderful time too, especially with the lavish buffet and all the delicious gourmet food. He helped keep everyone fueled and motivated at the shoot as we stayed up until the wee hours of the morning (5 a.m.), the soft warm nighttime breeze made staying up all night very comfortable.

 It was a whirlwind of excitement and creativity with sparkling bright lights and action. Bruno and I walked near the elegant Lexus car when the director said, "lights, camera, action!" Bruno was a natural actor and was at home on the set. The combination of luxury, hard work, and camaraderie was an unforgettable experience. All the actors loved having a poodle on set and he helped cheer people up during down time. In between takes he hopped on the white leather sofa and made himself at home.

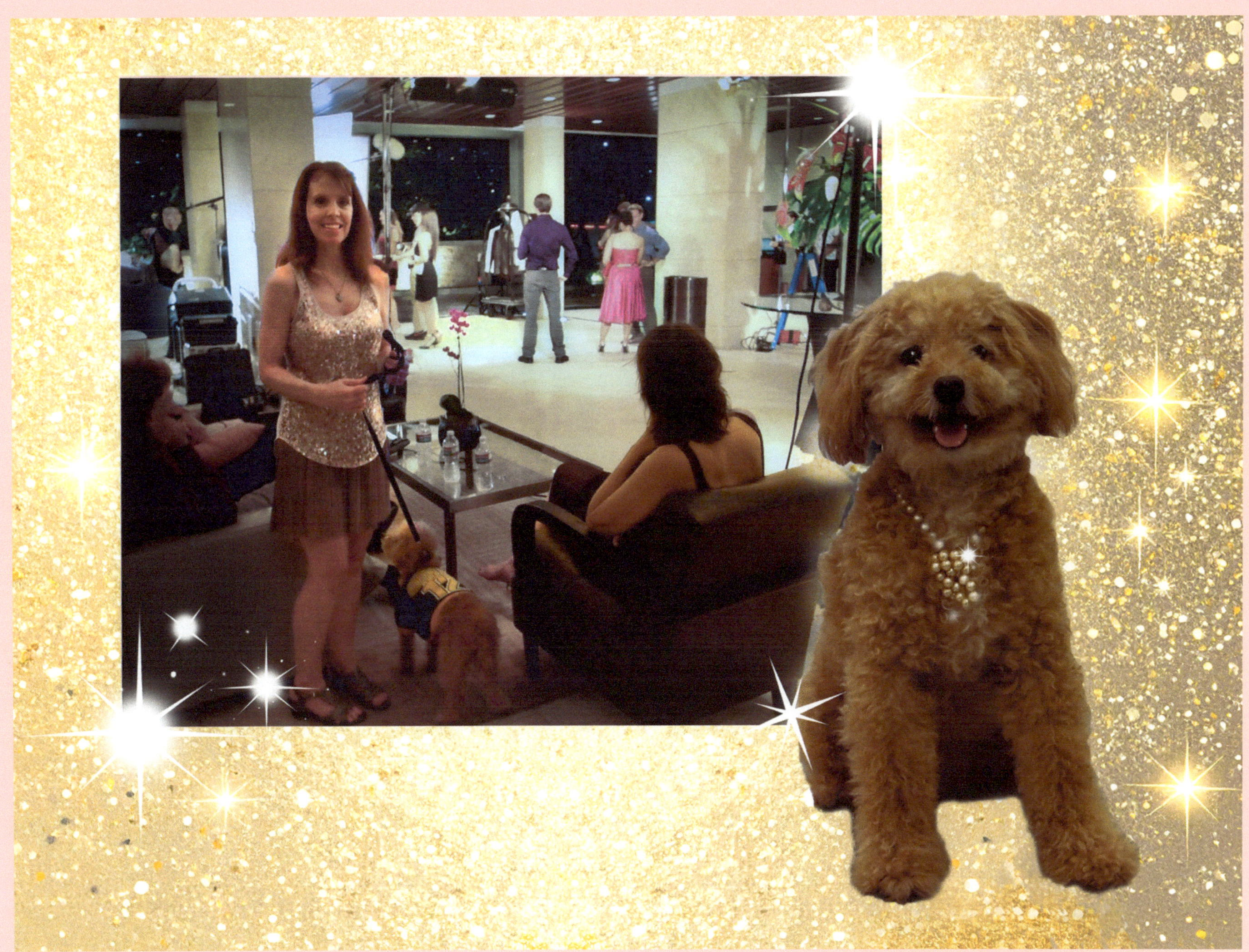

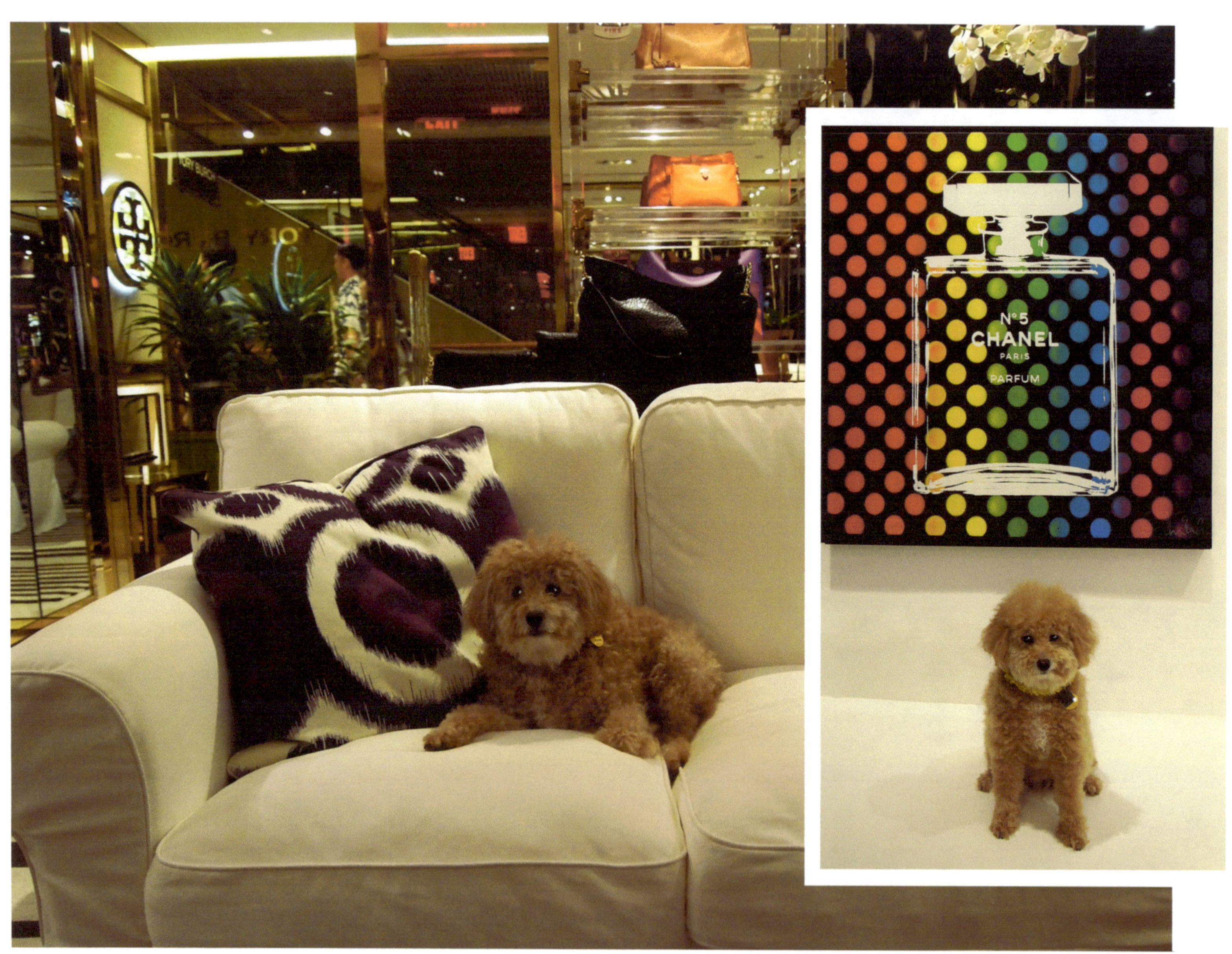

N°5
CHANEL
PARIS
PARFUM

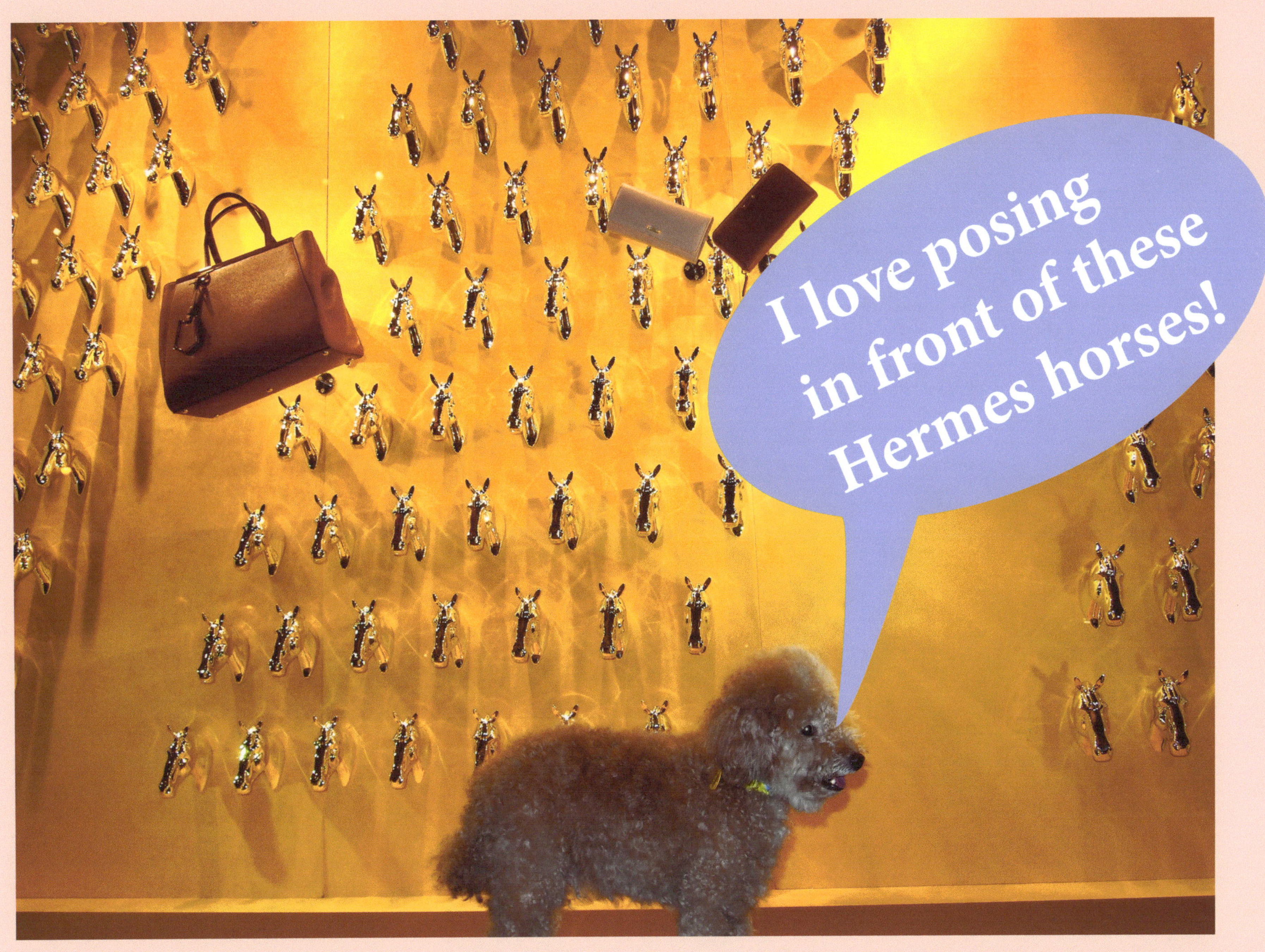

I love posing in front of these Hermes horses!

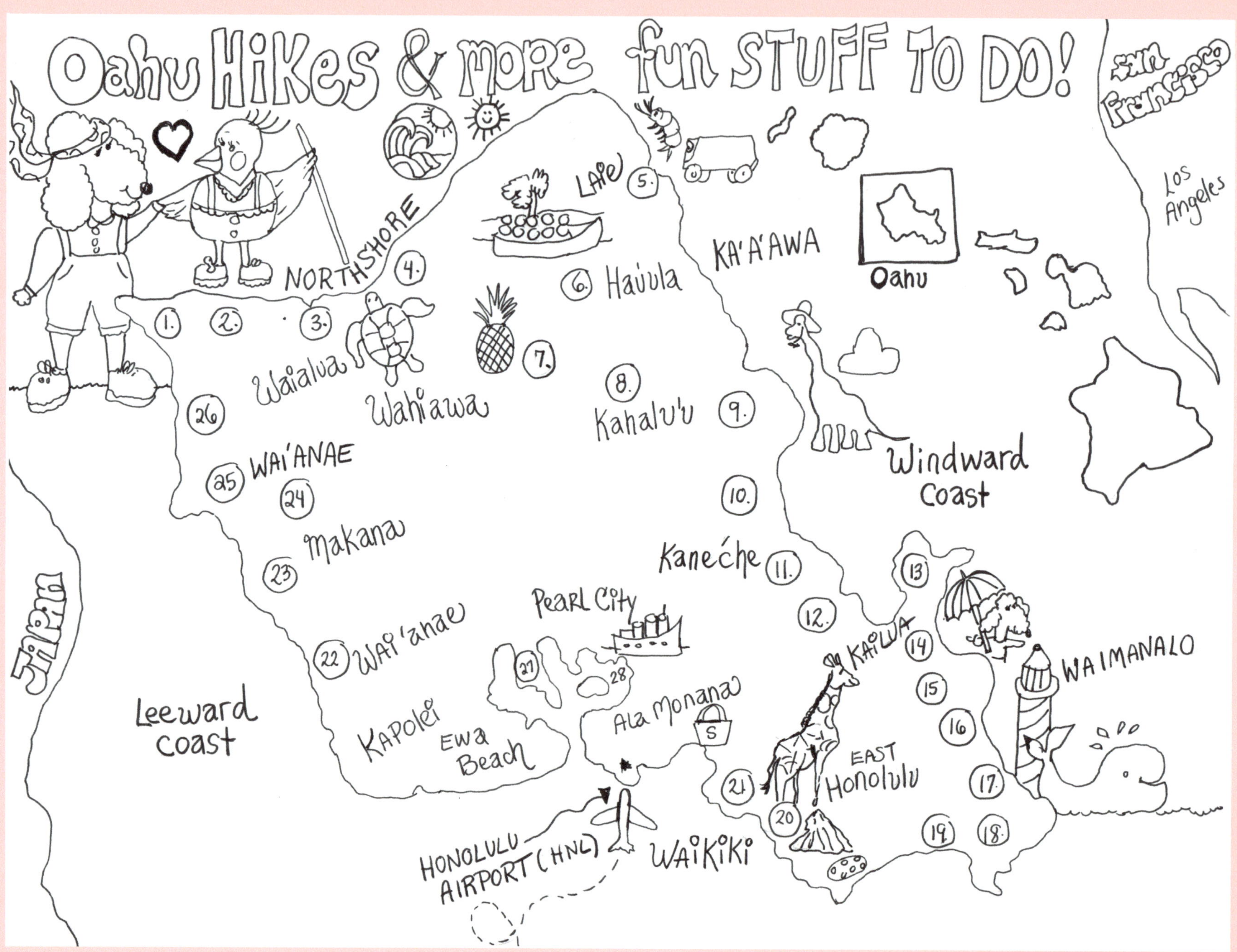
Oahu Hikes & more fun STUFF TO DO!
San Francisco
Los Angeles
NORTHSHORE
LAIE
5.
KA'A'AWA
Oahu
4.
6. Haiula
1. 2. 3.
Waialua
Wahiawa
7.
26
8.
9.
Kahalu'u
25 WAI'ANAE
Windward
Coast
24
Makana
23
Kaneohe
11.
13
10.
12.
Pearl City
22 WAI'anae
21
14
KAILUA
28
15
Leeward
coast
Kapolei
Ala Moana
S
16
WAIMANALO
Ewa
Beach
21
EAST
Honolulu
17
20
19 18.
HONOLULU
AIRPORT (HNL)
WAIKIKI
Oahu

1. Ka'ena Point Trail
2. Kealia Trail
3. Mokule La Loop
4. Kammieland Trail
5. Papali To Poamoho
6. Hauula Forest Reserve
7. Kaipapau Forest Reserve
8. Pu'u Ōhulehule Trail
9. Mokoli'i Island Trail
10. Pu'u Ohulehule (south)
11. Pu'u Maelieh Trail
12. Friendship Gardens Trail
13. Marine Corps Base Hawaii Kaneone
14. Kailua Bay Beach Walk
15. Kayak Tomoku Nui
16. Kaiwa Ridge
17. Makapu'u Point Lighthouse
18. Ko Ko Crater Tramway
19. China Wall & Spitting

20. Diamond Head Crater
21. Waikiki Beach Walk
22. Pu'u Oholu Trail
23. Mount Ka'ala Trail
24. Kole Kole Trail
25. Makaha Ice Ponds
26. Puu Ōhikilolo Trail
27. Pearl Harbor
28. USS Missouri

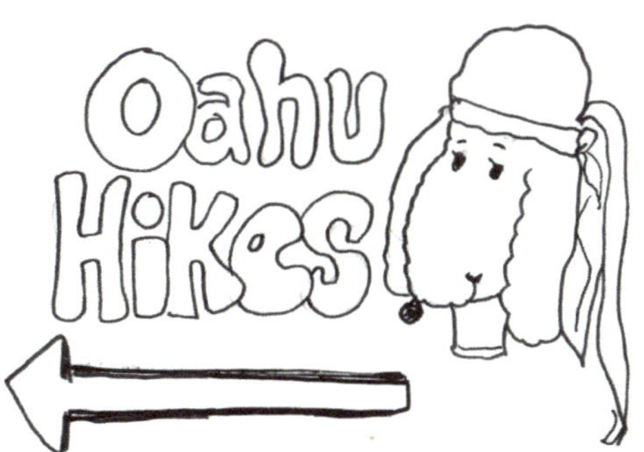

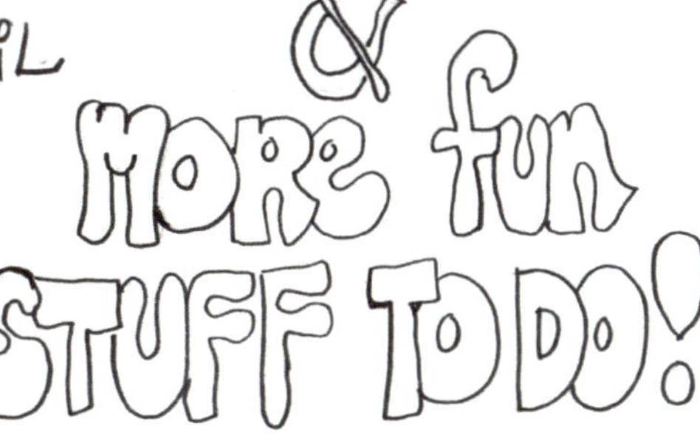

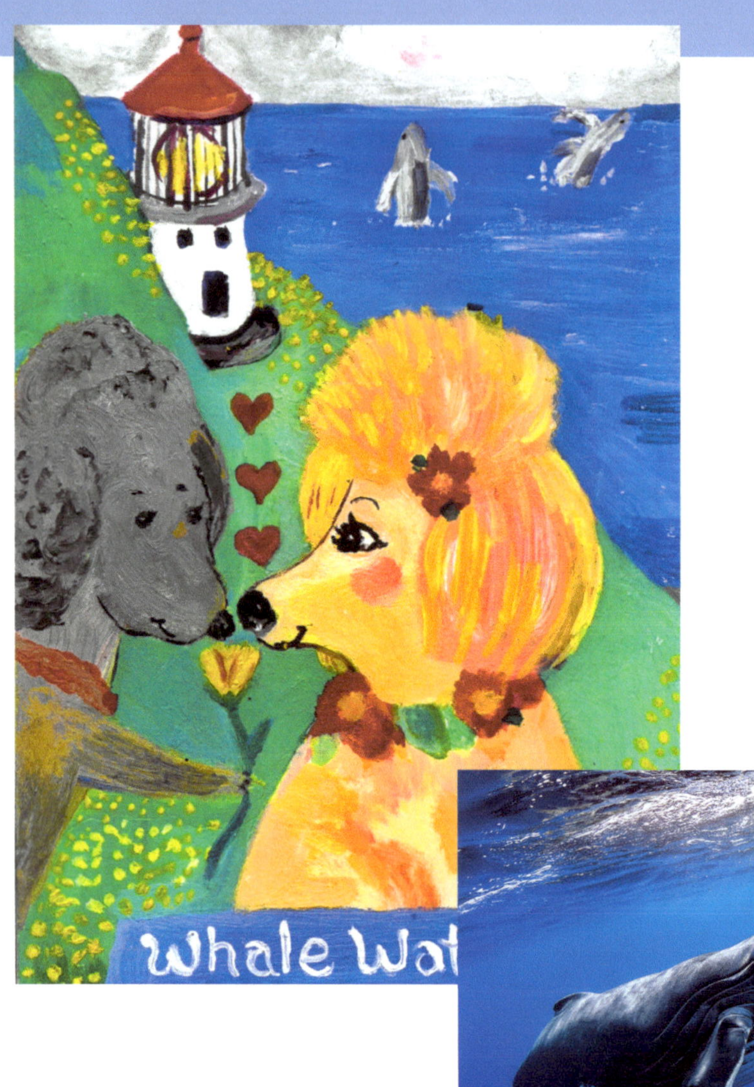

Makapu'u Point - O'ahu

Makapu'u Point, located on O'ahu's southeastern coast, is a prime spot for observing humpback whales from the shore. Perched atop the cliffs overlooking the Pacific Ocean, you'll have a commanding view of the whales in their natural habitat. You can see humpback whales from December to May.

The Makapu'u Point Lighthouse Trail, located within Kaiwi State Scenic Shoreline, offers stunning panoramic views of O'ahu's southeastern coastline, including Koko Head and Koko Crater. The trail leads to the summit at Makapu'u Head, where hikers are rewarded with spectacular views of the windward coast and nearby offshore islets.

The historic Makapu'u Lighthouse, sits atop the point, and although the lighthouse itself is off-limits to visitors, it makes for a beautiful photo backdrop against the deep blue sea below. On clear days, you may catch glimpses of Moloka'i and Lana'i in the distance. Built in 1909, the lighthouse has been a vital navigation aid for vessels approaching Honolulu from the American West Coast. In 1977, it was added to the National Register of Historic Places.

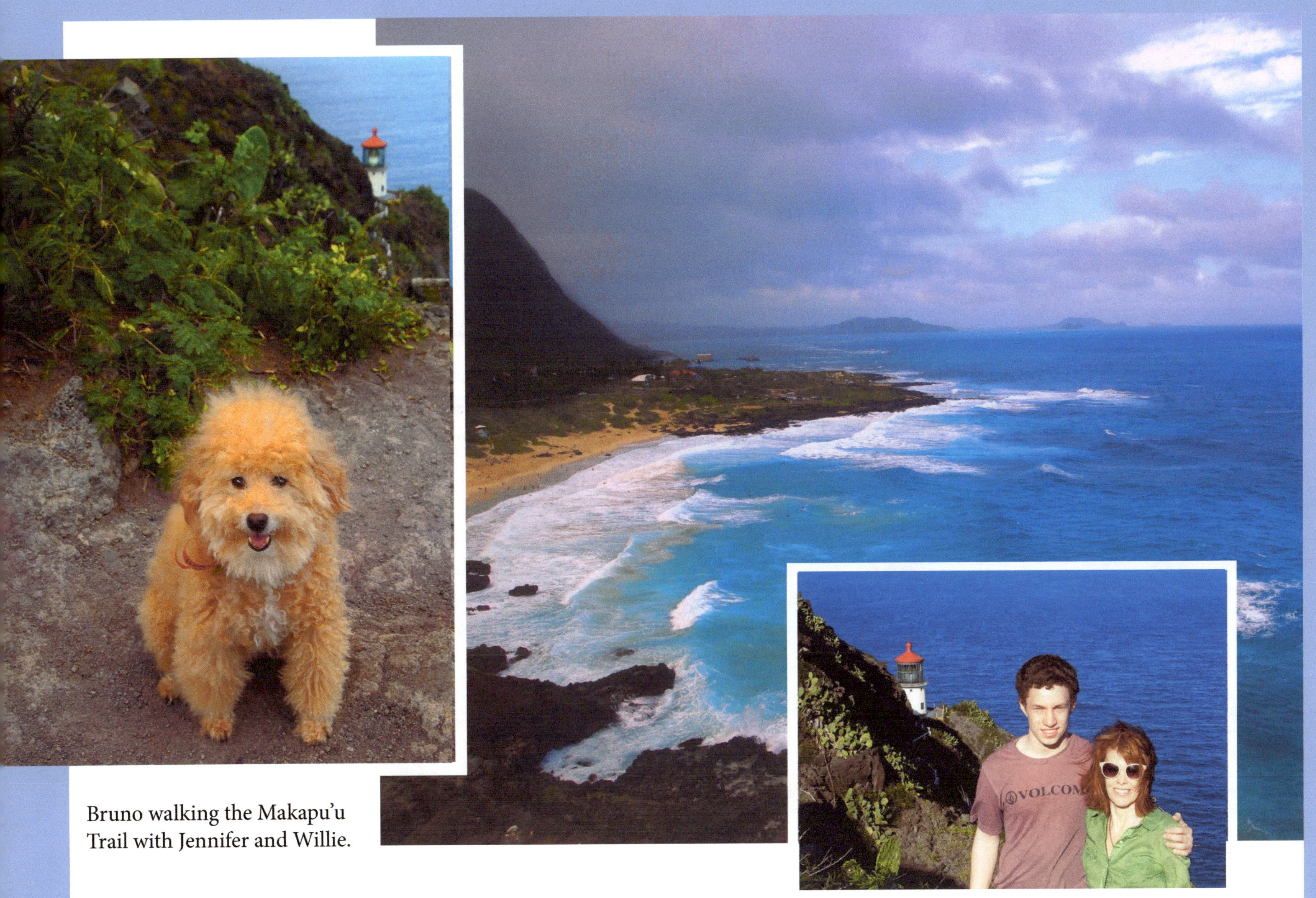

Bruno walking the Makapu'u
Trail with Jennifer and Willie.

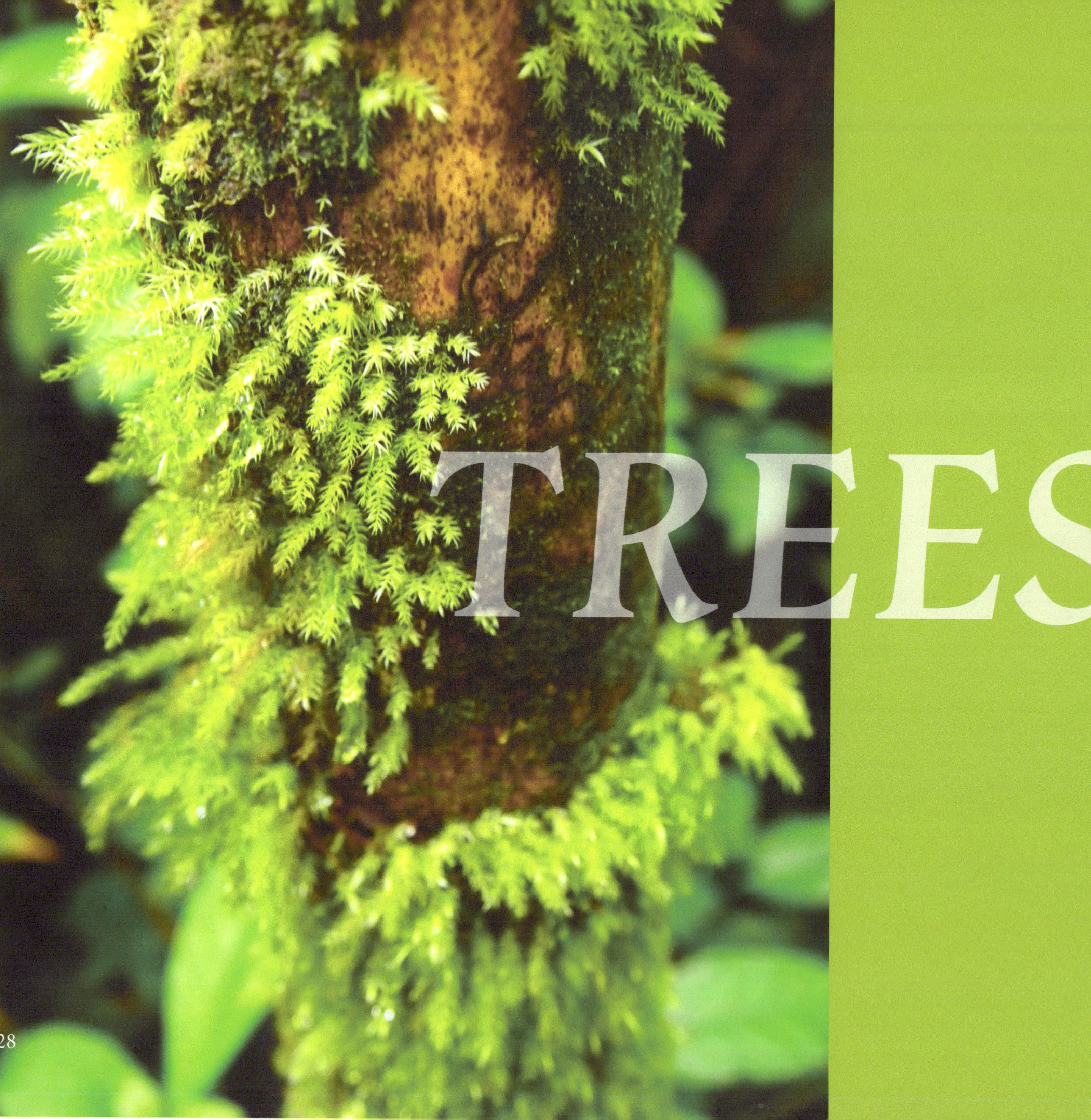
TREES

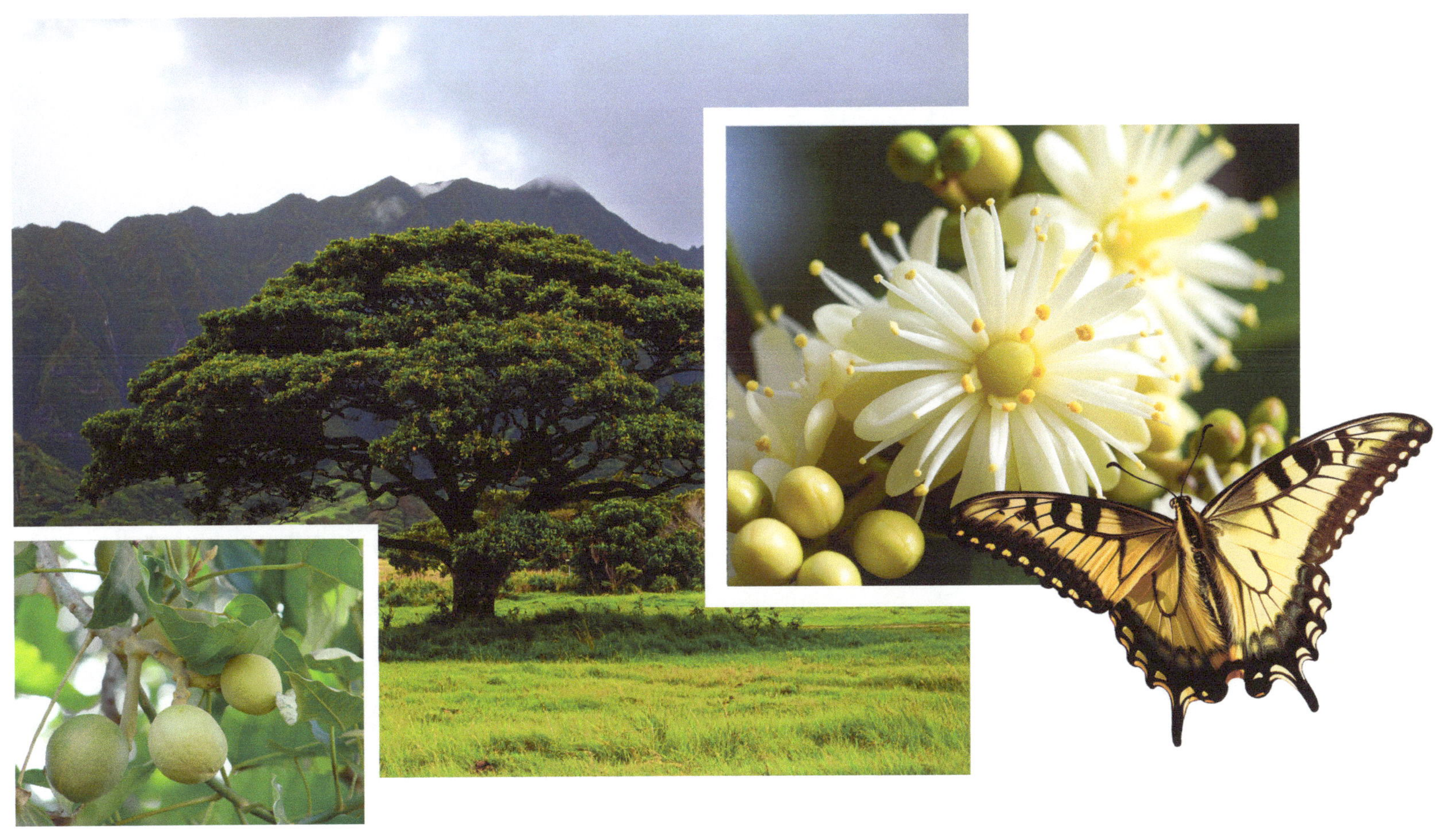

The Kukui tree (*Aleurites moluccanus*) is the official state tree of Hawai'i, revered for its cultural and ecological significance. The Kukui tree is perhaps most famous for its seeds, also known as candlenuts, which have been used by Native Hawaiians to create beautiful jewelry and crafts.

The Kukui tree is not just the state tree of Hawai'i—it is a symbol of resilience, adaptability, and cultural pride. Its contributions to both Hawaiian tradition and the natural world make it a beloved and essential part of the islands' identity.

Banyan Drive in Hilo, Hawai'i, is a scenic and historically rich tree-lined street, famous for its stunning banyan trees that line the shoreline. The street has earned the nickname "Hilo Walk of Fame" because of the banyan trees planted by celebrities over the years, creating a unique tribute to notable figures. These trees, some over a century old, have become a symbol of resilience, having withstood several tsunamis that have devastated the town.

One of the most famous trees along Banyan Drive is the Babe Ruth Banyan Tree, planted by the legendary baseball player himself. Ruth visited Hilo in 1933, and his tree remains a lasting tribute to his legacy, standing tall in the face of time and natural disasters.

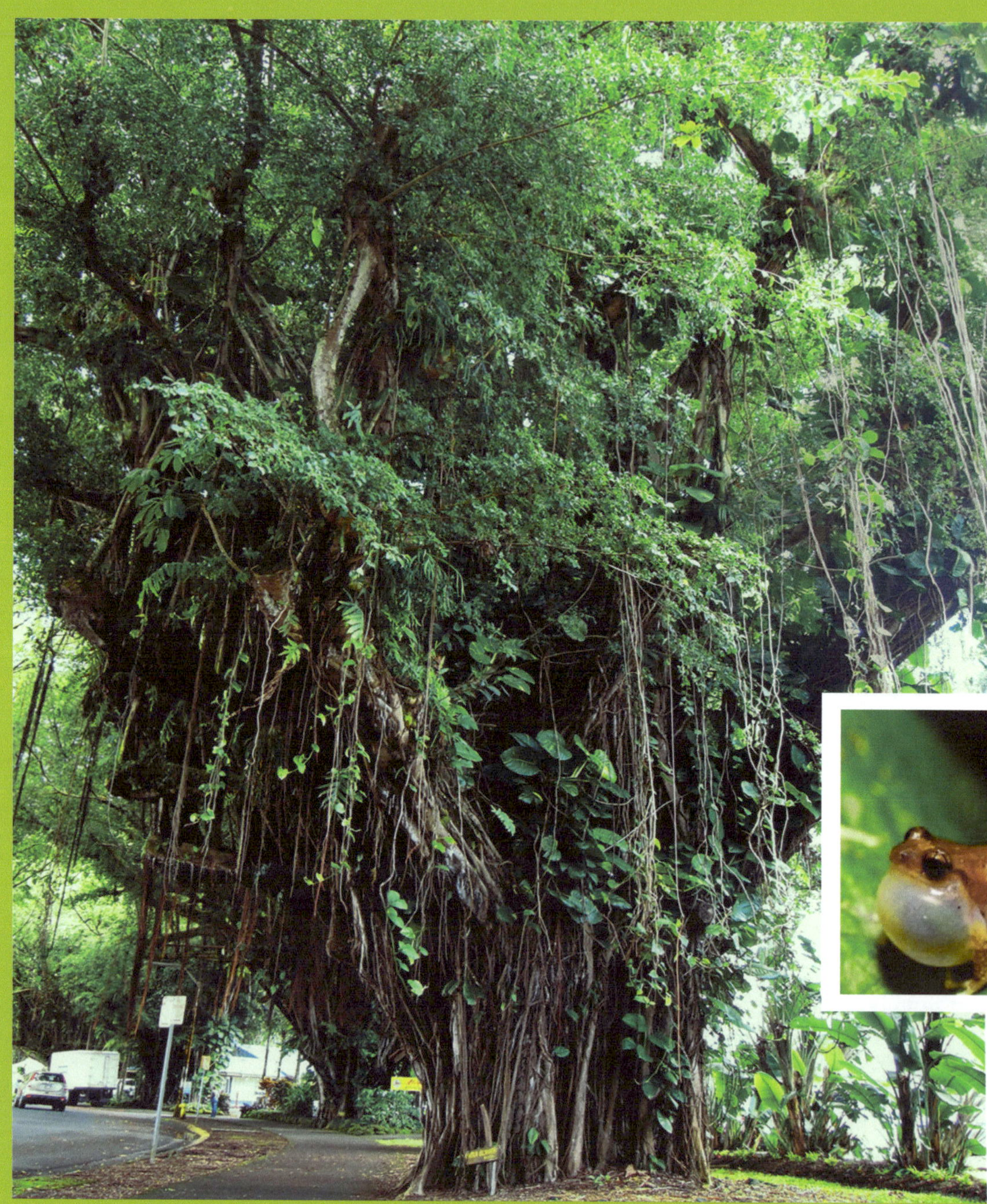

While Banyan Drive is known for its beauty and history, it is also home to a more unusual presence: the coqui frogs. These small, tree-dwelling frogs were accidentally introduced to Hawai'i from Puerto Rico.

The frogs are known for their loud, distinctive "KO-kee" calls, which can reach up to 100 decibels, making them a significant noise nuisance in the area.

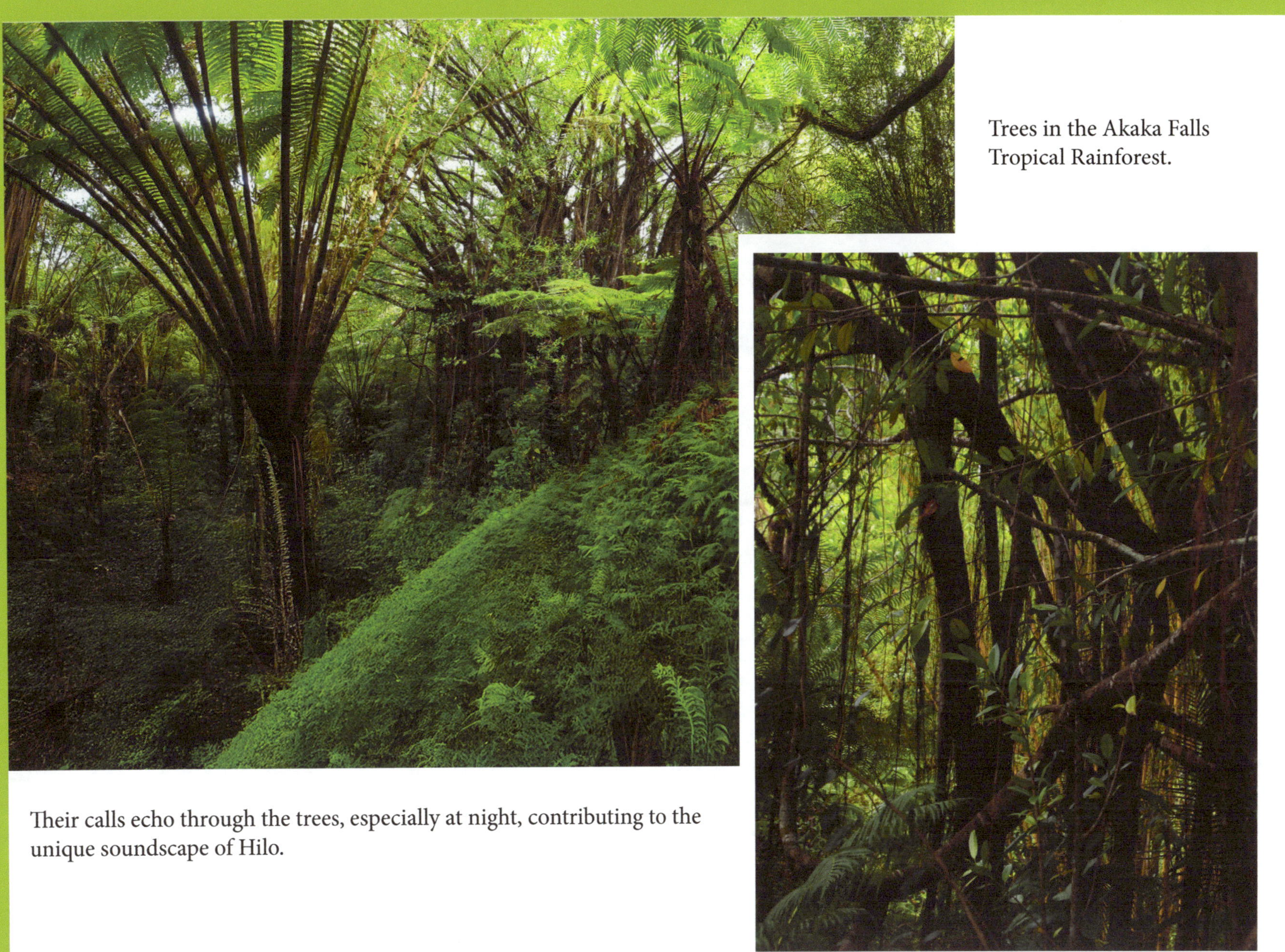

Trees in the Akaka Falls Tropical Rainforest.

Their calls echo through the trees, especially at night, contributing to the unique soundscape of Hilo.

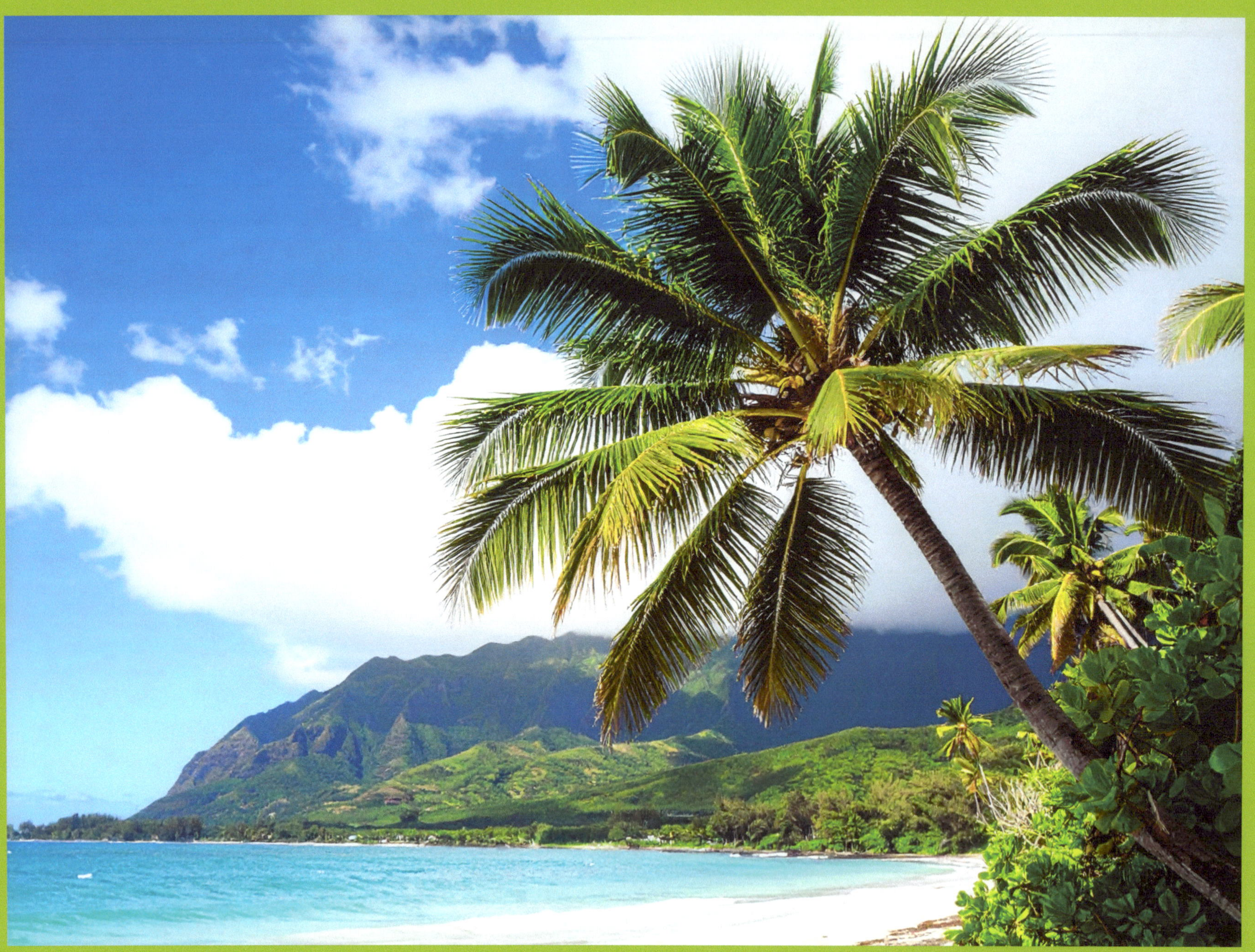

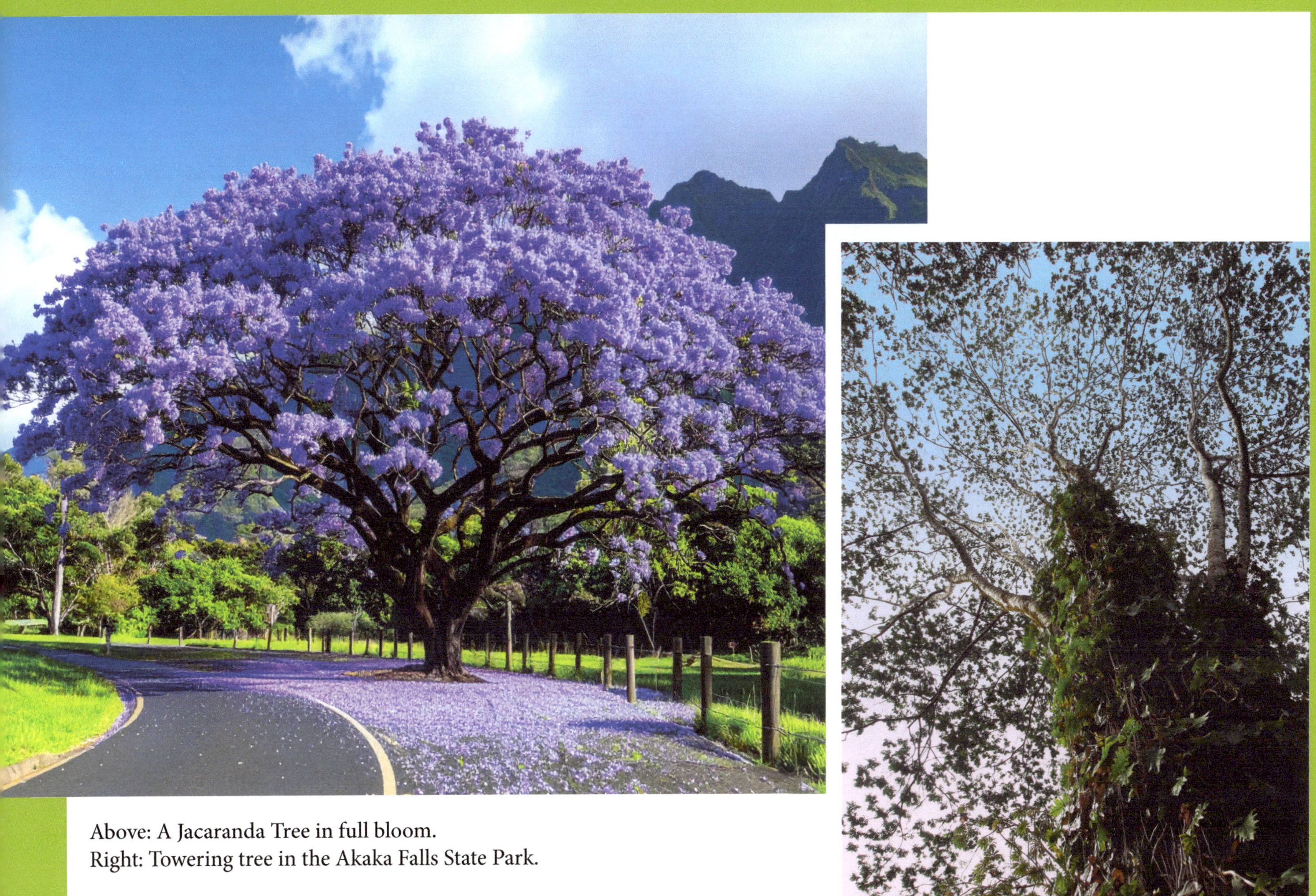

Above: A Jacaranda Tree in full bloom.
Right: Towering tree in the Akaka Falls State Park.

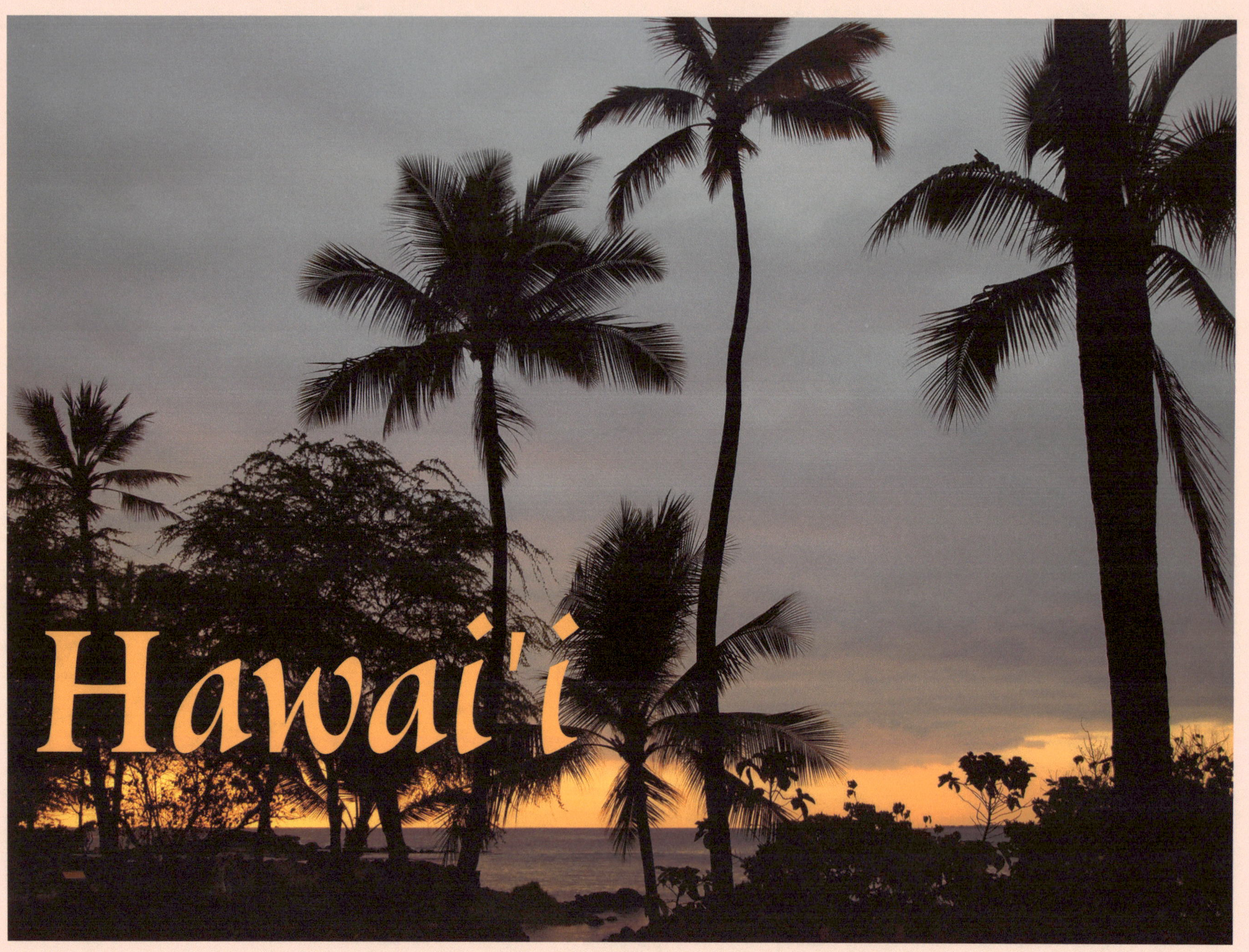
Hawai'i

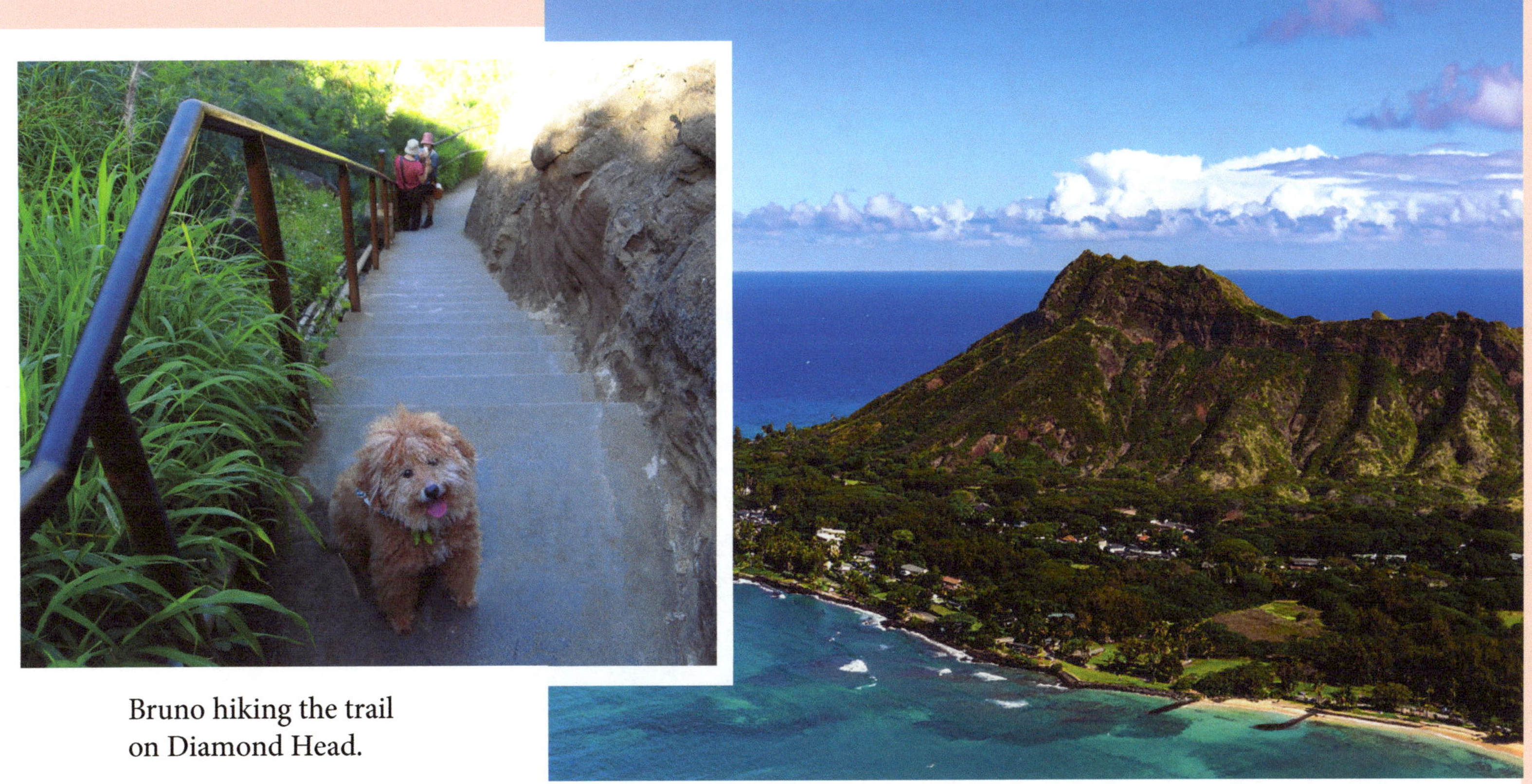

Bruno hiking the trail
on Diamond Head.

Diamond Head is a volcanic tuff cone located on the island of O'ahu, Hawai'i. It is one of the most iconic landmarks in Hawai'i, offering panoramic views of Waikīkī and Honolulu. Known in Hawaiian as **Lēʻahi**, the name likely comes from a combination of "lae" (promontory or browridge) and "ahi" (tuna), due to the mountain's ridgeline resembling the dorsal fin of a tuna. The English name "Diamond Head" was given by British sailors in the 19th century, who mistook the calcite crystals found on its nearby beach for diamonds.

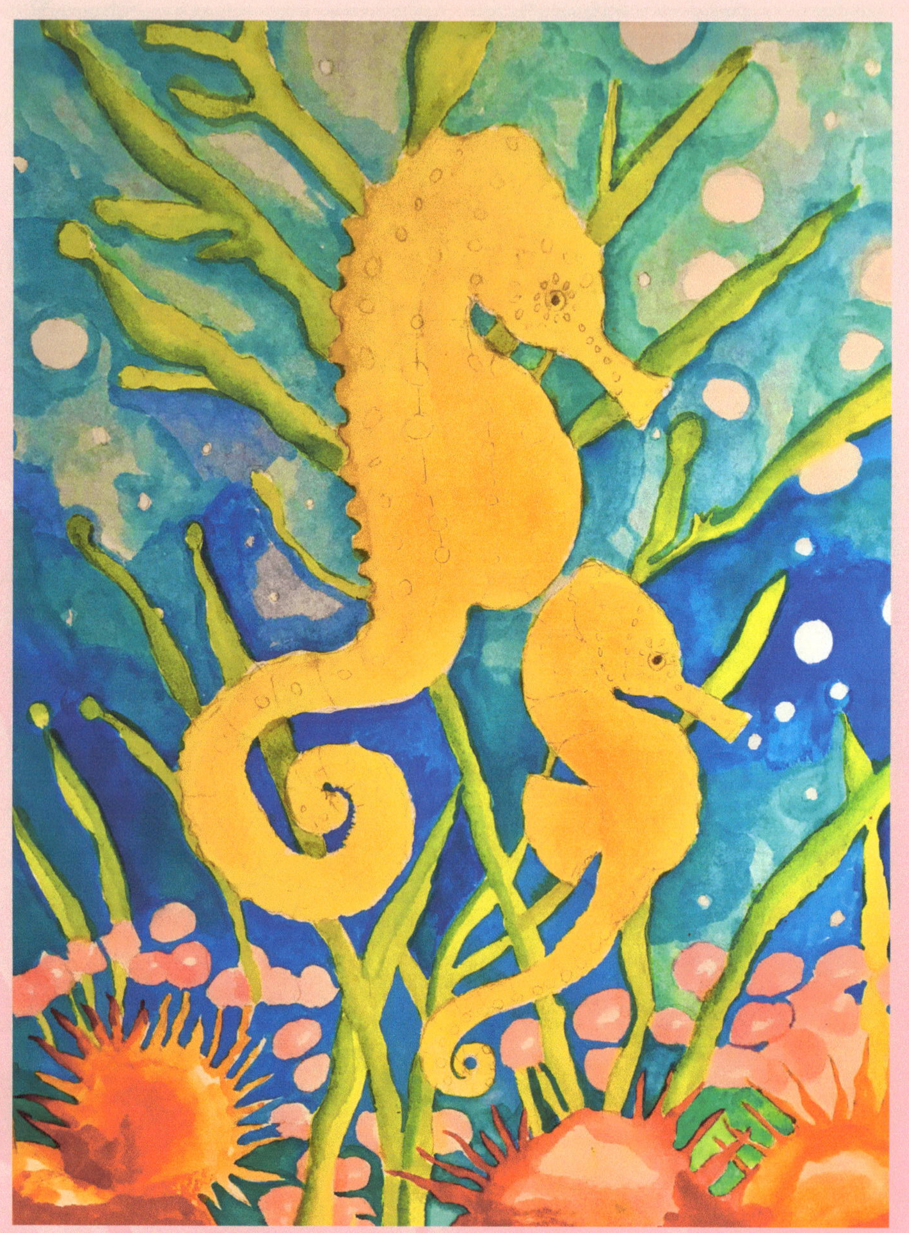

Ocean Rider Seahorse Farm – Kona, Hawai'i (The Big Island)

Farm-Raised Seahorses and Marine Life for Personal and Commercial Aquariums

Acclaimed & Recognized Since 1998

Located on the beautiful Big Island of Hawai'i, Ocean Rider Seahorse Farm is an organic aquaculture farm that has been dedicated to raising seahorses and other marine life since 1998. Known for its commitment to sustainable farming practices and ocean conservation, Ocean Rider has earned recognition as one of Hawai'i's top attractions, with multiple Trip Advisor Certificate of Excellence awards. The farm not only supports the well-being of seahorses but also plays a crucial role in protecting endangered species, ensuring that these remarkable creatures thrive for future generations.

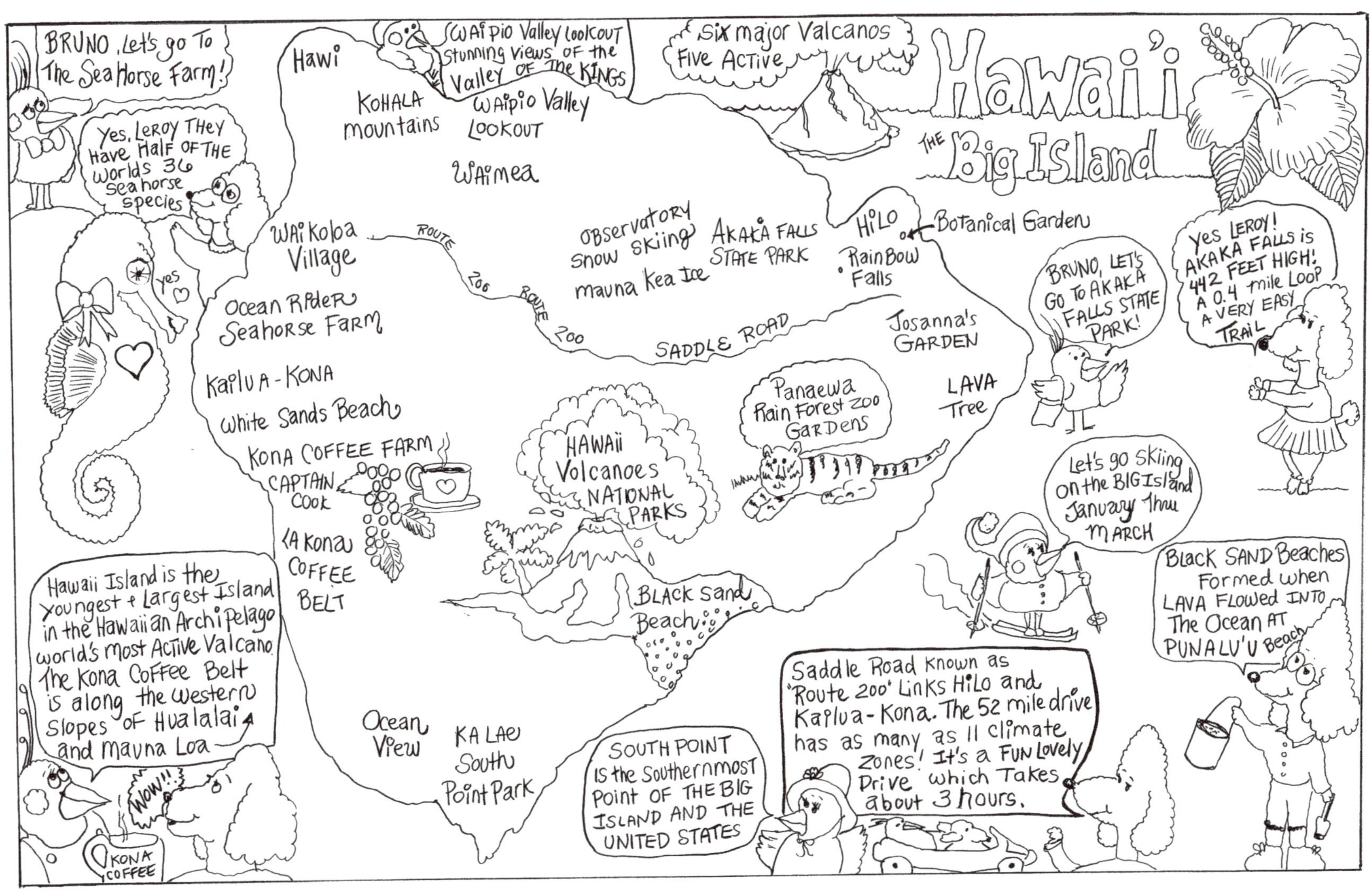

BRUNO, let's go to The Sea Horse Farm!
Yes, Leroy they have HALF OF THE worlds 36 seahorse species
yes
Hawi
KOHALA mountains
WAipio Valley lookout stunning views of the Valley of the KINGS
WAipio Valley Lookout
Six major Valcanos Five Active
Hawai'i
THE Big Island
Waimea
Waikoloa Village
ROUTE 200
ROUTE 200
Observatory snow skiing
mauna kea Ice
Akaka Falls State Park
Hilo
Botanical Garden
Rainbow Falls
BRUNO, LET'S GO TO AKAKA FALLS STATE PARK!
Yes LEROY! AKAKA FALLS is 442 FEET HIGH! A 0.4 mile LOOP A VERY EASY TRAIL
Ocean Rider Seahorse Farm
Kailua - KONA
White Sands Beach
Kona COFFEE FARM
CAPTAIN Cook
SADDLE ROAD
Josanna's GARDEN
LAVA Tree
Panaewa Rain Forest zoo Gardens
HAWAii Volcanoes NATIONAL PARKS
Let's go skiing on the BIG Island January thru MARCH
La Kona COFFEE BELT
Hawaii Island is the youngest & largest island in the Hawaiian Archipelago world's most Active Valcano. The kona COFFEE Belt is along the western slopes of Hualalai and Mauna Loa
BLACK Sand Beach
Black SAND Beaches Formed when LAVA FLOWED INTO The Ocean AT PUNALU'U Beach
Ocean View
KA LAE South Point Park
SOUTH POINT IS the southernmost Point OF THE BIG ISLAND AND THE UNITED STATES
Saddle Road Known as "Route 200" Links Hilo and Kailua- Kona. The 52 mile drive has as many as 11 climate zones! It's a FUN lovely Drive which Takes about 3 hours.
WOW!!!
KONA COFFEE

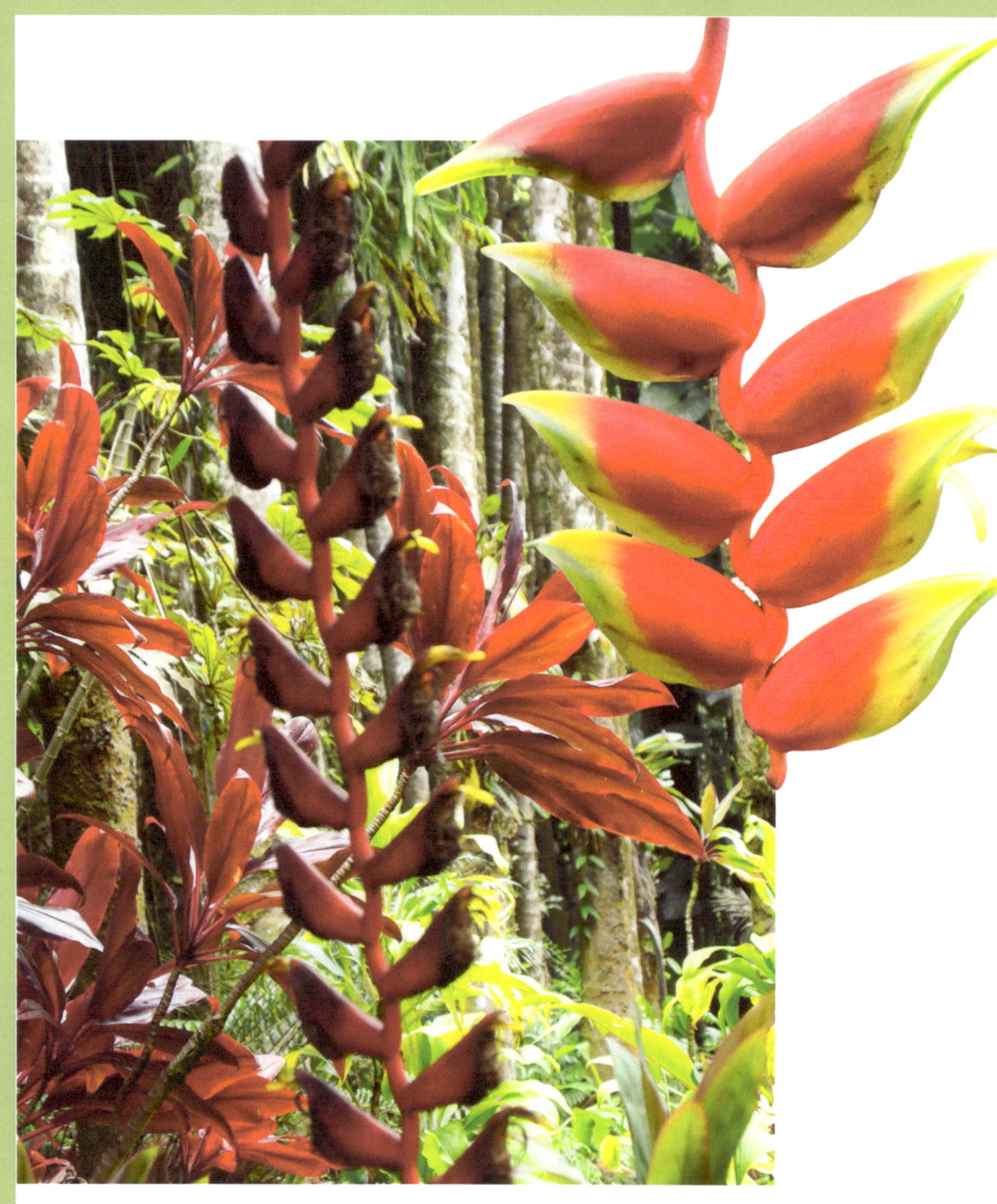

Hilo

Hilo is the second-largest census-designated place (CDP) in the state of Hawai'i and the largest settlement on the island of Hawai'i, with a population of 44,186 as of the 2020 census. It serves as the county seat of Hawai'i County and is in the South Hilo District, overlooking the picturesque Hilo Bay.

Hilo is situated near two major volcanoes: Mauna Loa, an active volcano, and Mauna Kea, a dormant one. These volcanic giants shape much of the region's landscape. Mauna Kea is also home to some of the world's best ground-based astronomical observatories due to its high altitude and clear skies.

During the early 19th century, King Kamehameha I unified the Hawaiian Islands and shifted the settlement to the shore, where it grew. The town

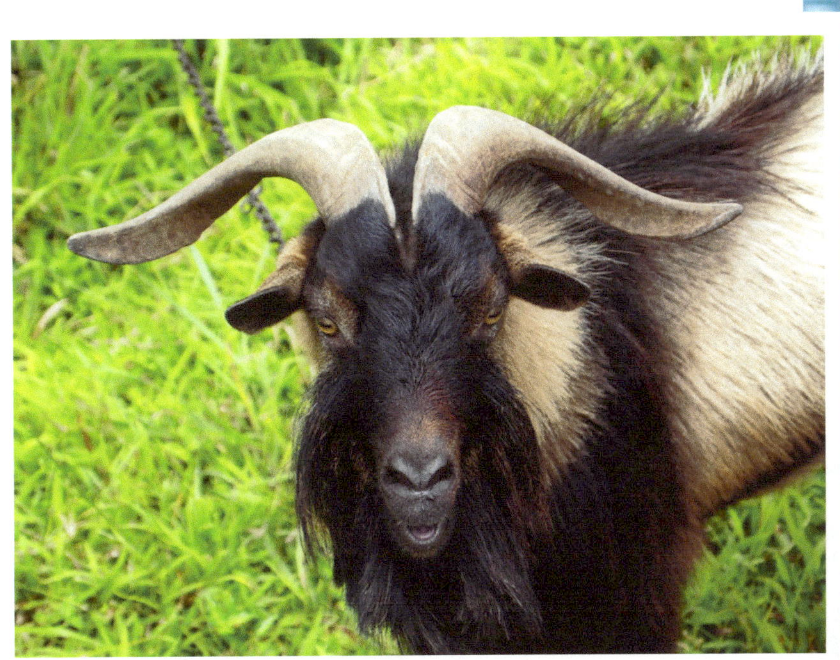

expanded further with the establishment of sugar plantations in the 19th and early 20th centuries.

These plantations attracted workers, particularly from Asia, making Hilo an important trading hub.

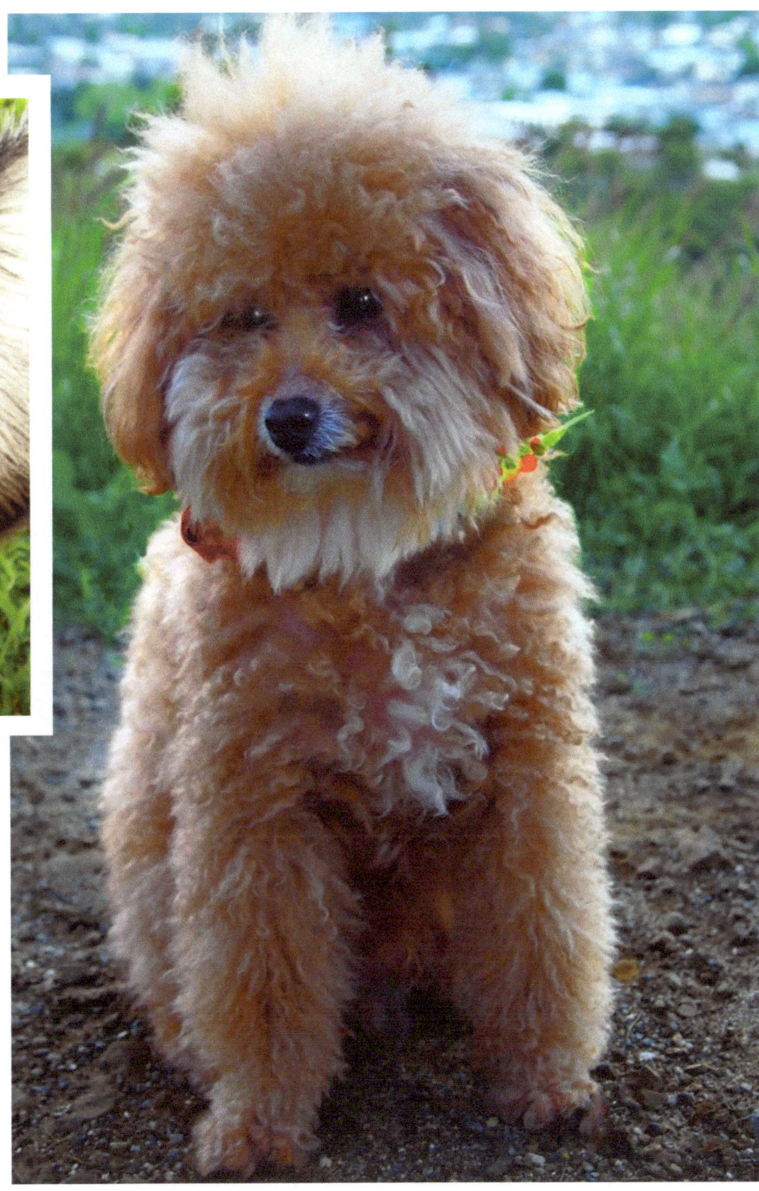

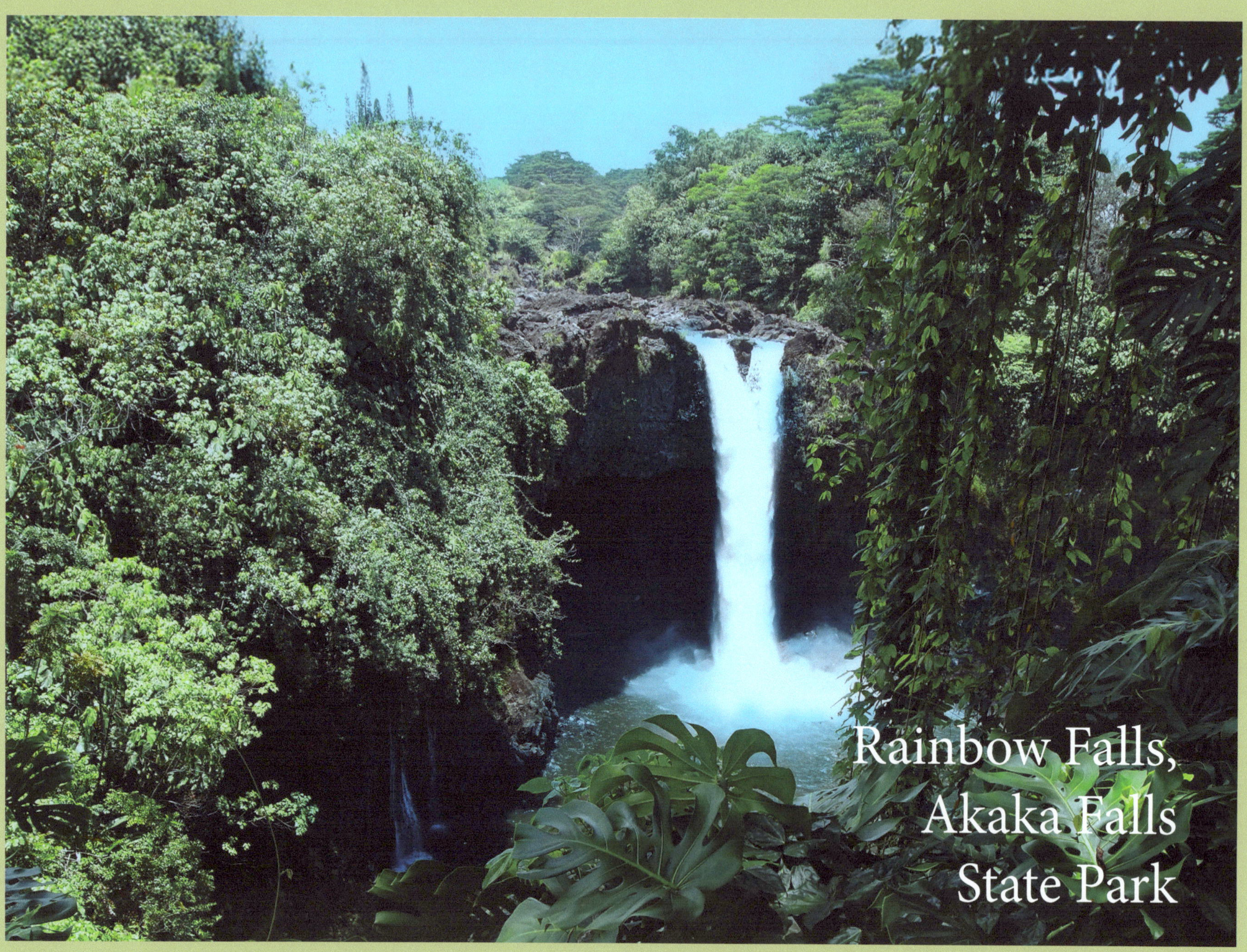
Rainbow Falls,
Akaka Falls
State Park

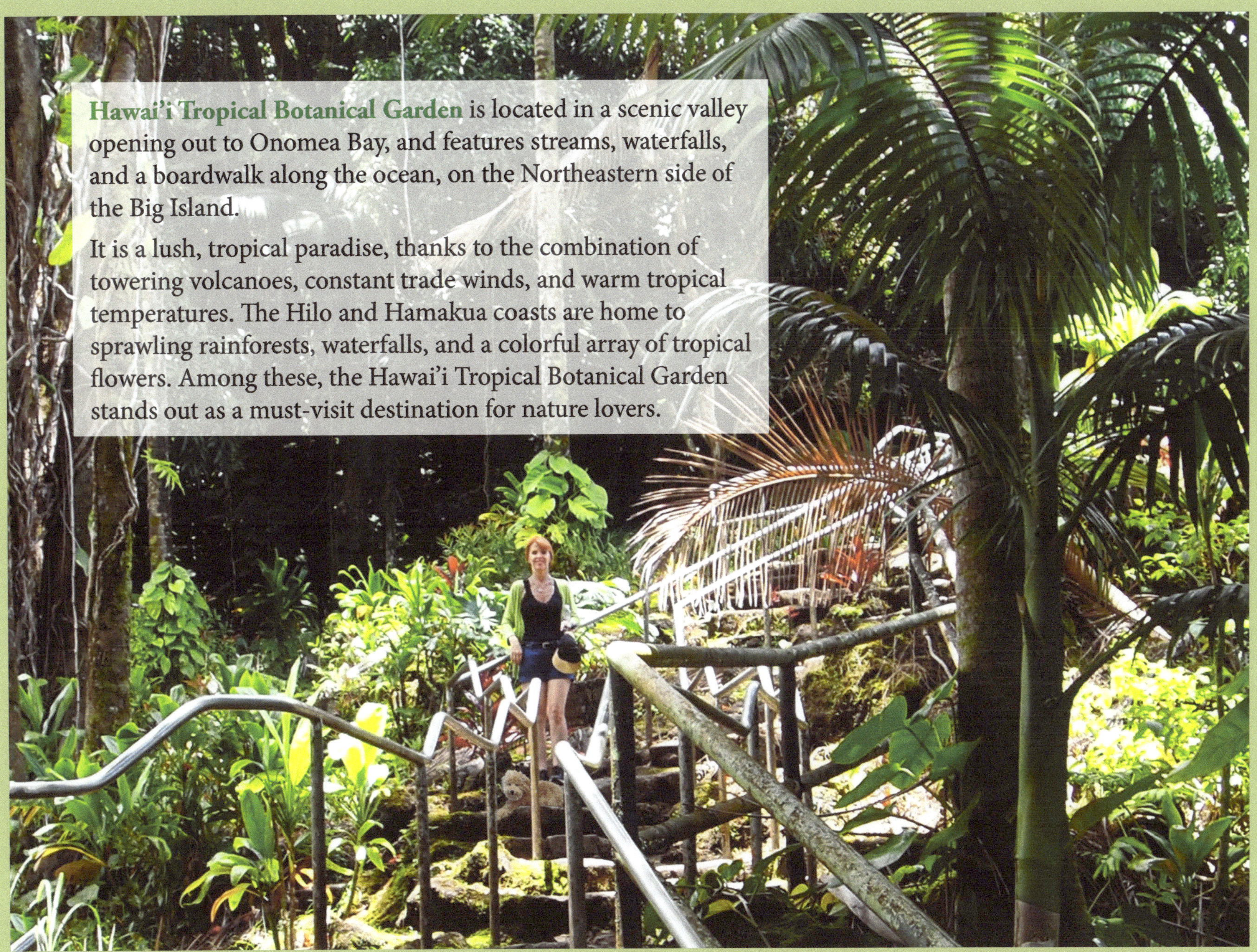

Hawai'i Tropical Botanical Garden is located in a scenic valley opening out to Onomea Bay, and features streams, waterfalls, and a boardwalk along the ocean, on the Northeastern side of the Big Island.

It is a lush, tropical paradise, thanks to the combination of towering volcanoes, constant trade winds, and warm tropical temperatures. The Hilo and Hamakua coasts are home to sprawling rainforests, waterfalls, and a colorful array of tropical flowers. Among these, the Hawai'i Tropical Botanical Garden stands out as a must-visit destination for nature lovers.

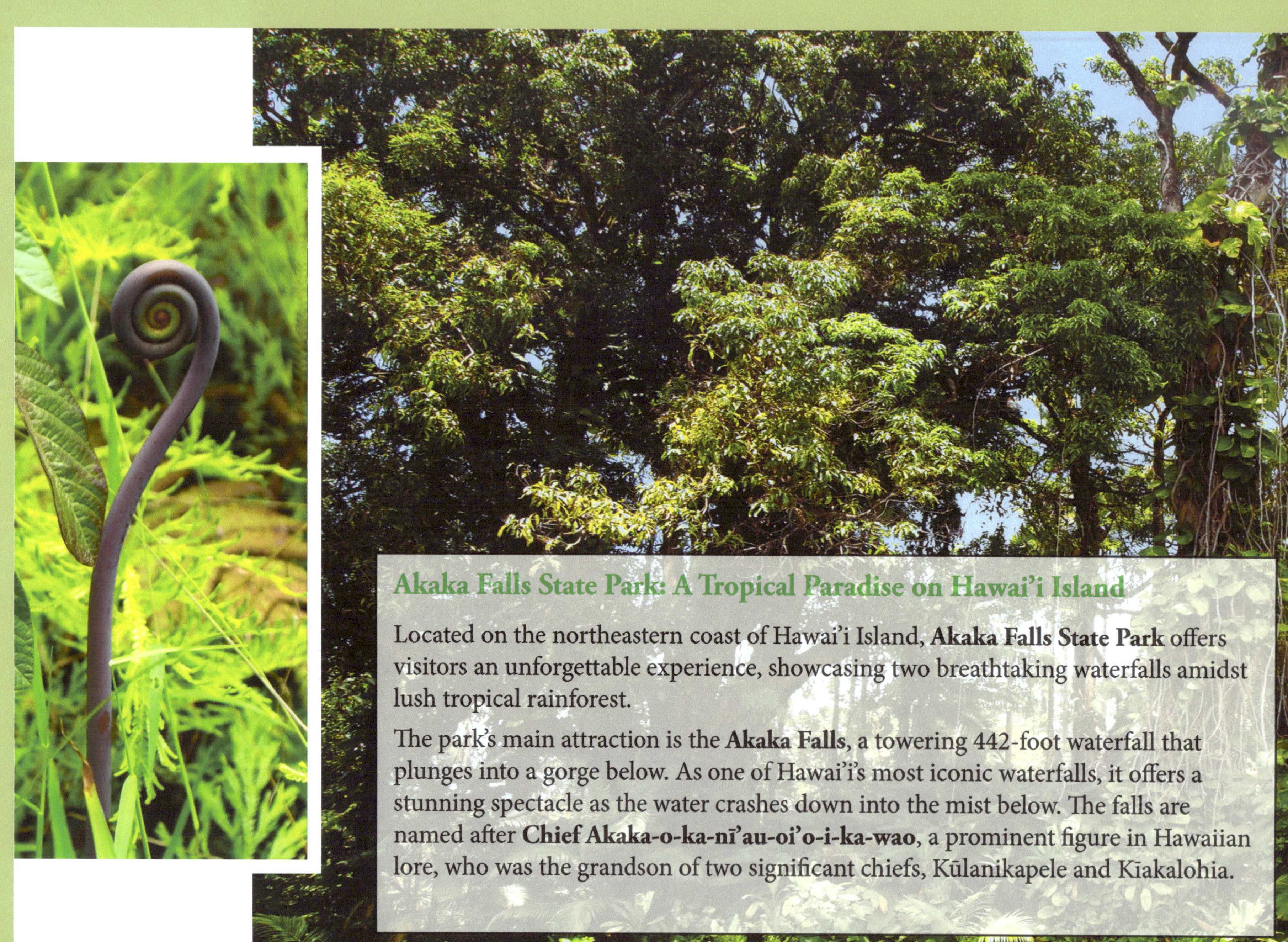

Akaka Falls State Park: A Tropical Paradise on Hawai'i Island

Located on the northeastern coast of Hawai'i Island, **Akaka Falls State Park** offers visitors an unforgettable experience, showcasing two breathtaking waterfalls amidst lush tropical rainforest.

The park's main attraction is the **Akaka Falls**, a towering 442-foot waterfall that plunges into a gorge below. As one of Hawai'i's most iconic waterfalls, it offers a stunning spectacle as the water crashes down into the mist below. The falls are named after **Chief Akaka-o-ka-nī'au-oi'o-i-ka-wao**, a prominent figure in Hawaiian lore, who was the grandson of two significant chiefs, Kūlanikapele and Kīakalohia.

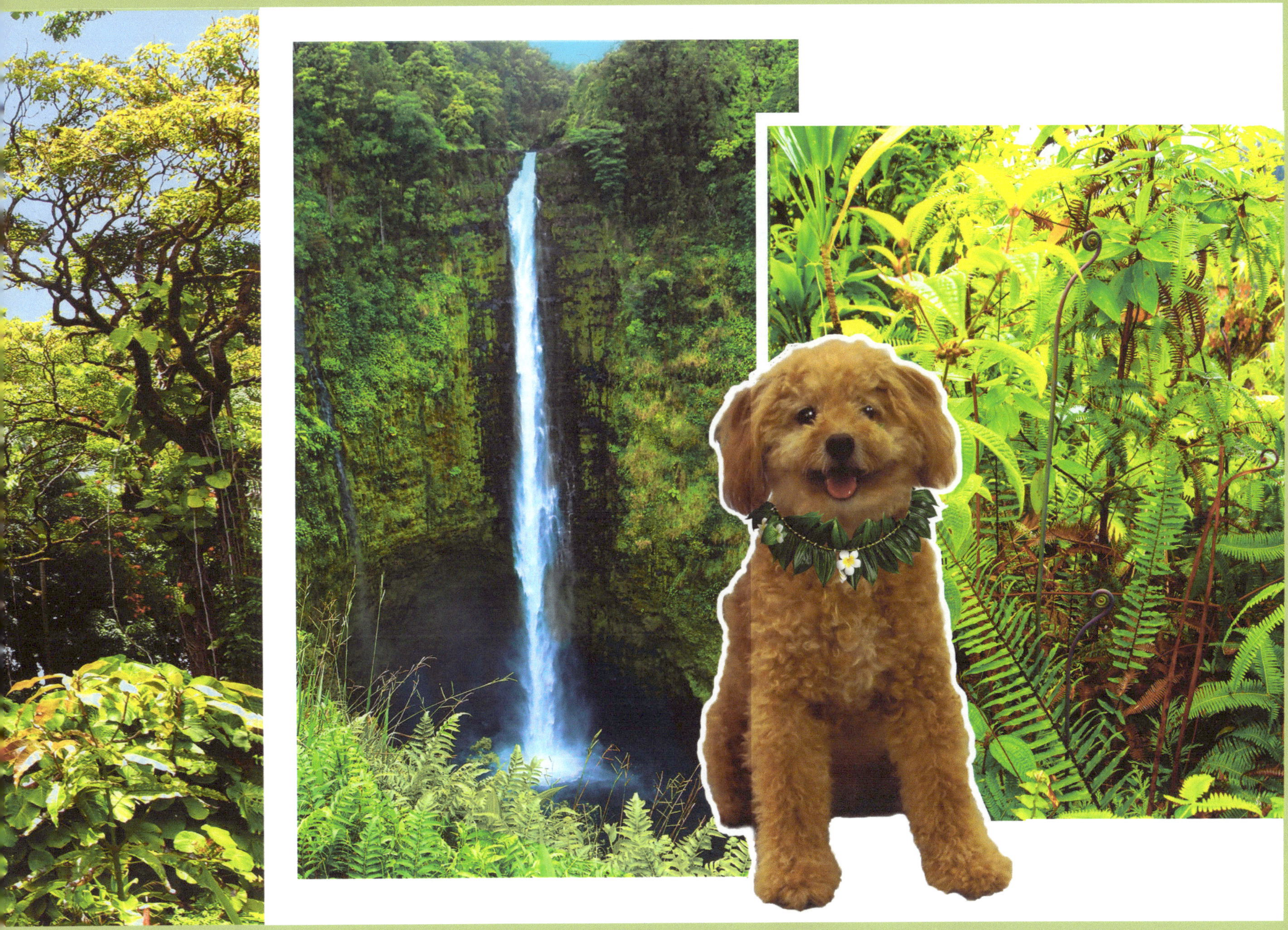

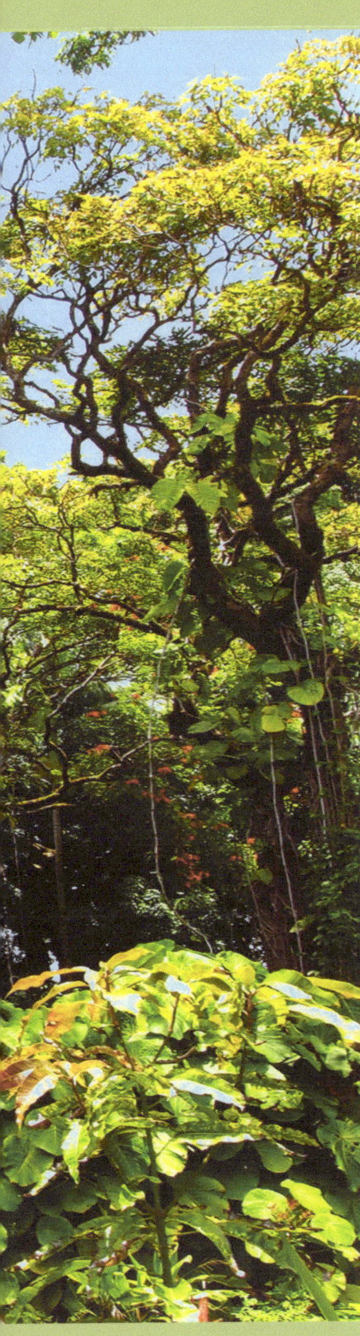

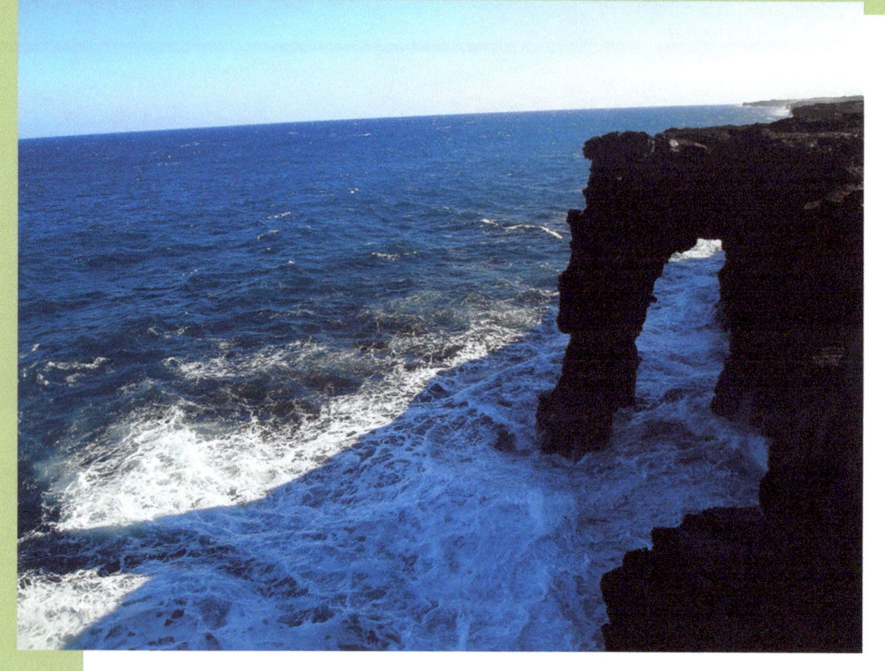

The Big Island of Hawai'i, also known as Hawai'i Island, is formed by the merging of six volcanoes: Mahukona,Kohala, Mauna Kea, Hualalai, Mauna Loa, and Kilauea. The ocean surrounding the island is the Pacific Ocean. The island itself is the result of volcanic activity over millions of years, with each volcano contributing to its unique landmass.

The ocean on the Hilo side of Hawai'i Island (also known as the Big Island) is the Pacific Ocean. Hawai'i Island and the entire Hawaiian archipelago are located in the North Pacific Ocean. Hilo is situated on the eastern side of the island and overlooks Hilo Bay, which is part of the Pacific.

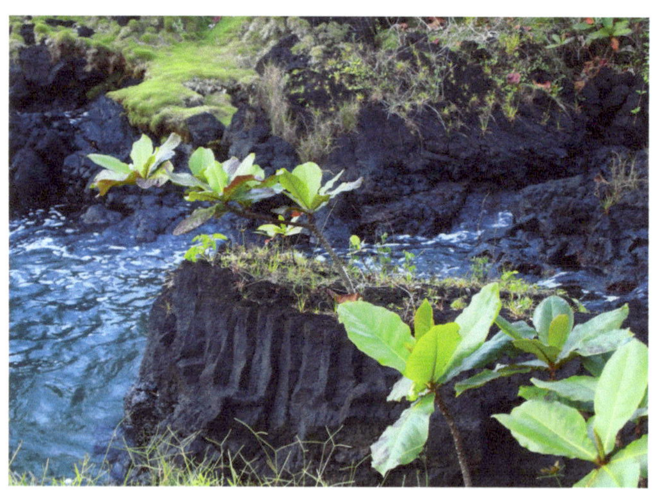

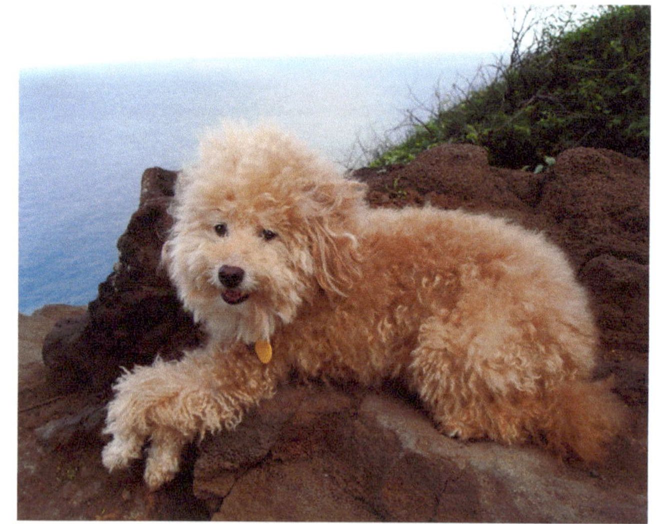

I'm lucky to call these talented artist's my friends—they share my heartfelt love and passion for Hawai'i."

—Jennifer Jordan

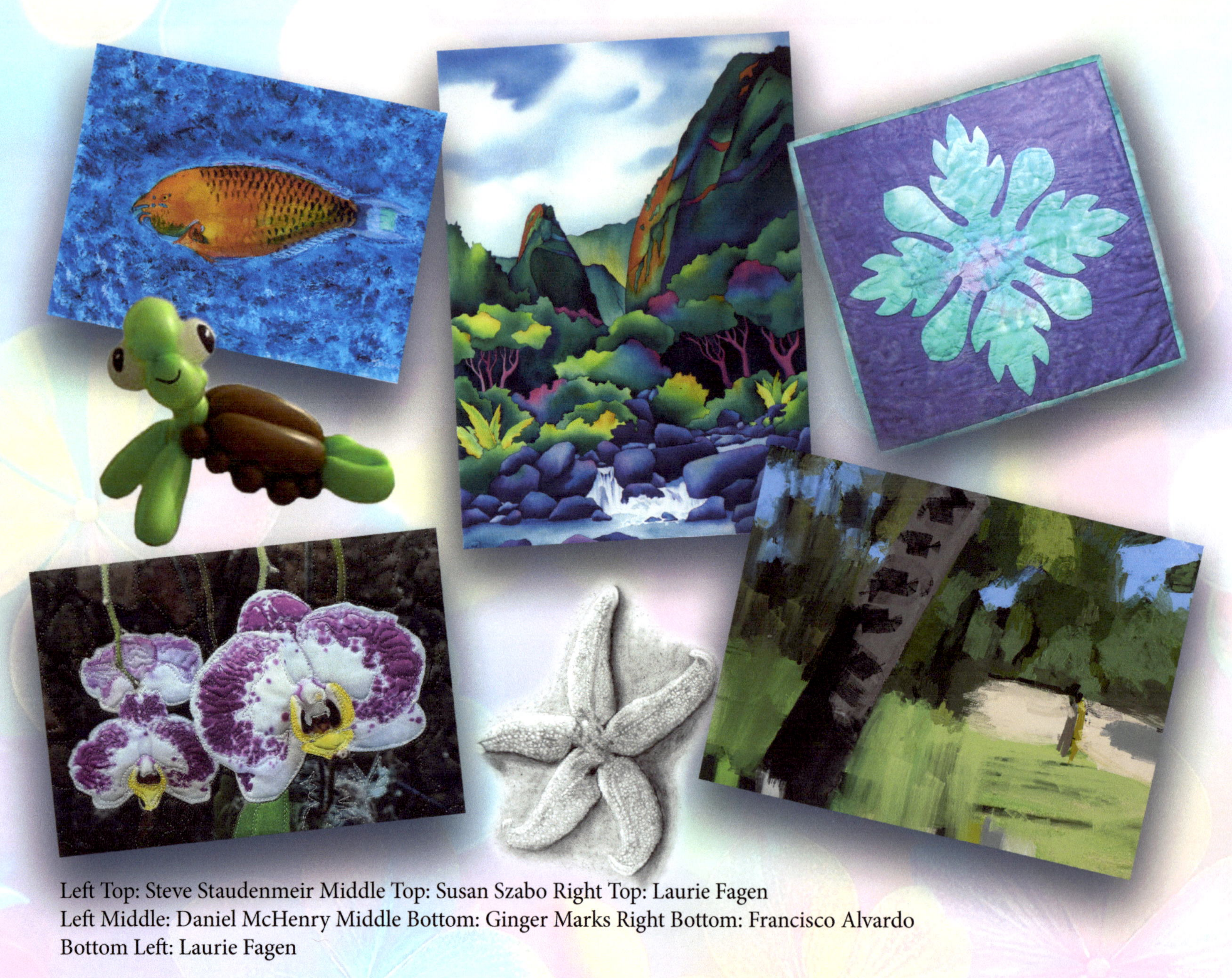

Left Top: Steve Staudenmeir Middle Top: Susan Szabo Right Top: Laurie Fagen
Left Middle: Daniel McHenry Middle Bottom: Ginger Marks Right Bottom: Francisco Alvardo
Bottom Left: Laurie Fagen

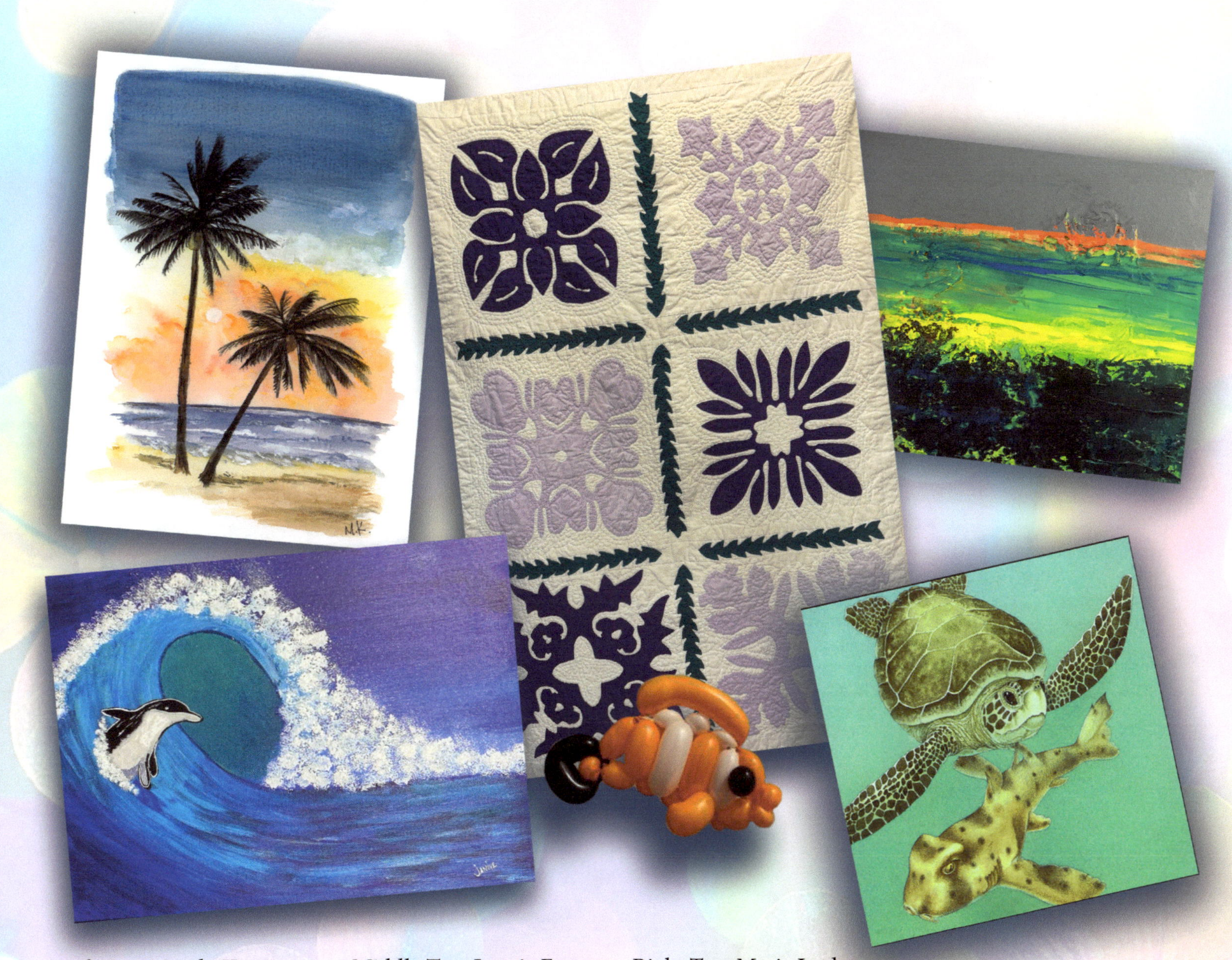

Left Top: Mandy Knapp   Middle Top: Laurie Fagen   Right Top: Marie Jordan
Left Bottom: Janine McIver   Middle Bottom: Daniel McHenry   Right Bottom: Jeannie Winston

Mandy Knapp

A self-taught artist, she is currently based in Milwaukee, Wisconsin.

Mandy was born in Taiwan and moved to the United States at the end of 2009. She studied Chinese music and had never taken any painting classes.

At the end of 2019, she discovered her passion for painting. As a self-taught artist, her curiosity drove her to experiment with different painting media and themes. Watercolor and acrylic are her most often used media. Limited drawing and language skills did not stop her.

Her paintings have been exhibited in the local hotel and several regional shows. She will continue to create and would love to share her art with more people.

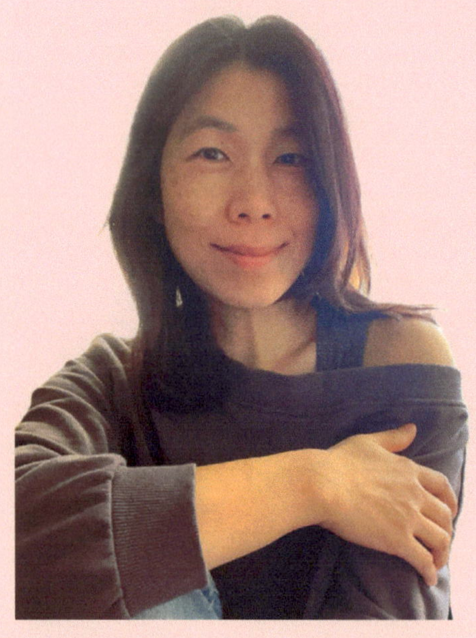

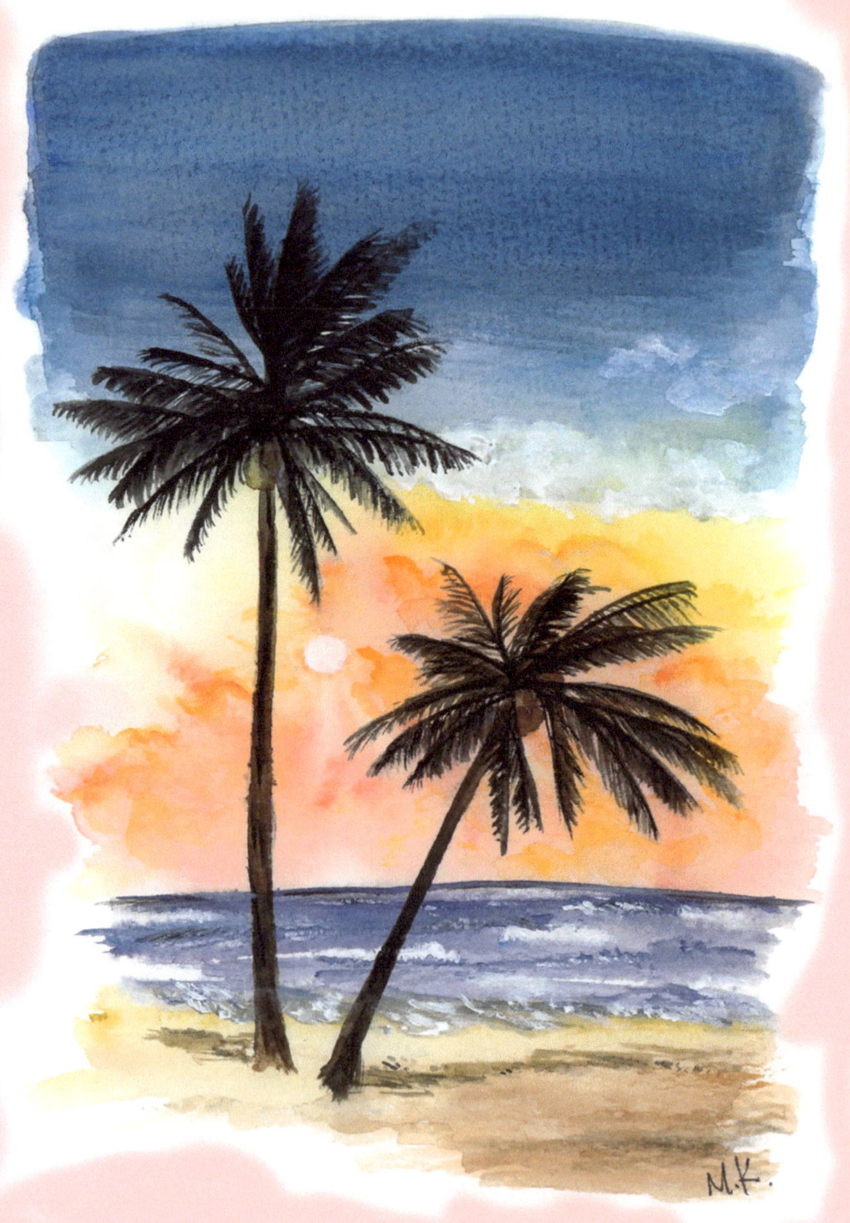

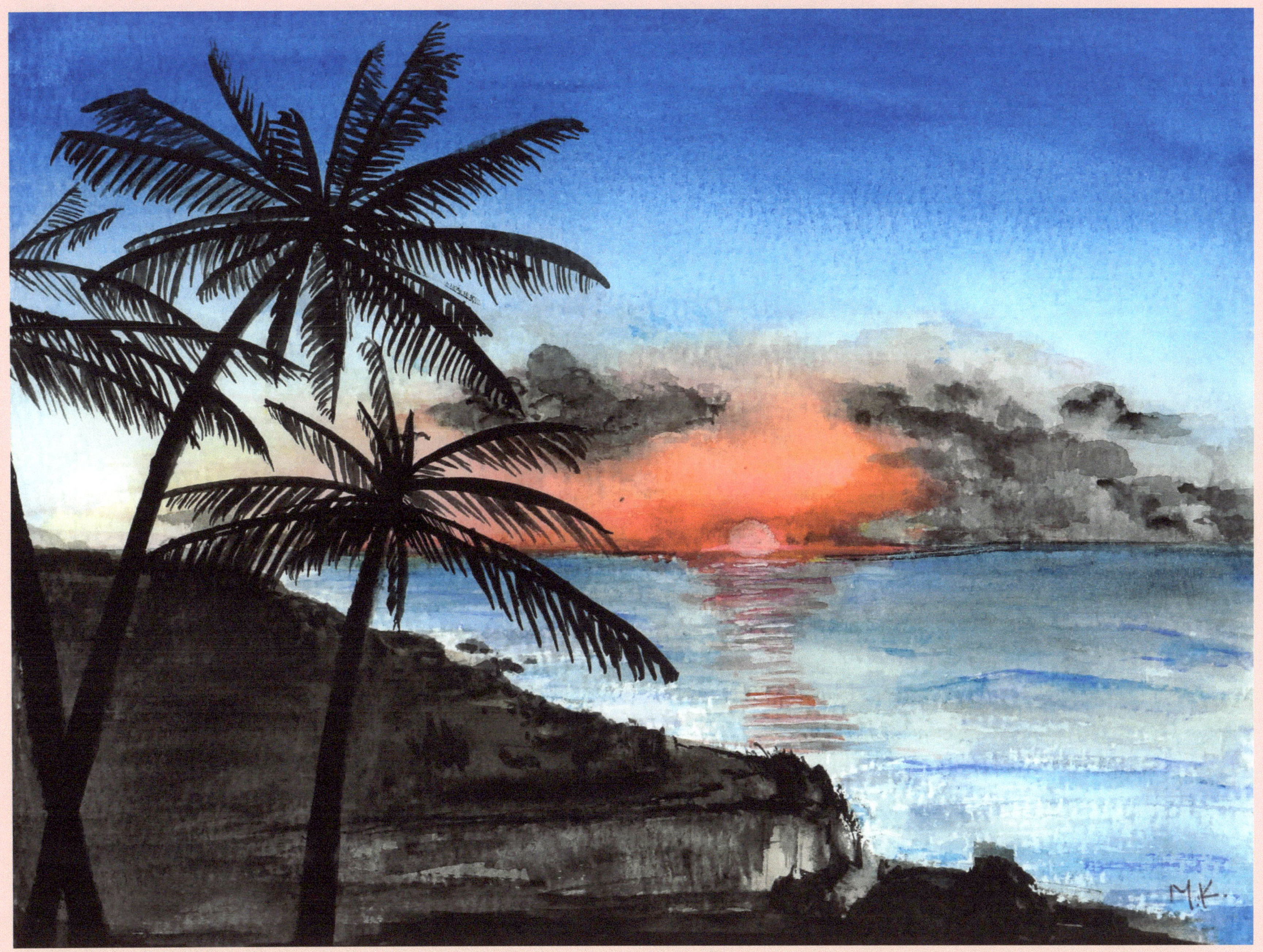

SUSAN SZABO

Susan Szabo's skilled use of colorful hues in elegant compositions has become her trademark as an artist. She is renowned for her ability to capture the essence of Hawai'i's nature and people in a personal palette of colors that expresses the spirit of her subjects. She is inspired by the power of the land, the ocean and all of nature, as well as the energy of Hawai'i's people.

She has been a featured artist for Hawaiian Airlines and Aloha Airlines, and she was the cover artist for Hawai'i's 1998/1999 phone directories. She has a highly enthusiastic following, with her paintings and fine art prints included in collections throughout the United States, Canada, Asia, Australia and Europe.

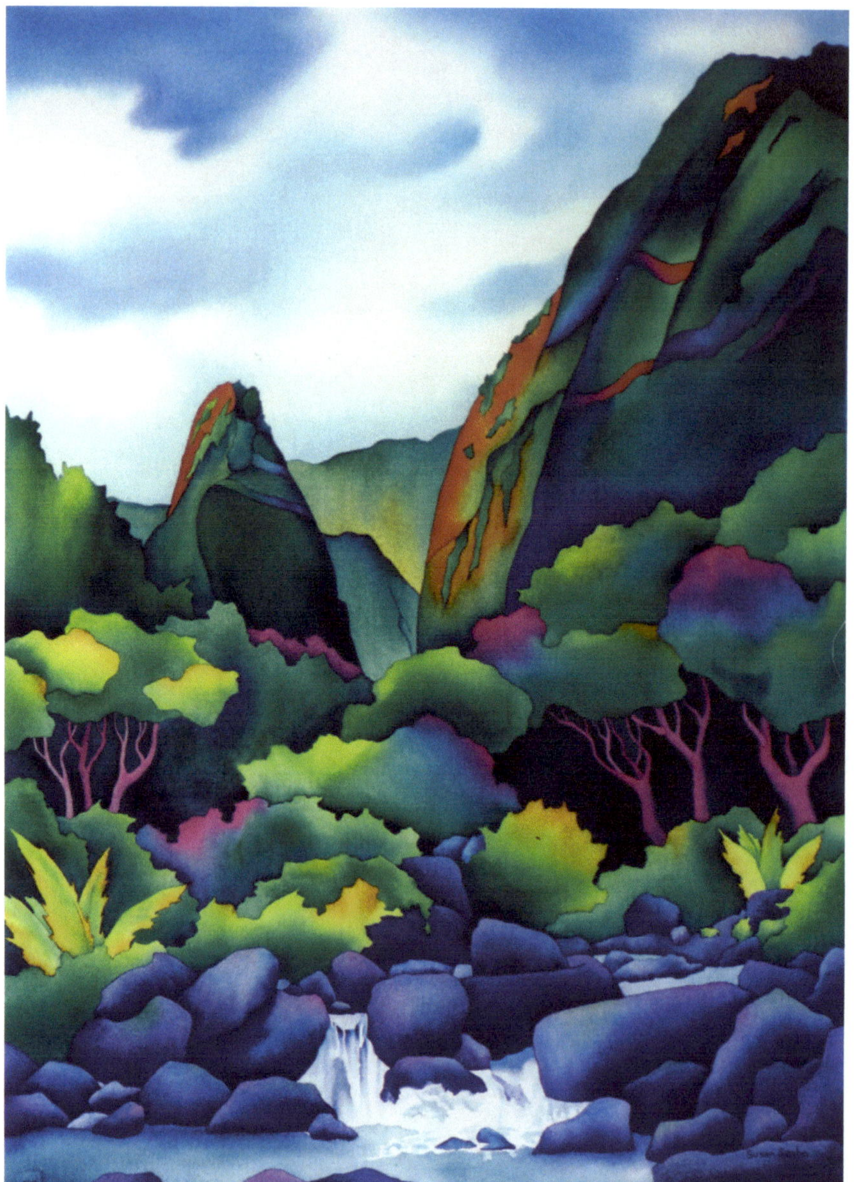

"'Īao Needle" © Susan Szabo.

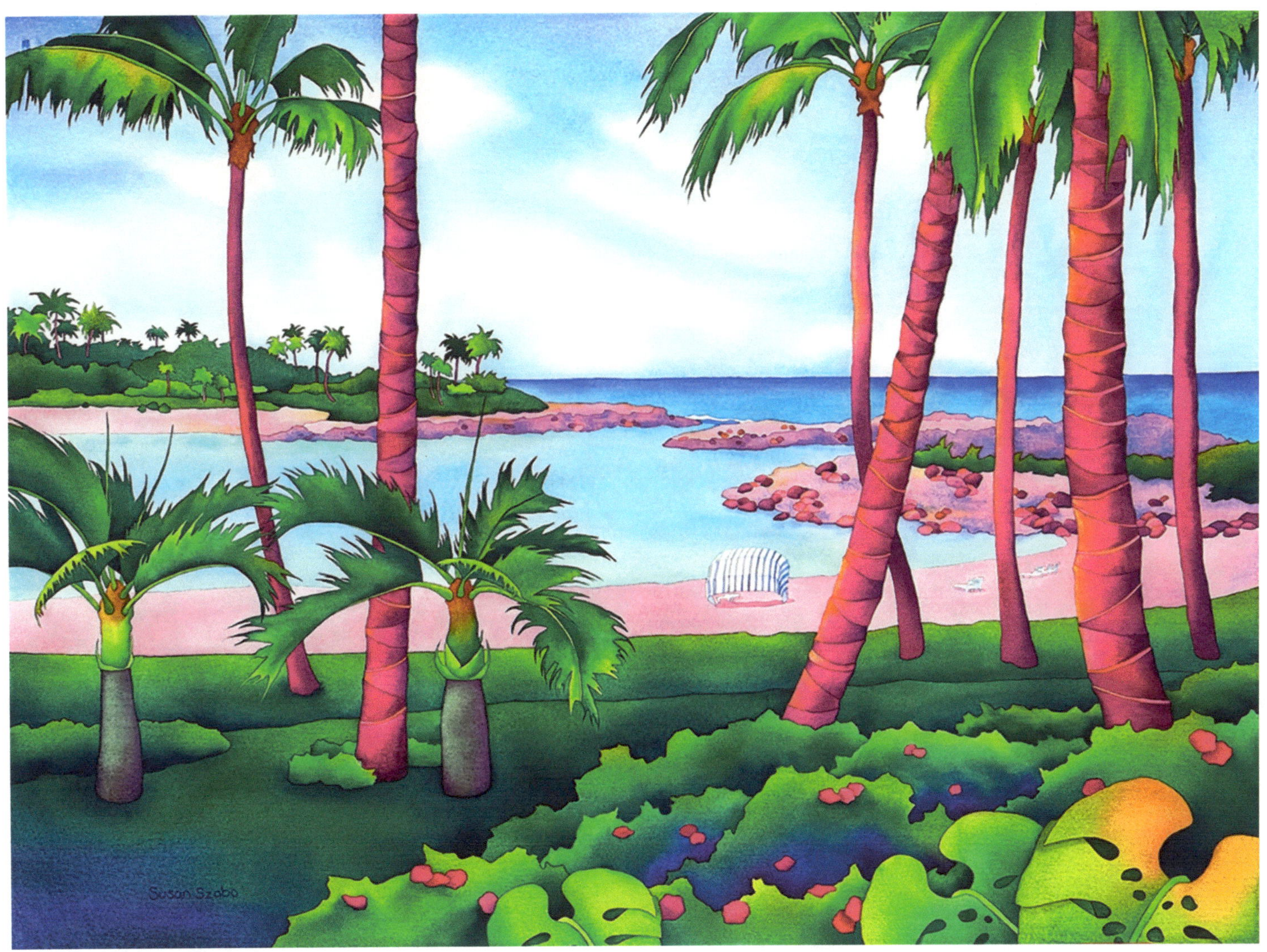

"Koolina Morning" © Susan Szabo

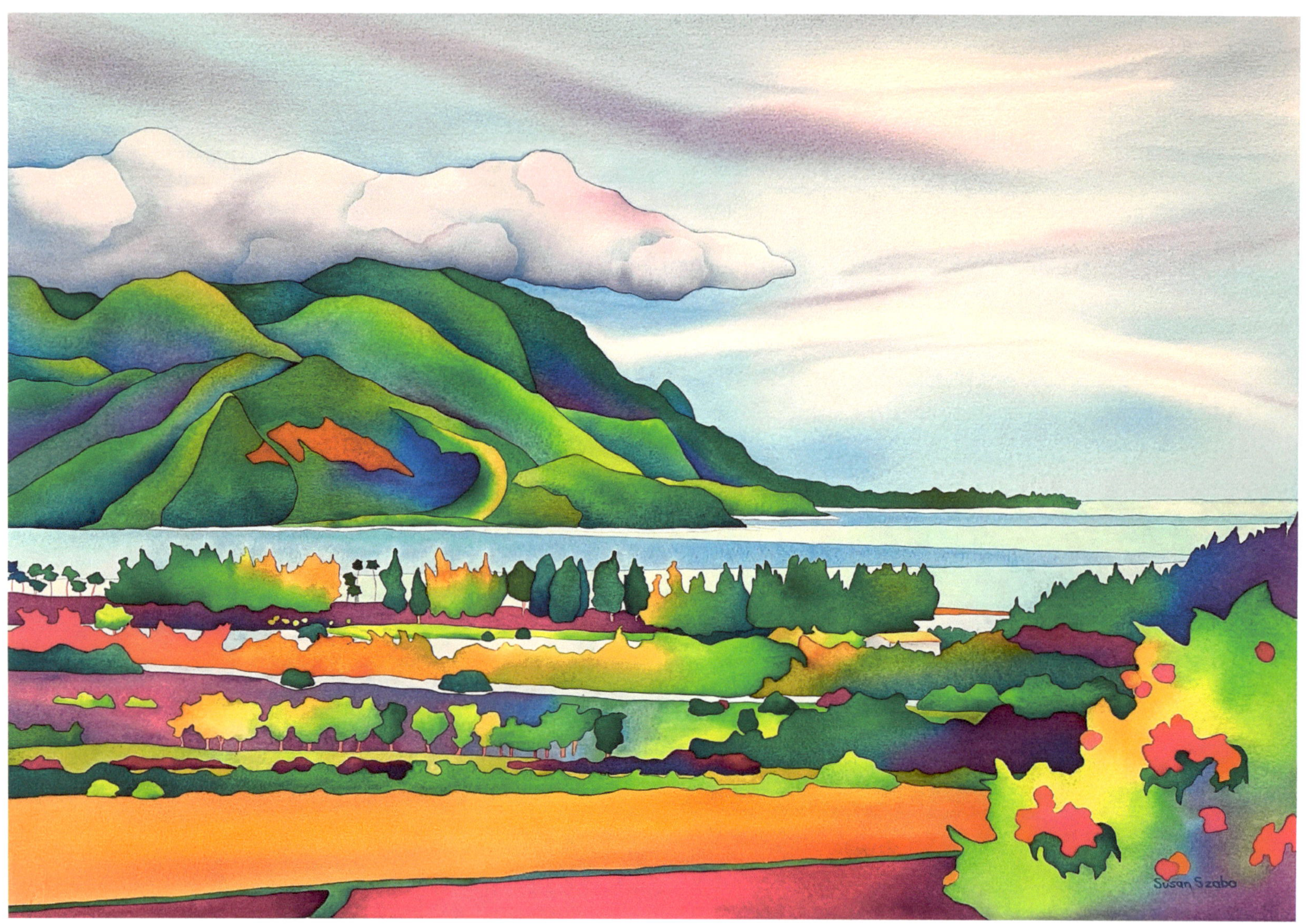

"Hanalei Bay" © Susan Szabo

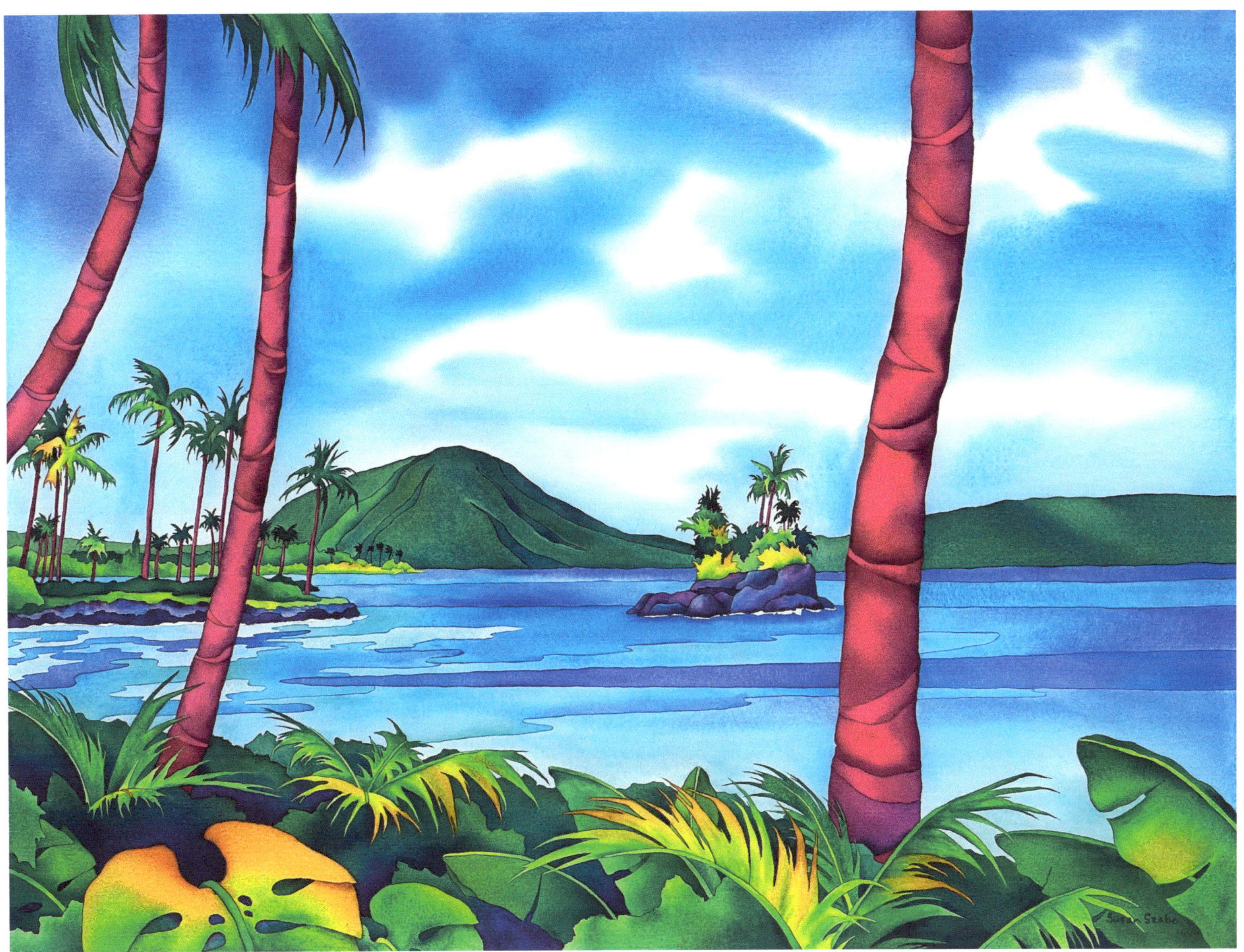

"Muanalua Bay" © Susan Szabo

Francisco Alvarado PAKO

A Journey Through Color and Abstraction

Francisco Alvarado PAKO is a versatile and dynamic artist whose work seamlessly bridges traditional and digital mediums. Born in Ecuador, Alvarado's formative years were shaped by his travels through the lush tropical forests and the Amazon jungle. These vivid experiences continue to inspire his colorful, layered compositions, which capture the essence of nature and human connection.

Calling himself an "outsider artist," Alvarado embraces a wide range of materials, from paper and canvas to wood, metal, cardboard, and found objects. At the same time, he leverages modern technology, crafting digital art on his iPad with the same improvisational spirit that defines his physical works. His radiant palettes and joyful abstractions reflect a life lived in pursuit of exploration and curiosity.

Balancing traditional and digital techniques, Alvarado's process often begins with sketches and color studies on his iPad, which he then translates into large-scale canvas paintings. While he values the precision and efficiency of digital tools, he finds unparalleled satisfaction in the tactile experience of working with physical materials.

Although Alvarado's artistic range includes figurative pieces, his true passion lies in abstraction. "For me, abstract work is like taking a walk through a colorful, fantastical landscape," he explains. His creations invite viewers to step into an imaginative world, where vibrant colors, intricate textures, and dynamic forms celebrate the beauty and energy of life.

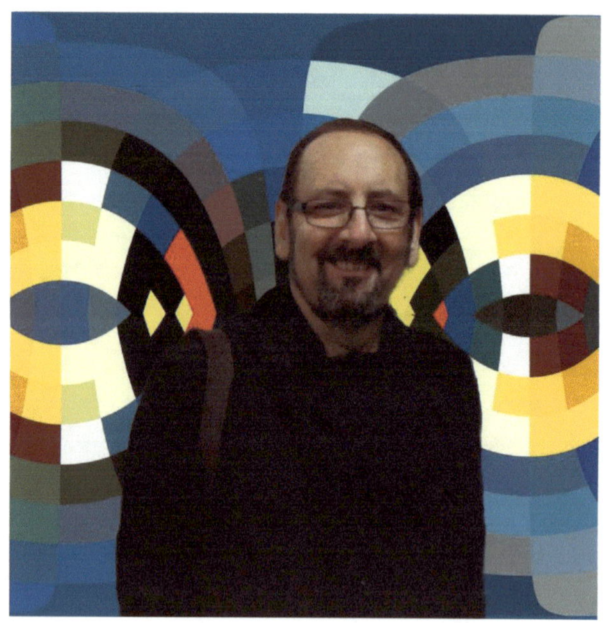

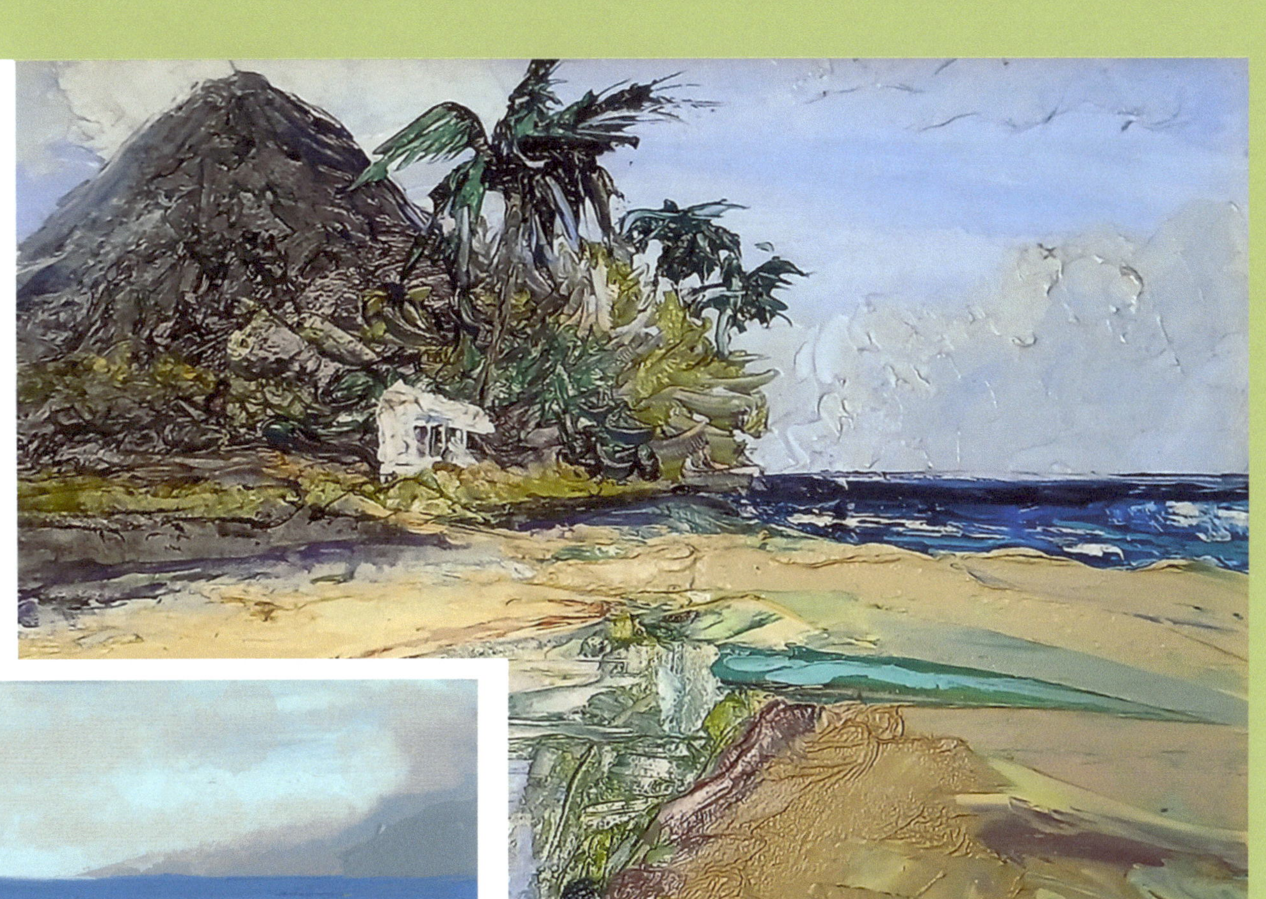

Left: "Open Space—Fly Maui" © Francisco Alvarado PAKO.
Top: "Haena Acrylic on Canvas (11x14)" © Francisco Alvarado PAKO.

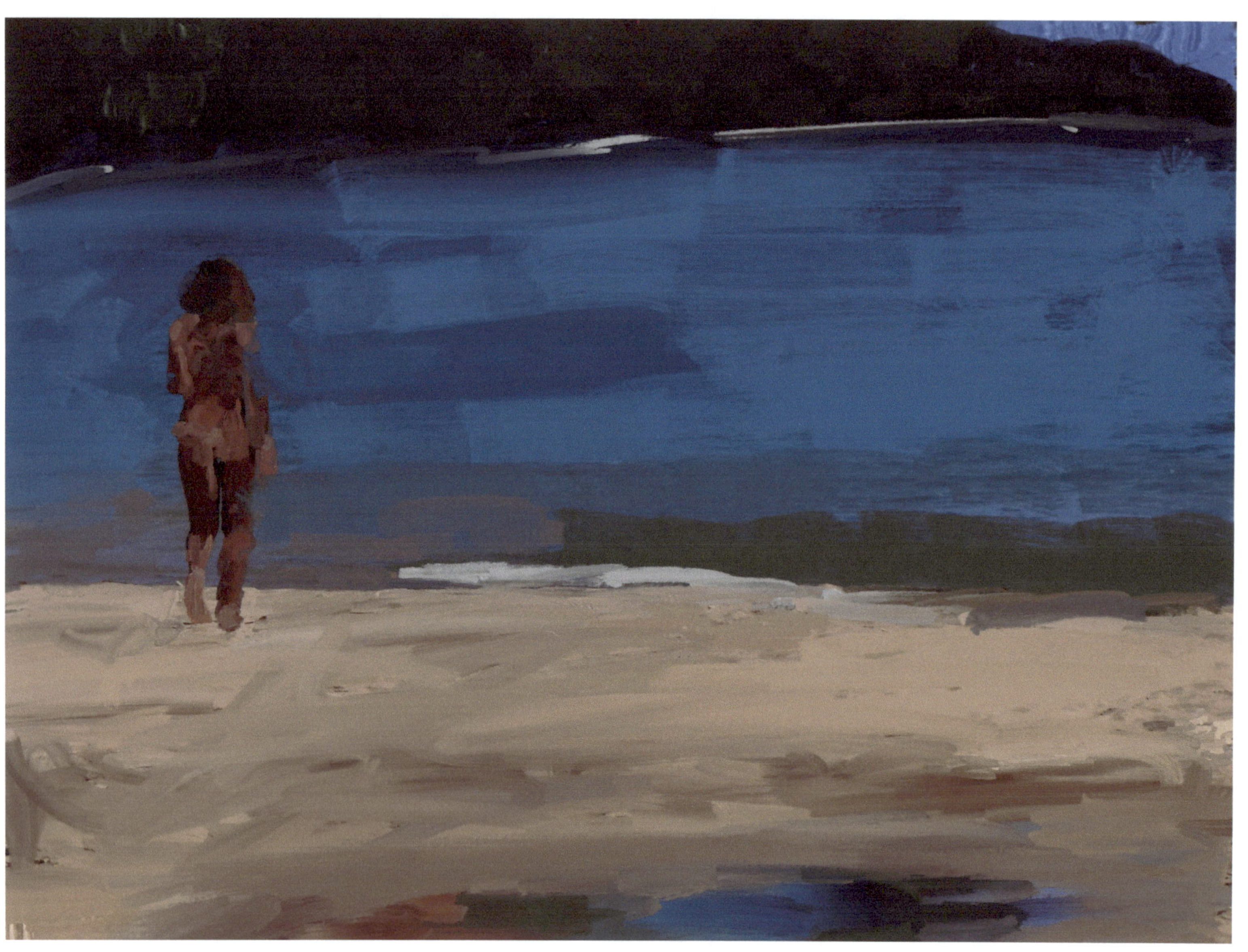

"Swimmer Kalapaki Beach, Digital Art" © Francisco Alvarado PAKO.

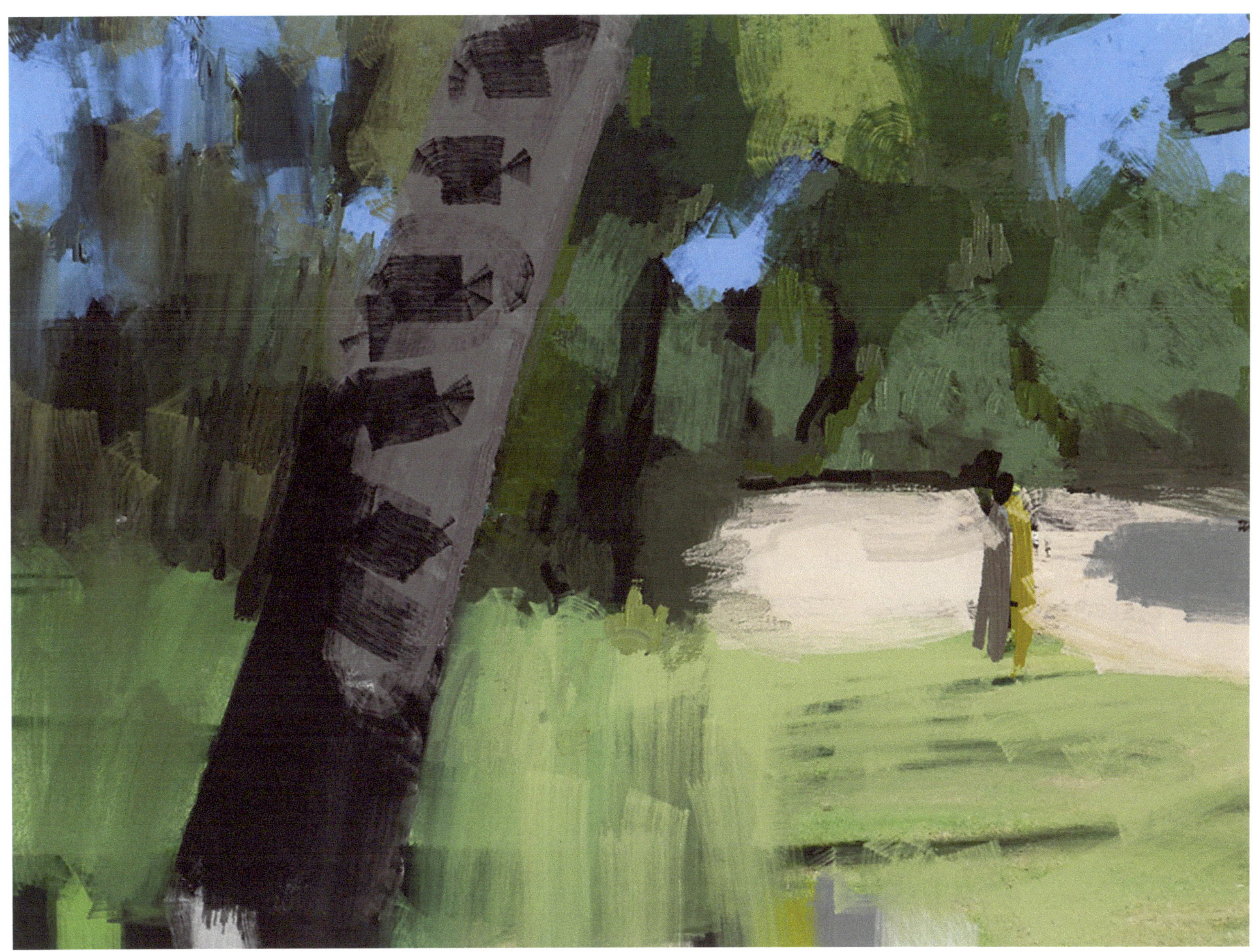

"Shade Spot Kalapaki Beach, Digital Art" © Francisco Alvarado PAKO.

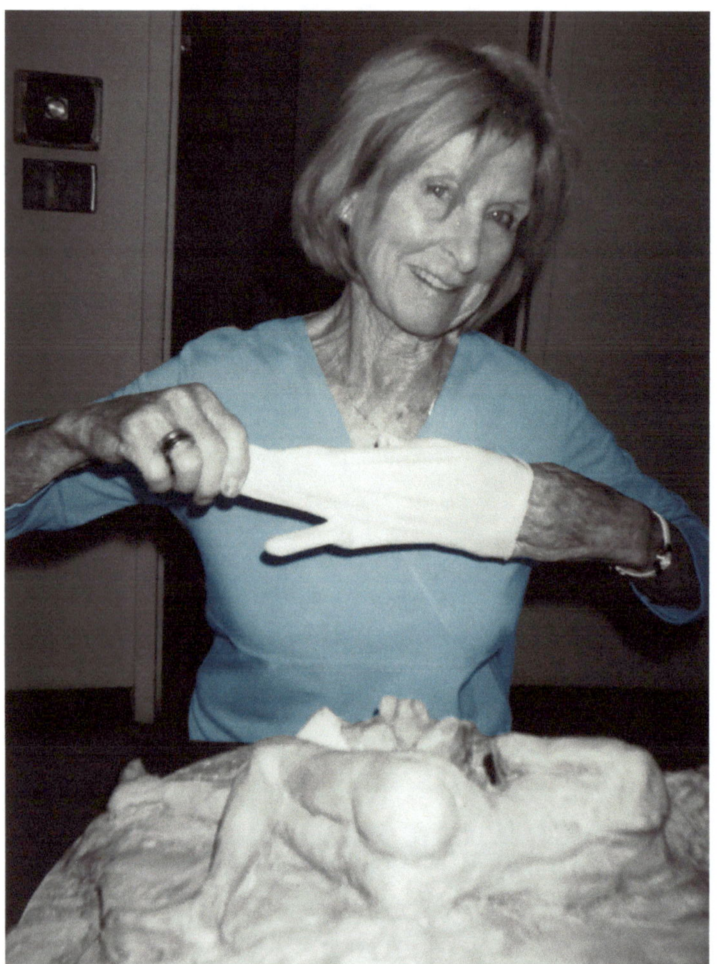

Marie Jordan was the esteemed Art Gallery Director for *The Designing Women,* an interior design studio located in La Cañada Flintridge, California. With a passion for both art and design, Marie played a key role in curating and showcasing the works of talented artists at the gallery, creating a unique space where art and interior design merged beautifully.

Marie had the privilege of traveling to meet many of the artists featured at *The Designing Women* gallery, building strong relationships and a deep appreciation for the creative process. Marie also had the opportunity to feature art in conjunction with The Pasadena Tour of Homes, an event that highlighted the intersection of art and interior design, where the gallery's pieces were showcased in stunning local homes.

In addition to her work as a gallery director, Marie was dedicated to her own artistic growth. She took classes at both Art Center College of Design and the Brand Library in Glendale, where she developed her skills in painting and sculpture. This personal passion for art informed her work at the gallery, giving her a deeper understanding of the artists she worked with and the pieces she showcased.

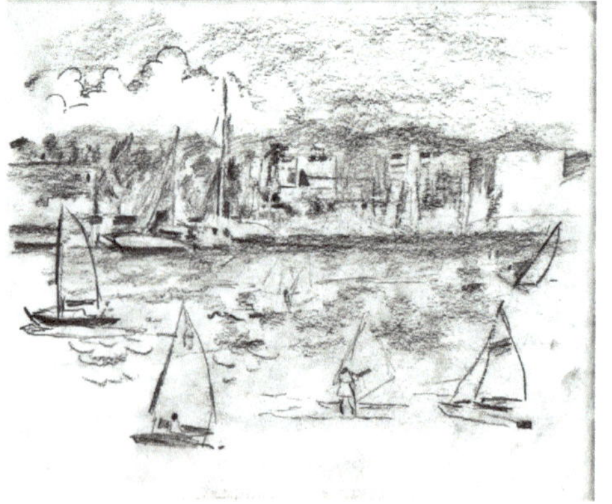

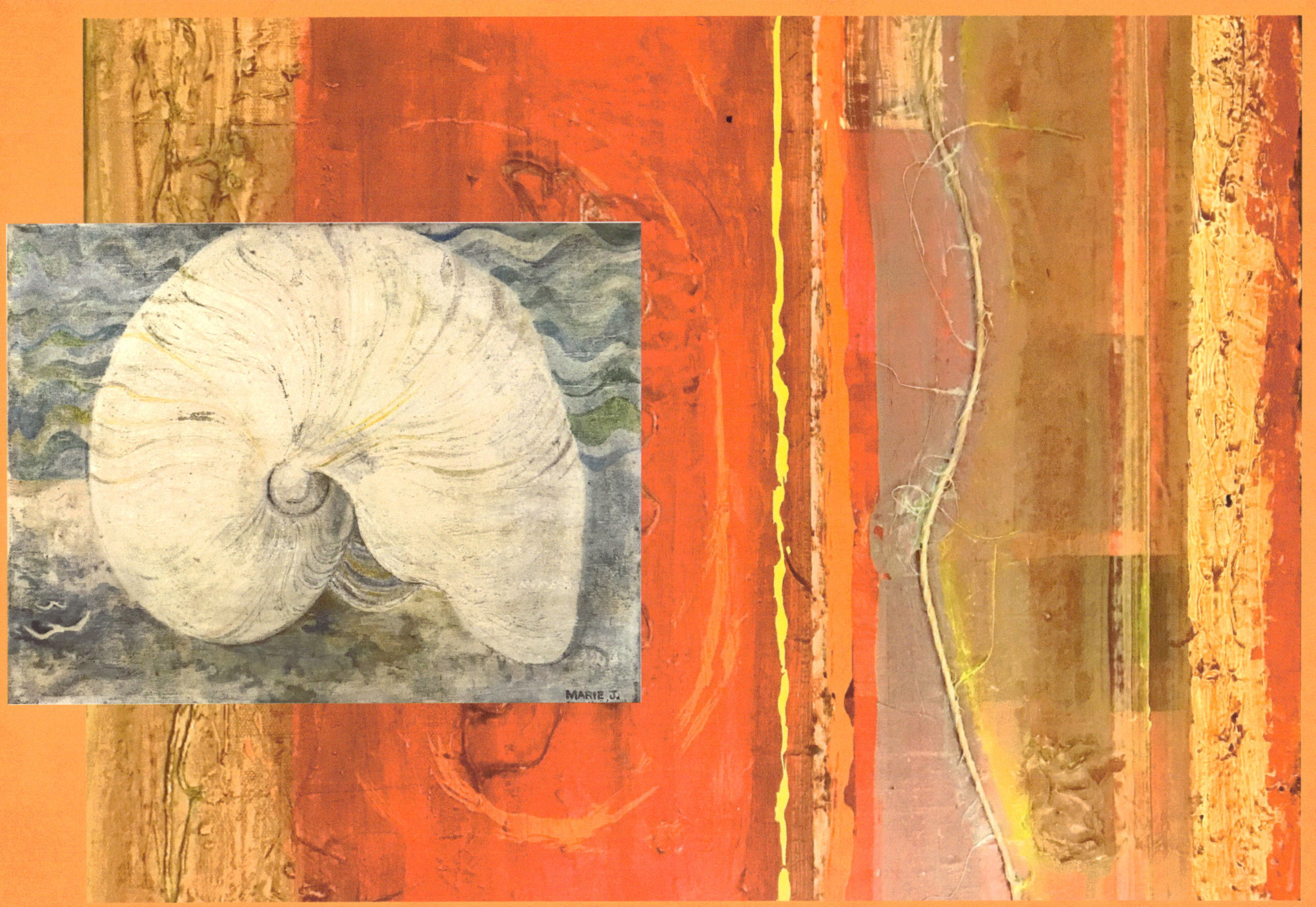

MARIE J.

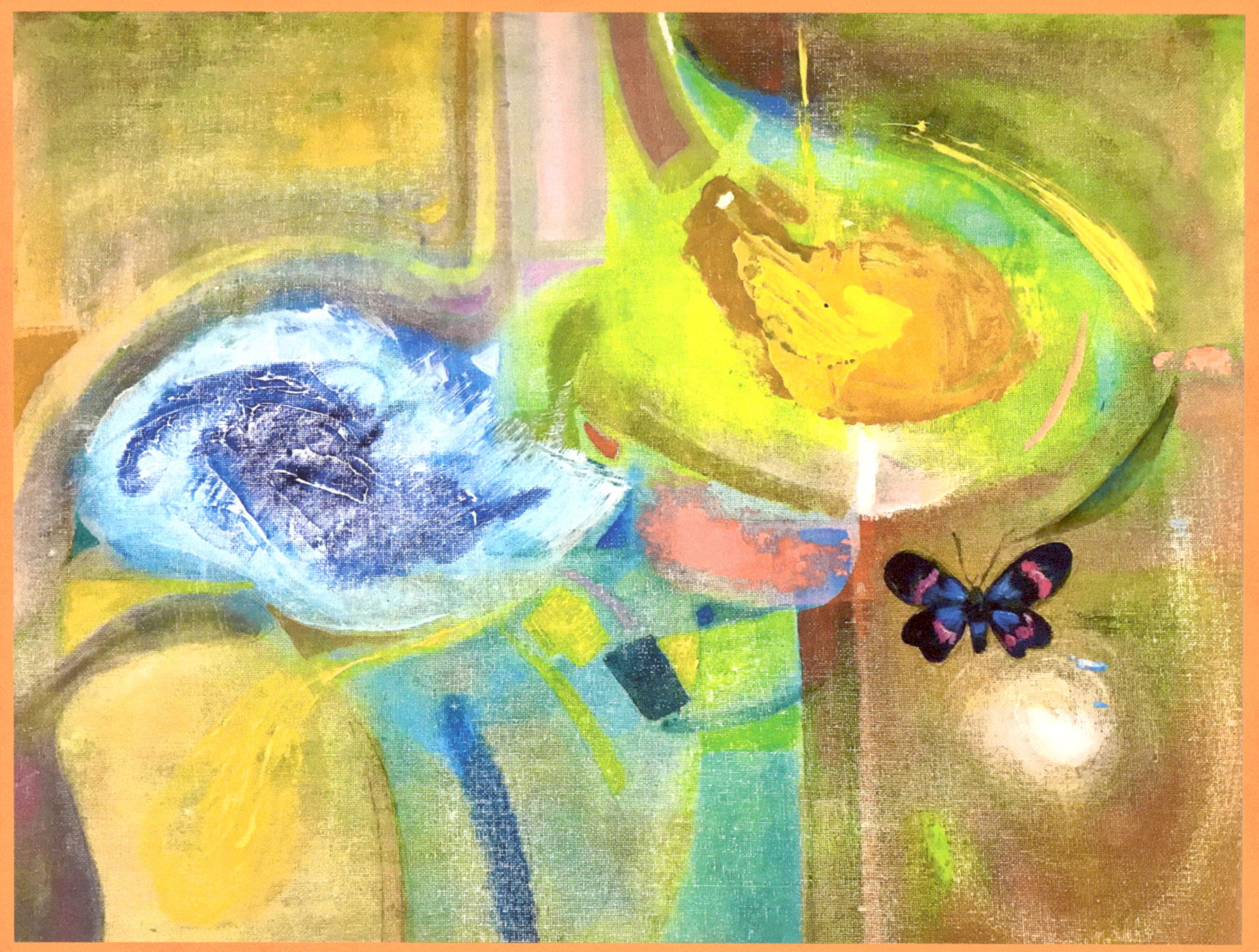

Laurie Fagen

Experimenting with a wide variety of fiber art techniques and designs, Laurie Fagen transfers original photos and stitches with metallic threads for a highly contemporary feel … takes bright fabrics and creates whimsy and fun … or paints whole cloth for a soft, elegant design.

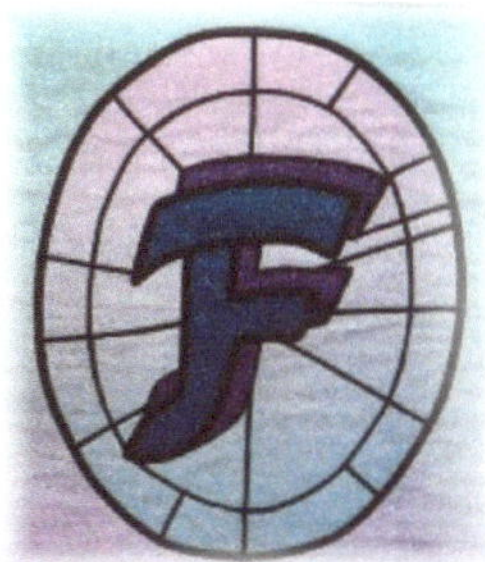

Fagen also creates fine silver jewelry and is certified as a Level 1 instructor in Art Clay. In addition, she creates one-of-a-kind polymer clay jewelry and often incorporates polymer into her fiber work, by custom designing beads and other surface design embellishments. Fagen is also working in fiber, clay and epoxy-sculpt resin clay for sculptures.

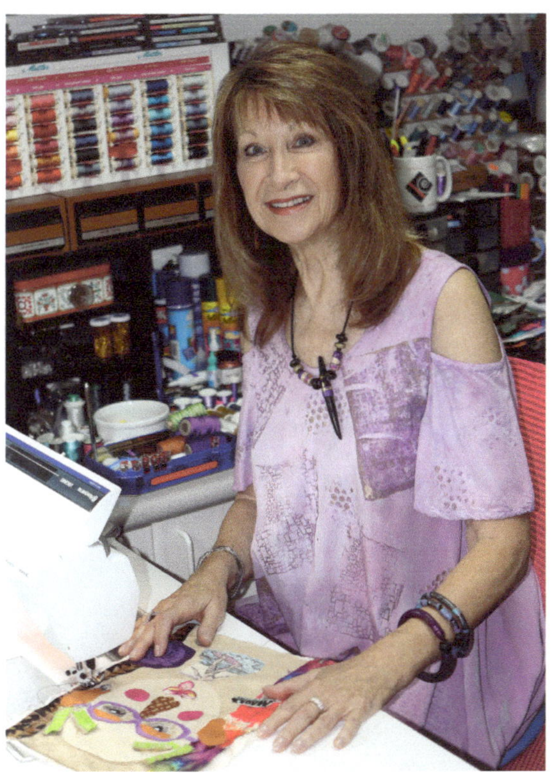

She's shown her work in galleries and shops including in Ireland, Arizona, Washington, D.C., Illinois, Nevada, North Carolina and Iowa, and welcomes commissions that are highly personalized in nature to the recipient.

"I enjoy experimenting with a wide variety of fiber art techniques and designs for original, one-of-a-kind wall art. I also love to create one-of-a-kind polymer clay jewelry, from statement pieces to bling rings and more.

Her work can be seen at www.FagenDesigns.com,

Instagram at https://www.instagram.com/lauriefagen/

Facebook at https://www.facebook.com/LaurieFagen/

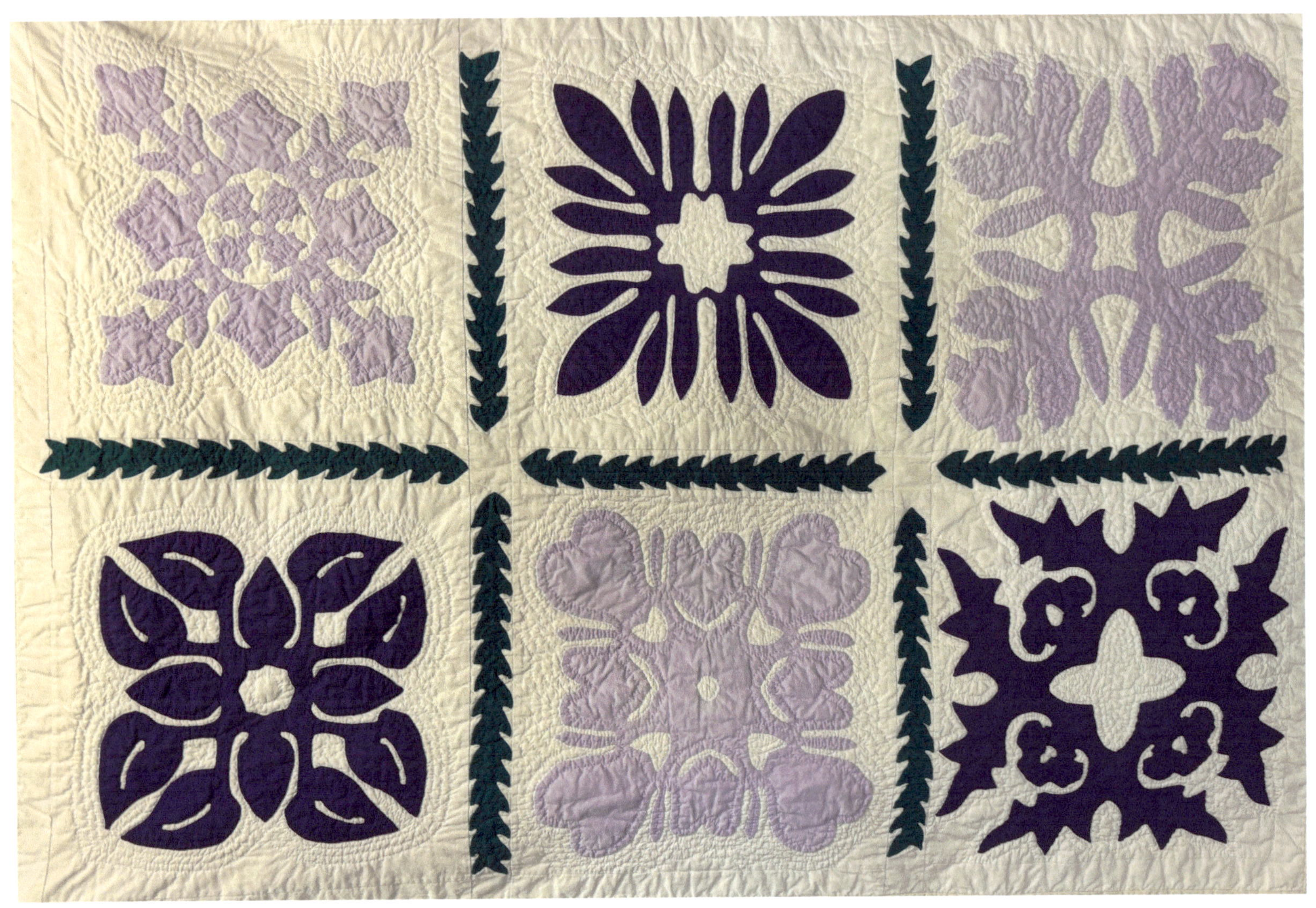

62

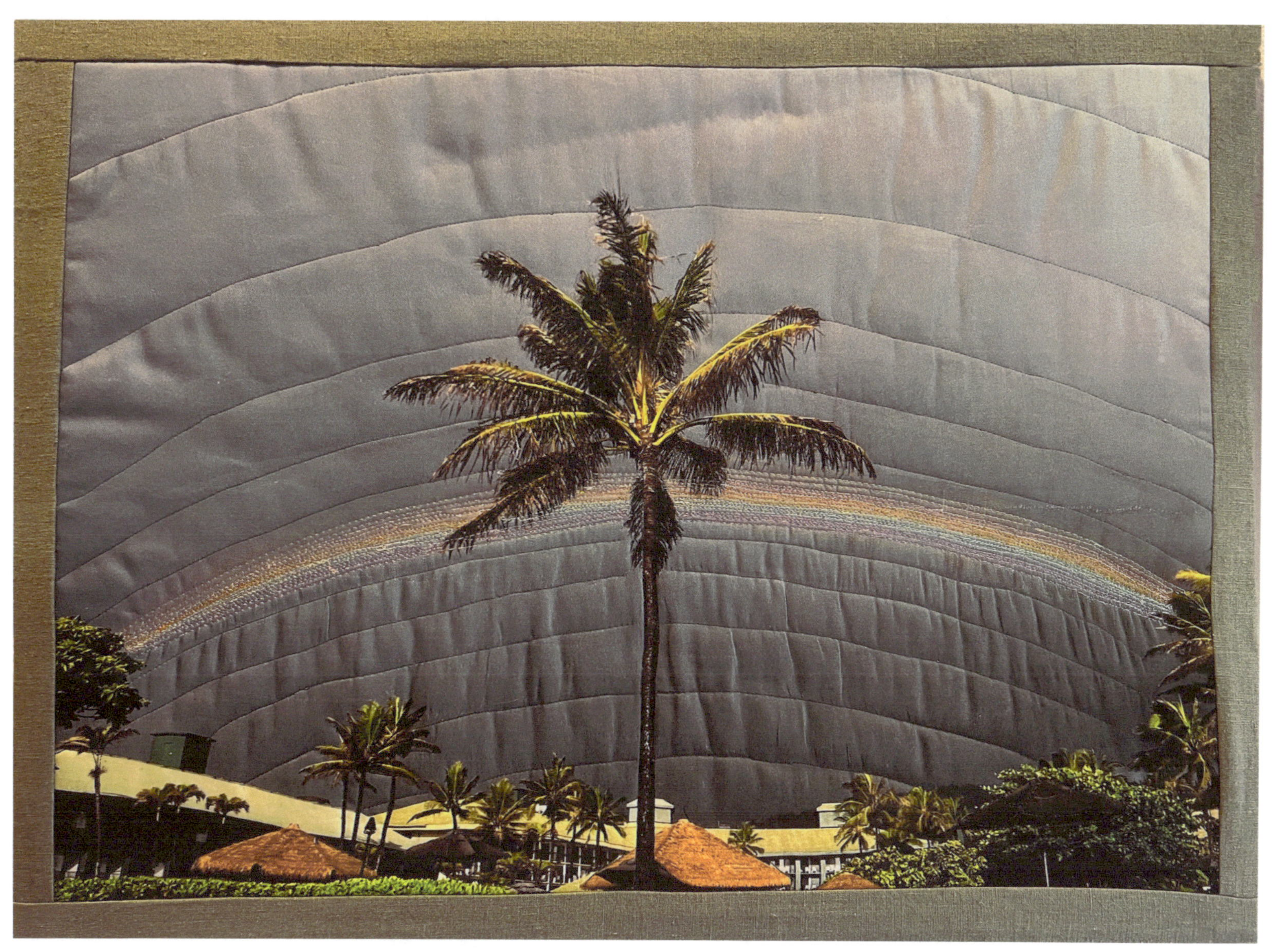

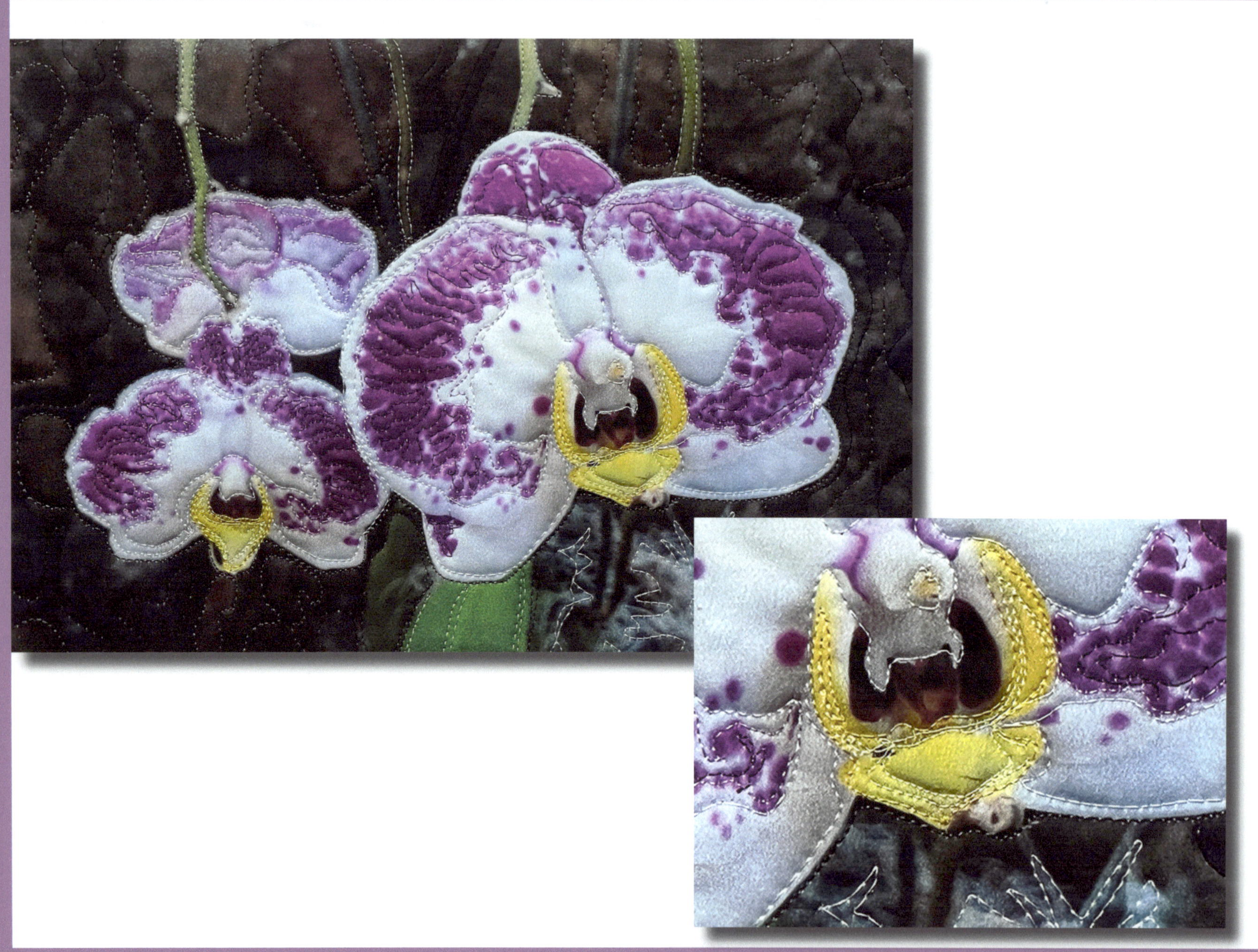

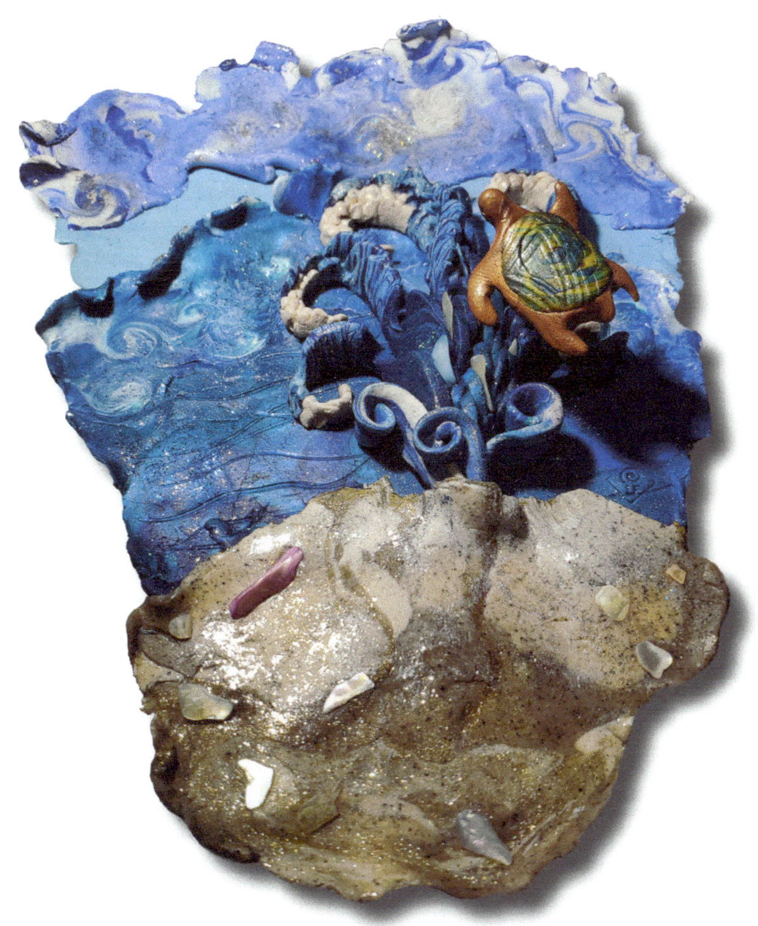

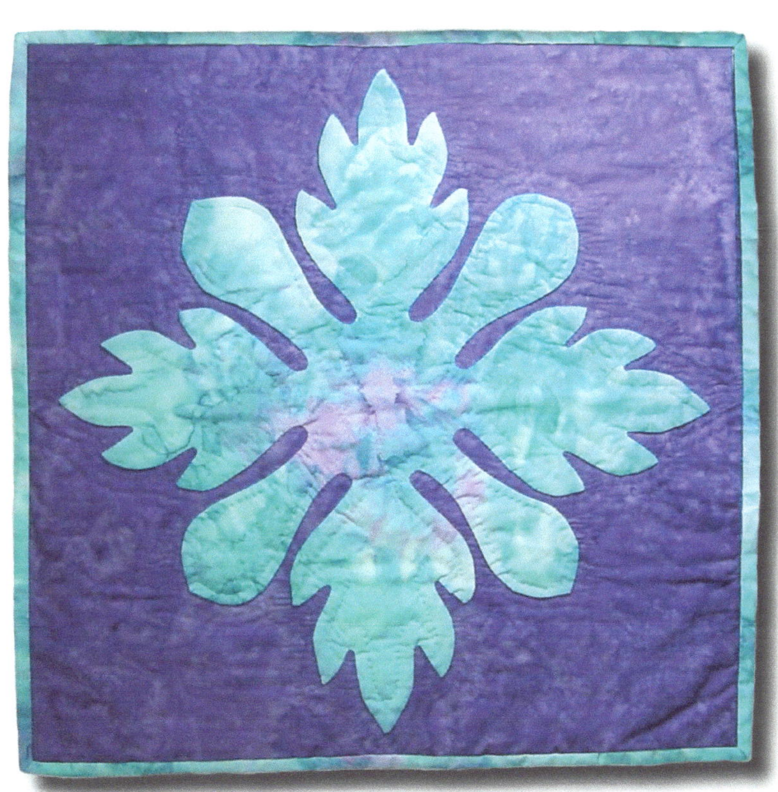

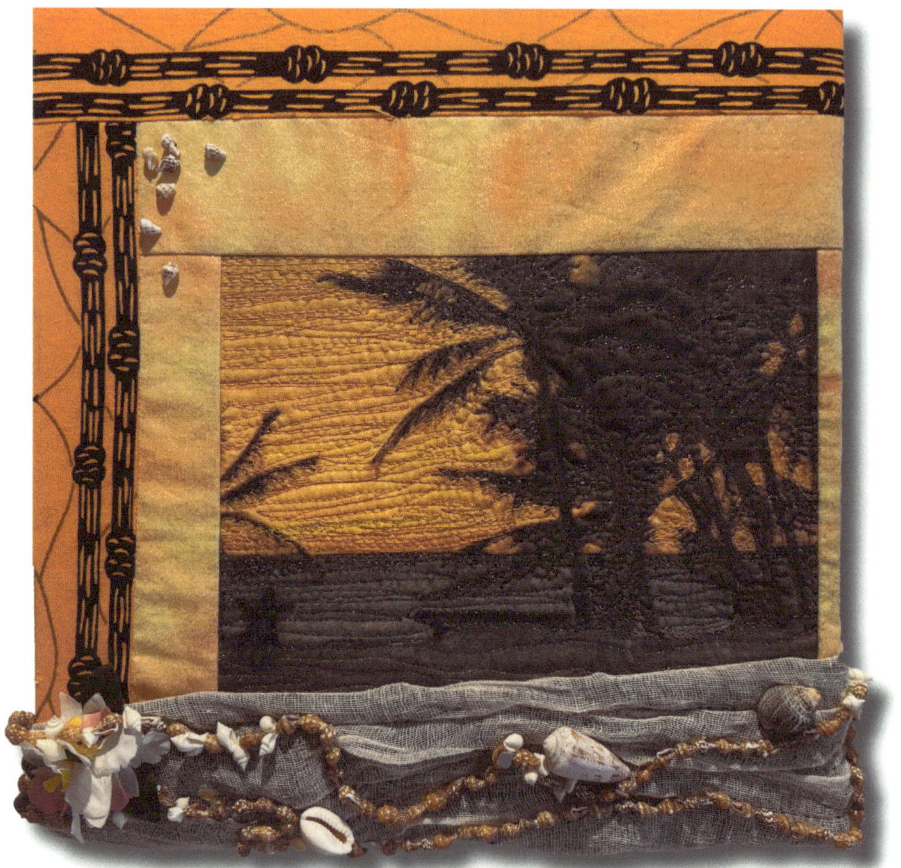

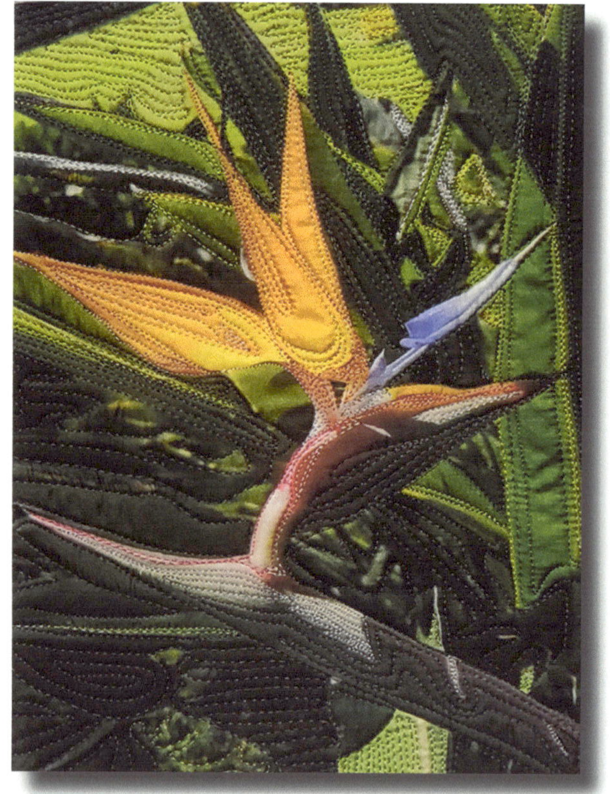

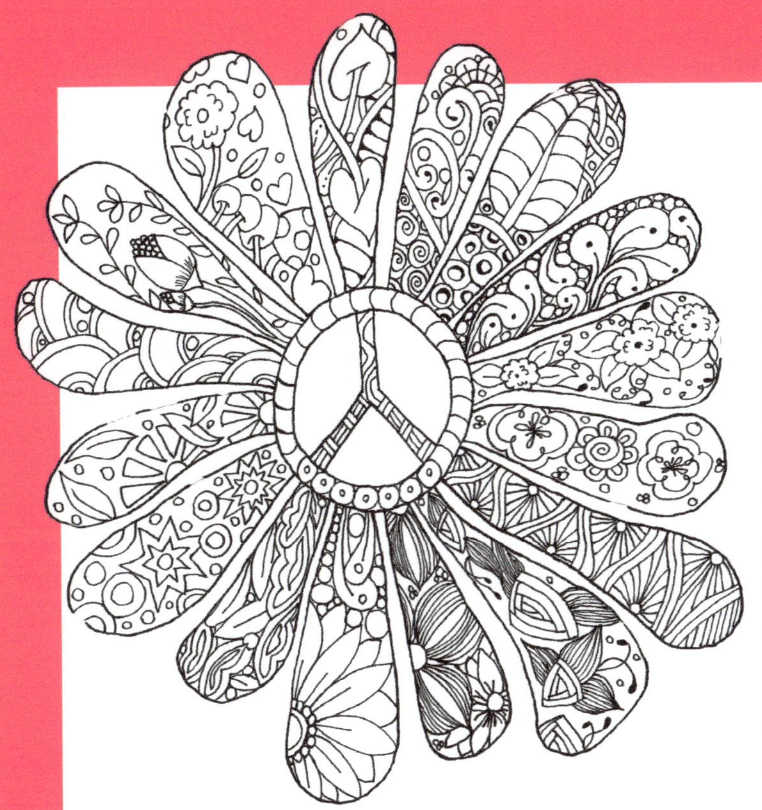

Ginger Marks

Born in Lansing, Michigan, Ginger Marks moved to the Tampa Bay Area of Florida in 1978. She began her career as a business owner in partnership with the medical profession. Marks owned and operated a multi-million-dollar surgical facility for 23 years with her late husband. After his passing, Ginger's drive to succeed led her to become a Financial Advisor while working on the side, for her own purposes, in the field of design with the founding of Graph Inc., which eventually became DocUmeant Designs.

Her love for writing and design has been the catalyst for her successful career in the publishing area. Coming from a family of published authors and speakers, it was no surprise when she, herself, embarked on the writing journey. She enjoys sharing from her vast expertise as a published author and business owner.

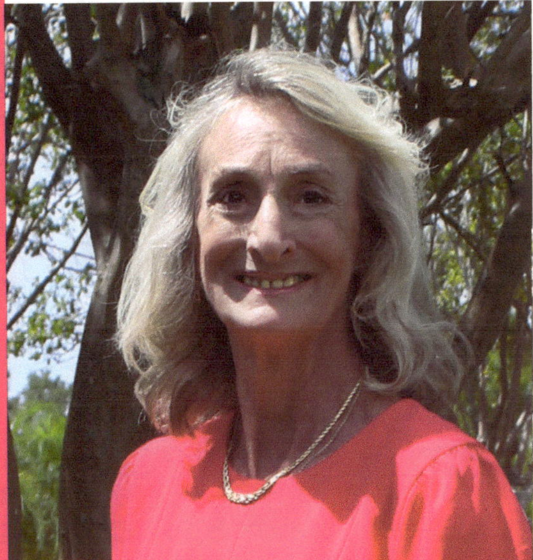

Ginger Marks is an award-winning author, publisher, and designer. Her books include two children's books as well as numerous business-related books. She is listed in Covington Who's Who Executive and Professional Registry, and Clearwater Business Hall of Fame. These awards confirm Mrs. Mark's commitment to excellence in the Publishing and Design services.

In 2017 Marks was honored by Women in eCommerce with the Golden Mouse award for publishing. Ginger is a member of International Book Publishers Association (IBPA), Association of Authors and Publishers for Special Sales (AAPS), and is on the board of the Florida Authors and Publishers Association (myFAPA.org). She served as their Design Chair from 2013–2023 and President in 2024–25. She is a platinum author on Ezine Articles and has also written for Huffington Post. In her spare time, she enjoys singing and crafts. She is a portrait artist and has recently delved into the art of *Zentangle* with her adult coloring book, *Color My World*. She pens a monthly ezine titled, "Words of Wisdom" which she invites you to register to receive and can be found at DocUmeantPublishing.com and DocUmeantDesigns.com.

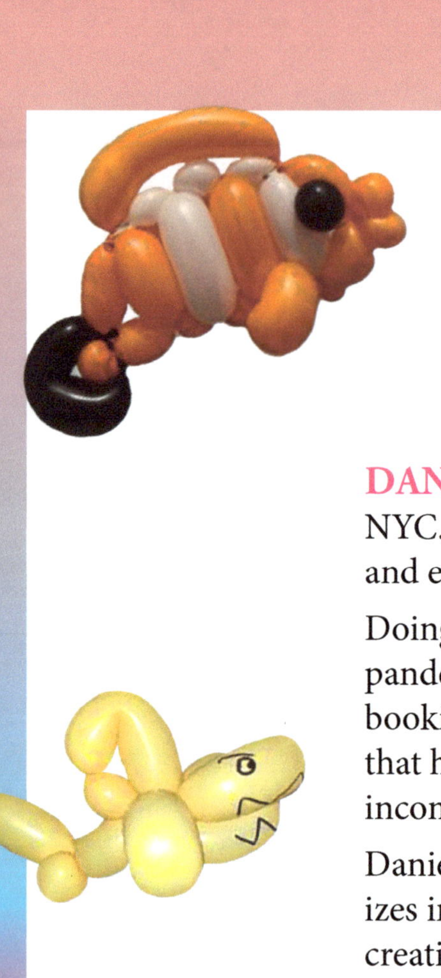

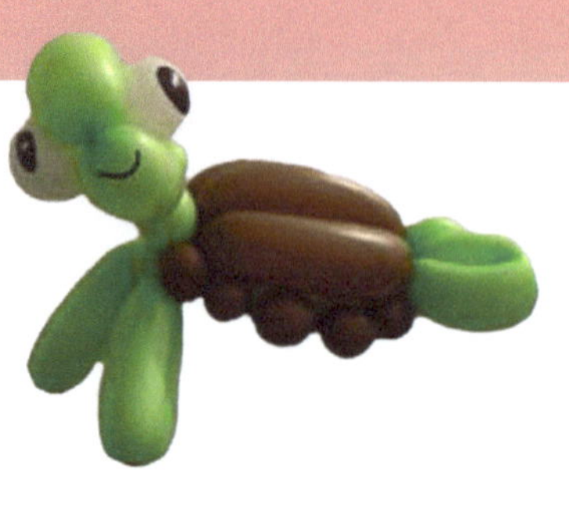

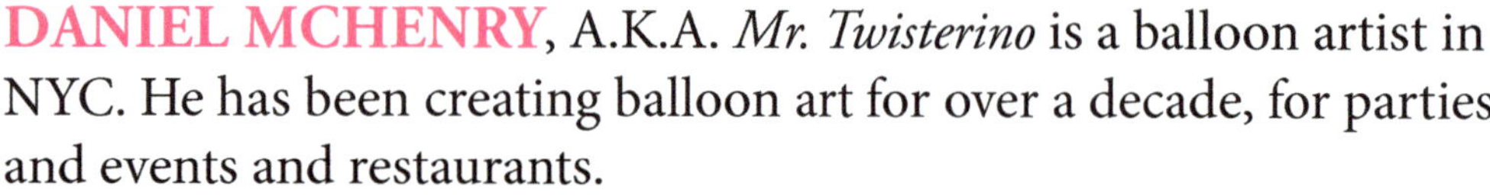

DANIEL MCHENRY, A.K.A. *Mr. Twisterino* is a balloon artist in NYC. He has been creating balloon art for over a decade, for parties and events and restaurants.

Doing balloons was always a side hustle for Daniel. Then, post pandemic, in Spring 2022 , on a whim he put up a bio on a party booking website. It took off and he began to get so many bookings that he no longer considered it a side hustle. It became a rewarding income stream and loves to earn money by bringing joy!

Daniel creates balloon themed art for special events. He specializes in all-occasion designs including Hawaiian-themed balloon creations bringing vibrant island flair to weddings, parties, and corporate events.

He can be found on:
IG: @mr.twisterino

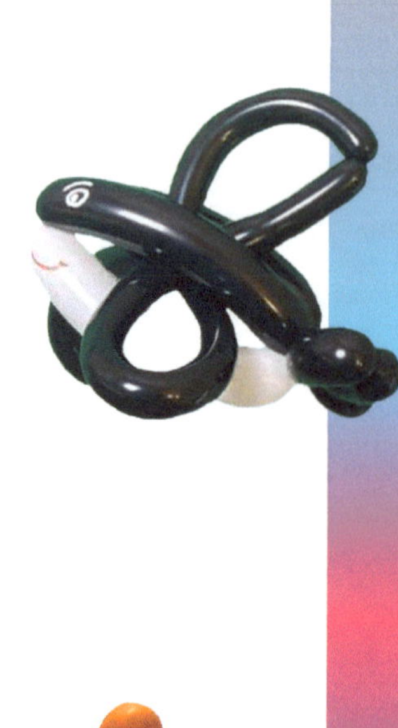

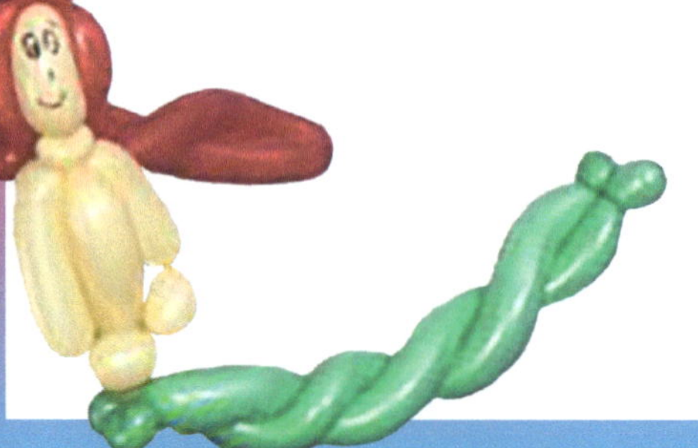

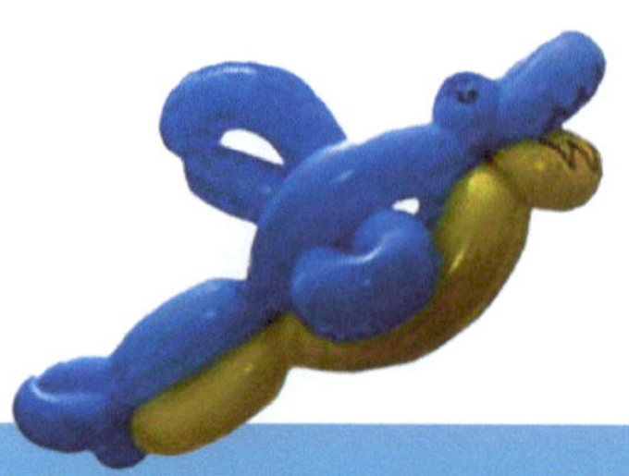

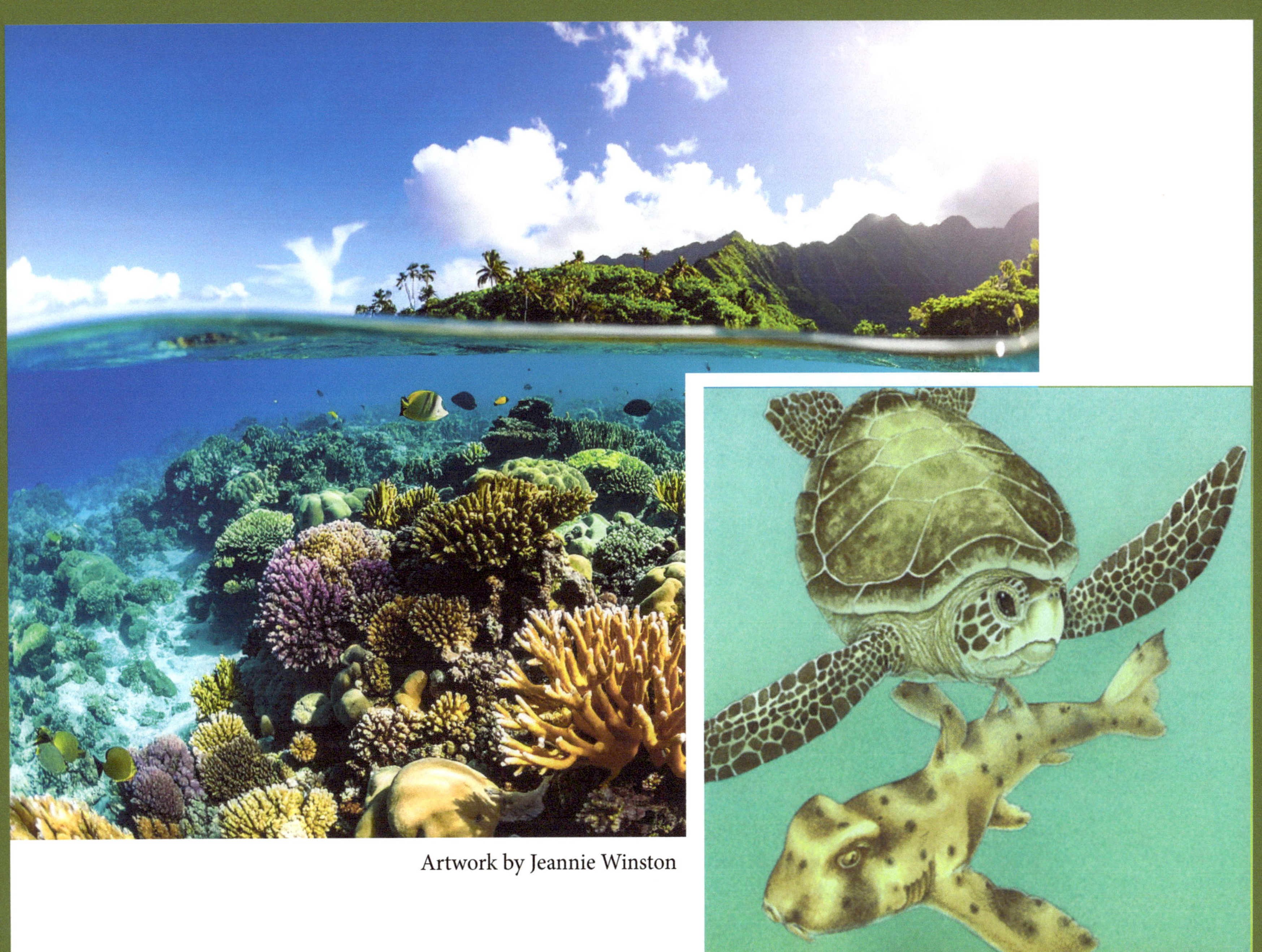

Artwork by Jeannie Winston

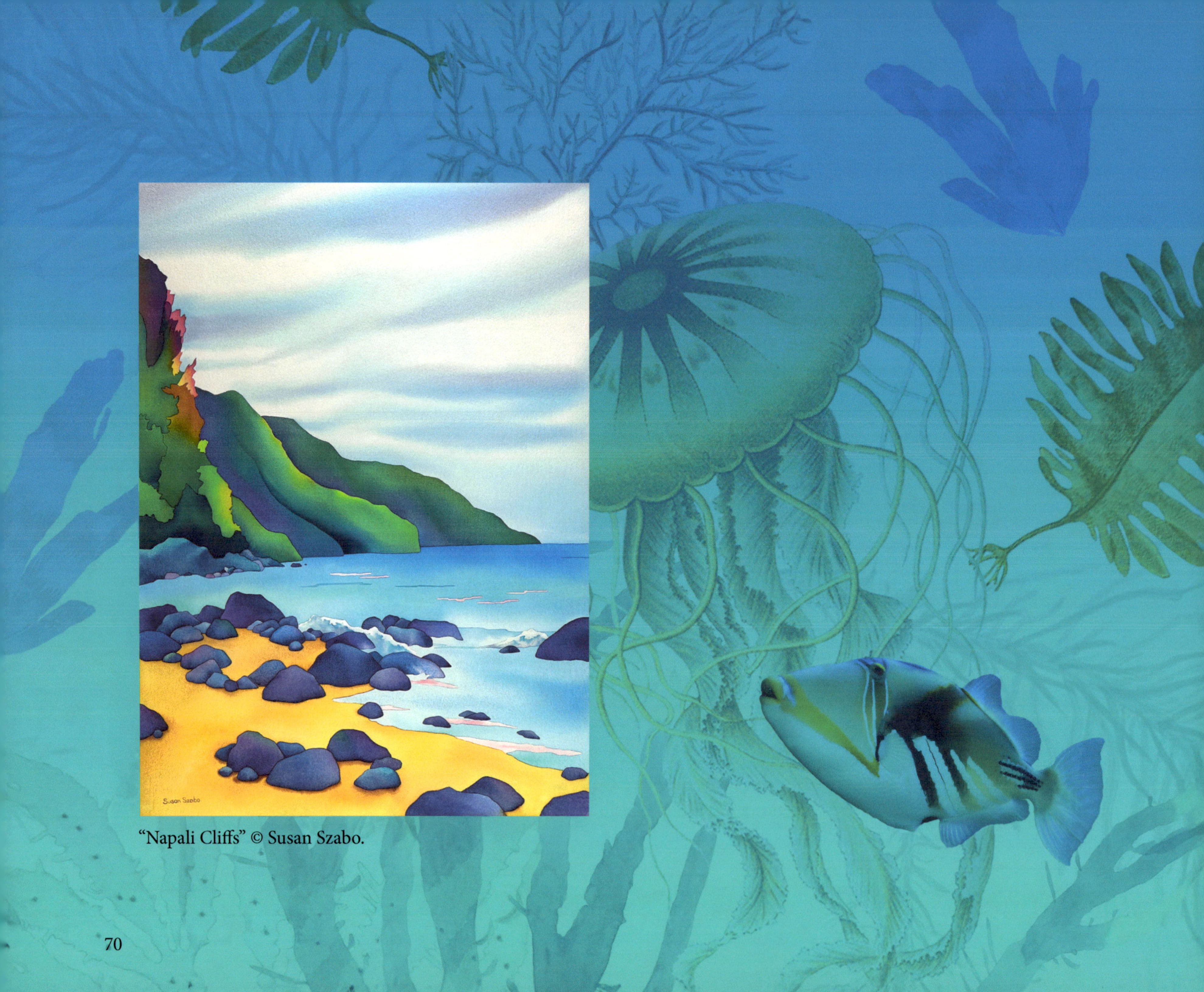

"Napali Cliffs" © Susan Szabo.

STEVE STAUDENMEIR began painting in watercolor when he retired after a successful career in Information Technology Management and Consulting. Painting was something he had always wanted to do but never had the time.

He found inspiration in drawings done by his artistic Grandmother and wondered if he might have some of her talent. He picked flowers to begin with as he enjoyed the shapes and beautiful colors. Focusing on flowers allowed him to learn many of the basics of watercolors.

From there Steve branched out into landscapes, city life and animal subjects. He feels fortunate to have received valuable help, support and encouragement from other more experienced artists. He belongs to the Temecula Valley Artists League and the Murrieta Gem of the Valley Art Association. He has received various awards and has had success selling his paintings and prints.

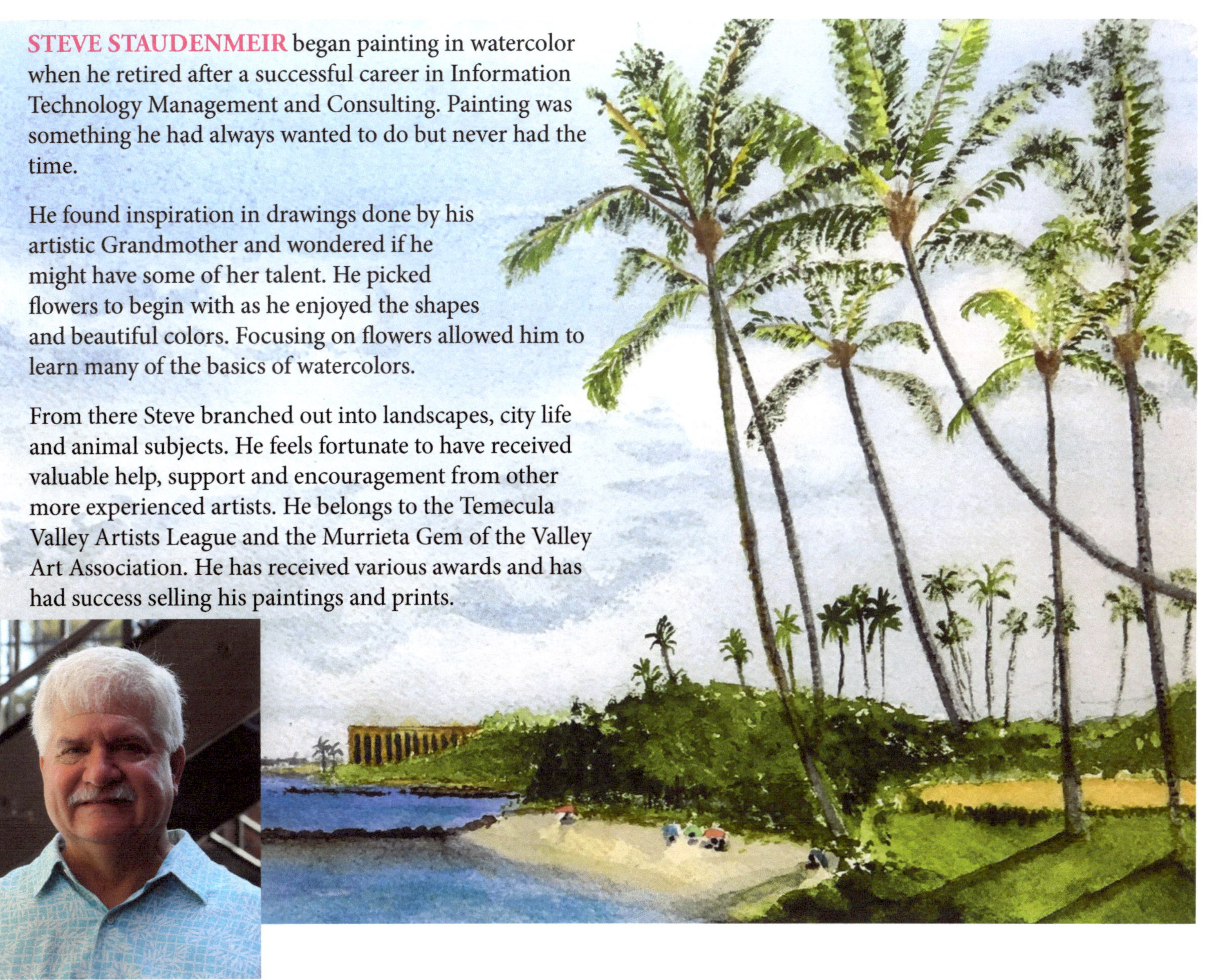

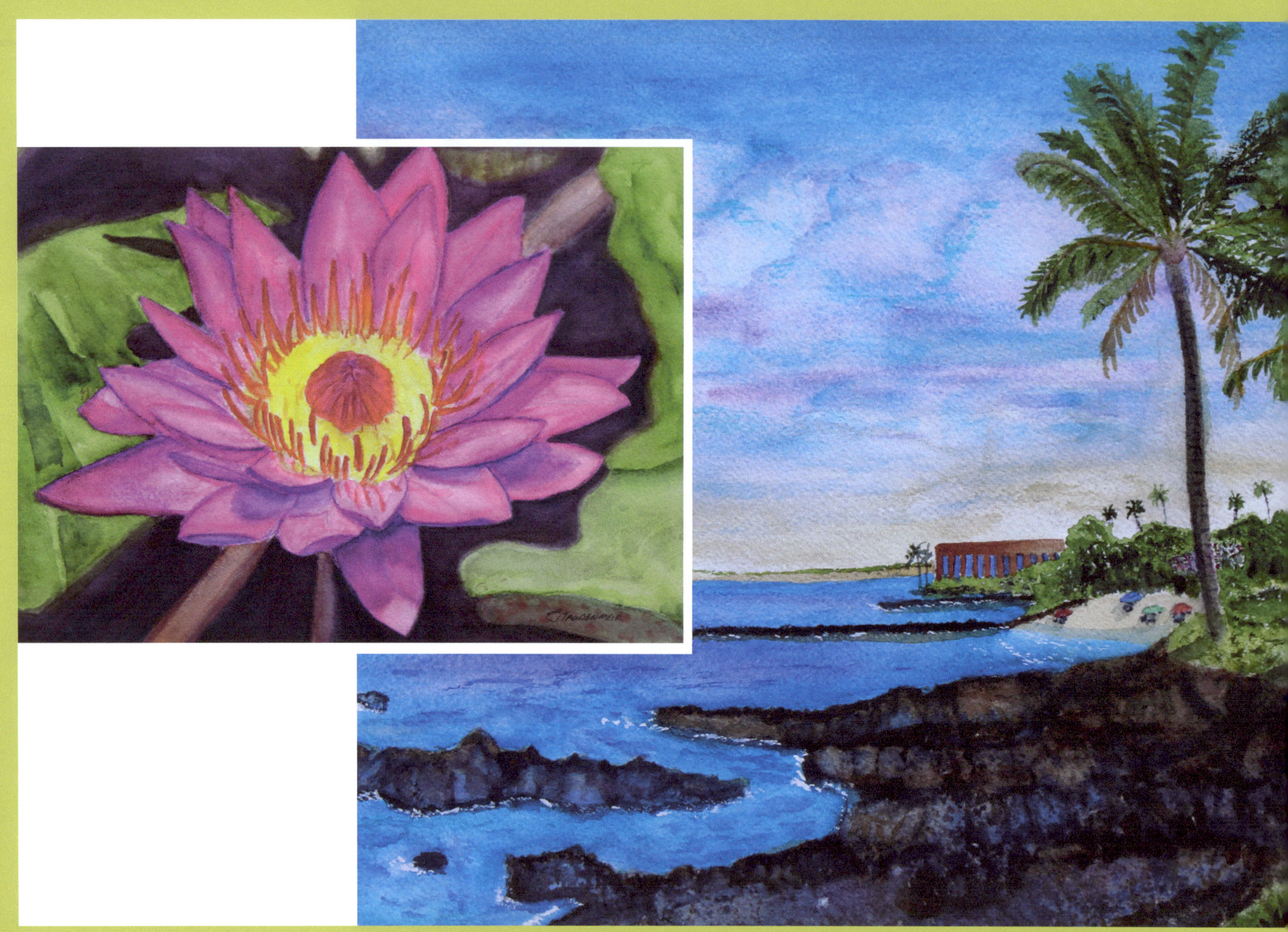

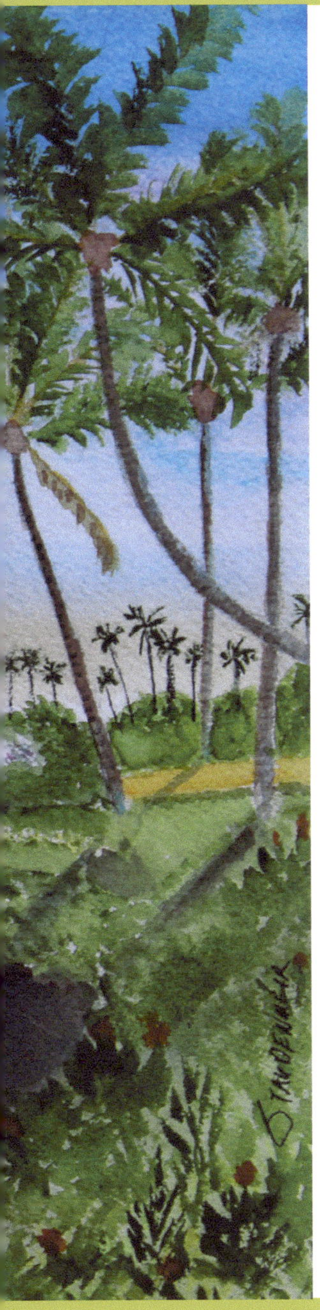

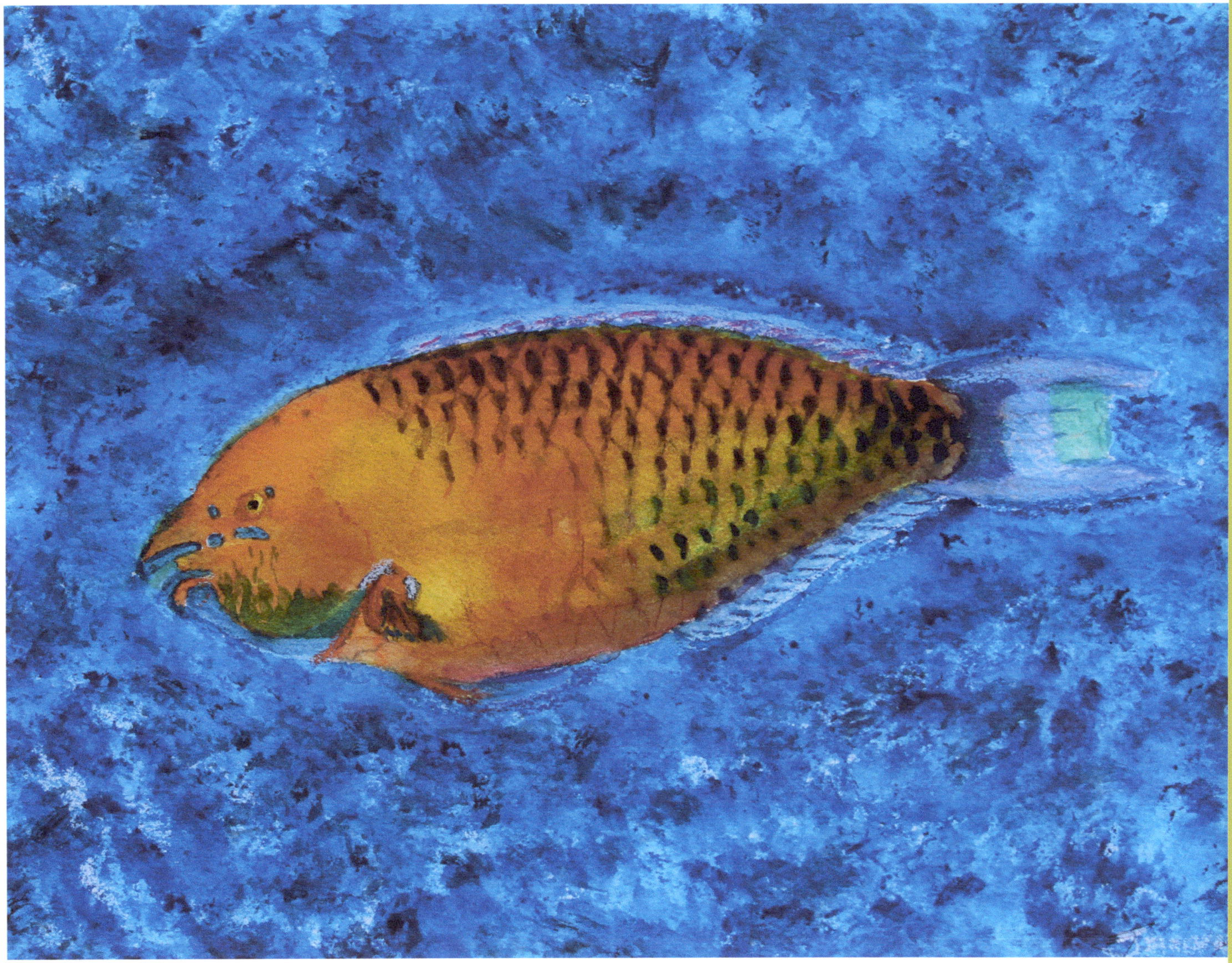

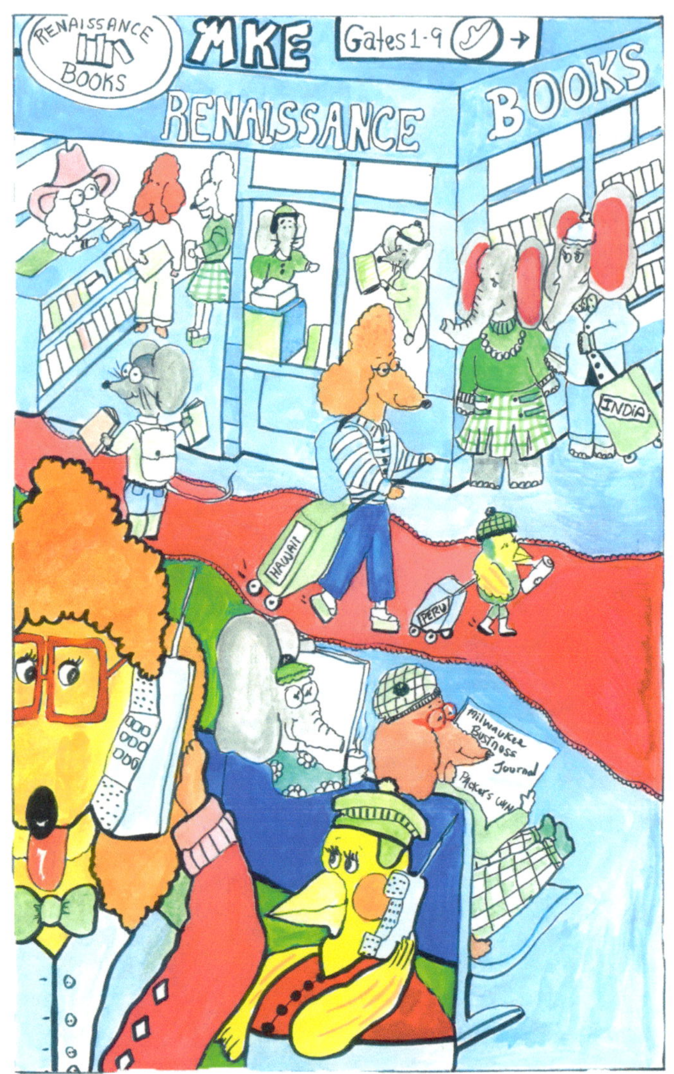

Bruno and Leroy at the Milwaukee Mitchell International Airport (MKE). They love finding books and magazines at the Renaissance Airport Bookstore.

Comics by Jennifer Jordan: Comic Books Coming Soon!

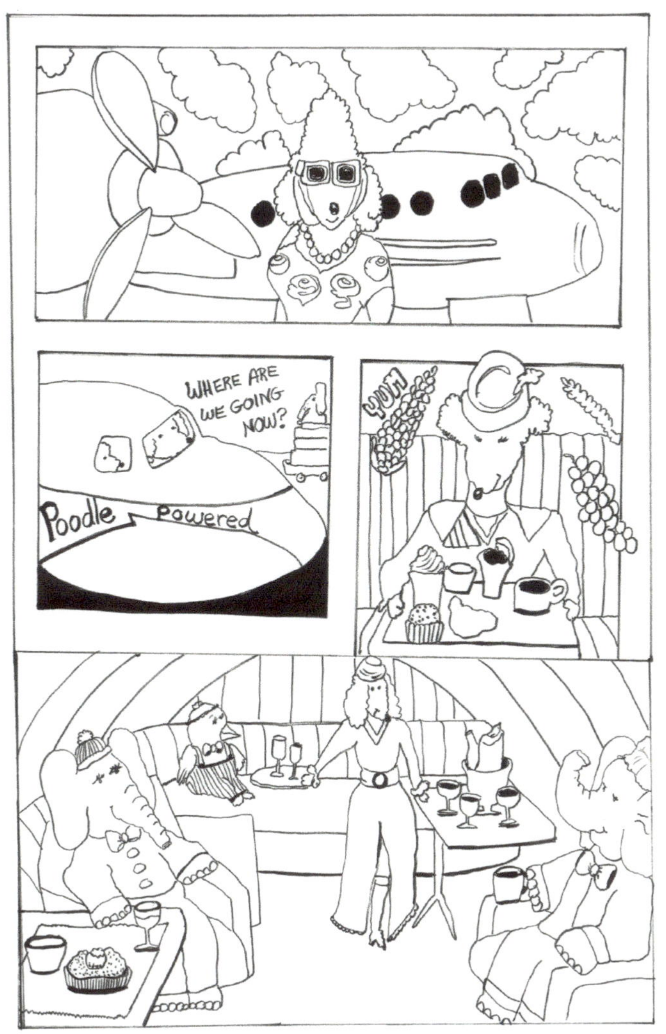

Wings and Maps: Bruno & Leroy's Travel Conundrum.

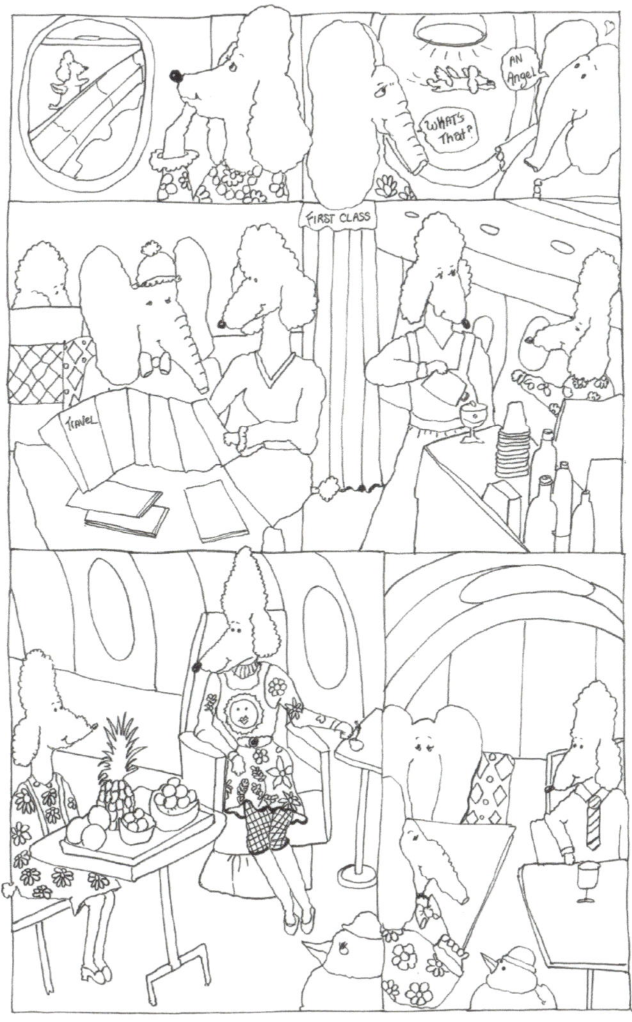

Bruno's friends, Ellie the elephant and Toby the Mouse, invented a new electronic car that flies. Uncle Martin developed a new electric jet pack that is environmentally friendly!

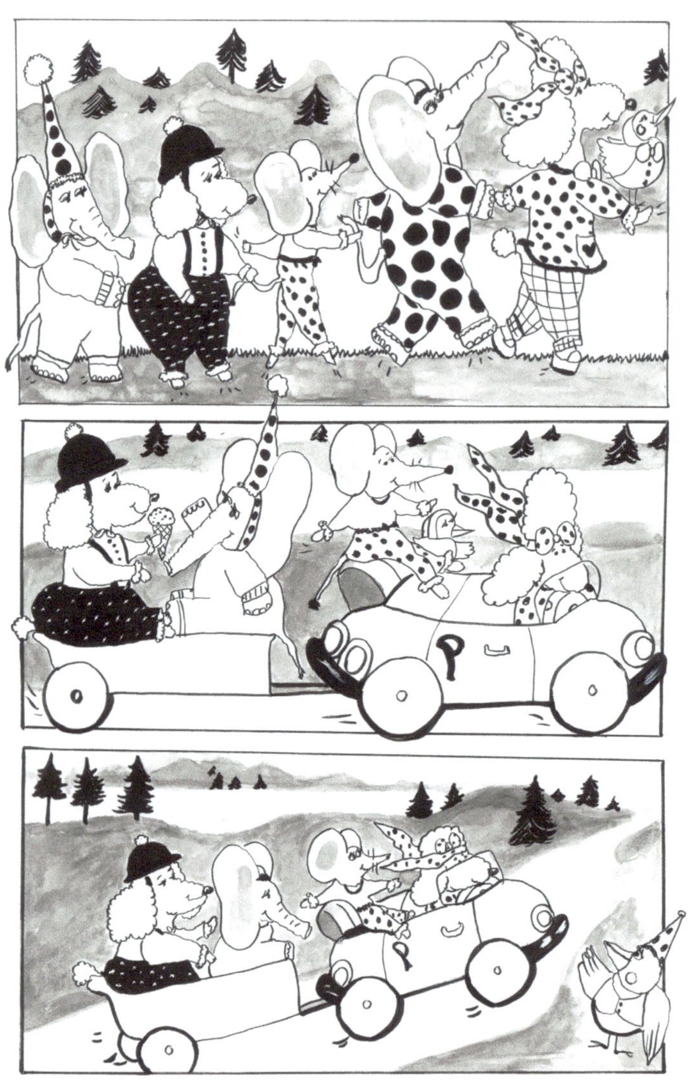

Bruno and friends, Leroy, Ellie, Toby and Aunt Juanita are on a road trip!

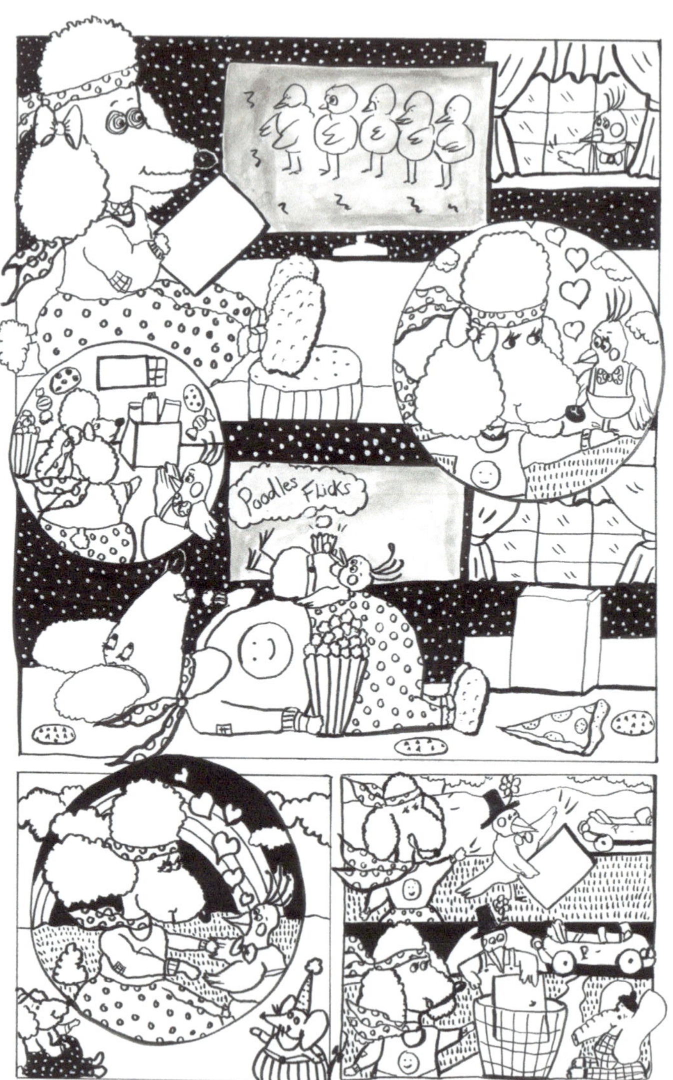

Bruno and Leroy are getting cabin fever...

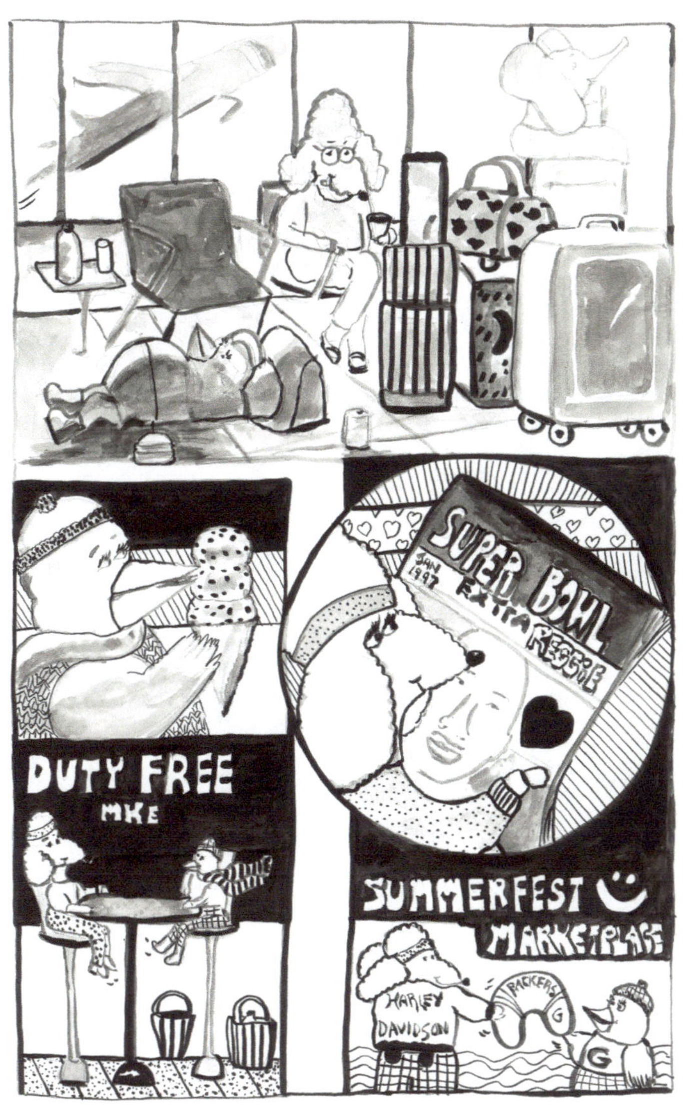

Bruno and Leroy living their best lives waiting at MKE--treats, naps on deck. Nothing like a little R&R before takeoff!

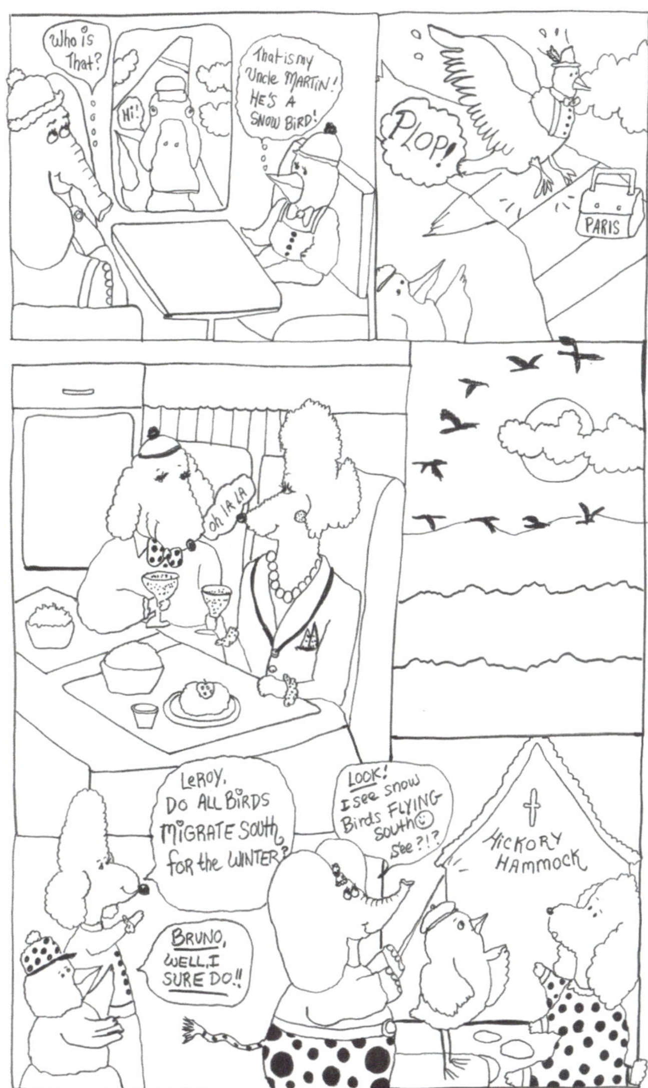

Uncle Martin, like most birds, wants to escape the cold winter.

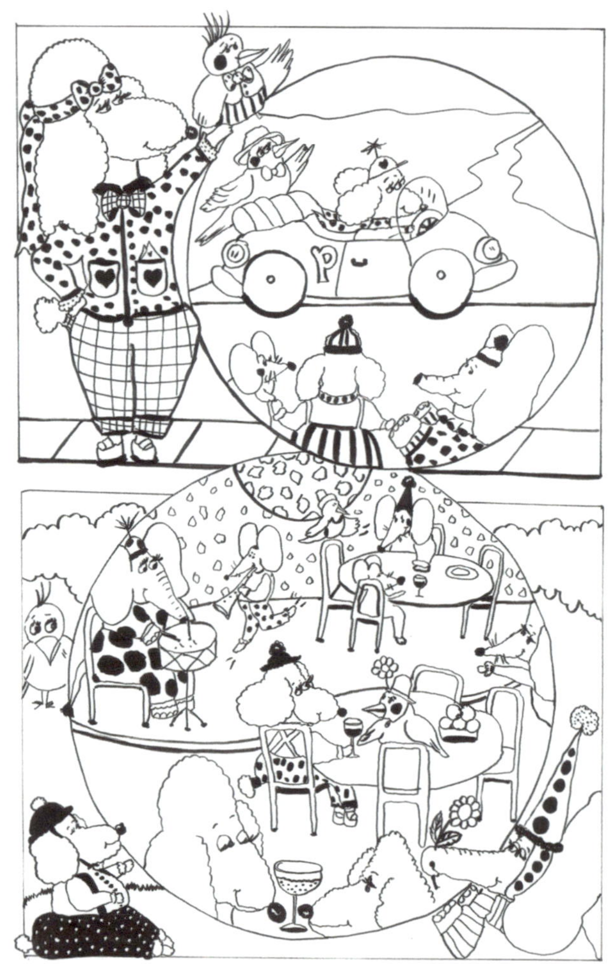

Top: Bruno and Leroy are dreaming about their travels.
Bottom: Bruno and Leroy's friends threw a big extravaganza at the Moose Lodge, wishing them safe travels. Ellie the elephant and Toby the Mouse's Band came to entertain everyone!

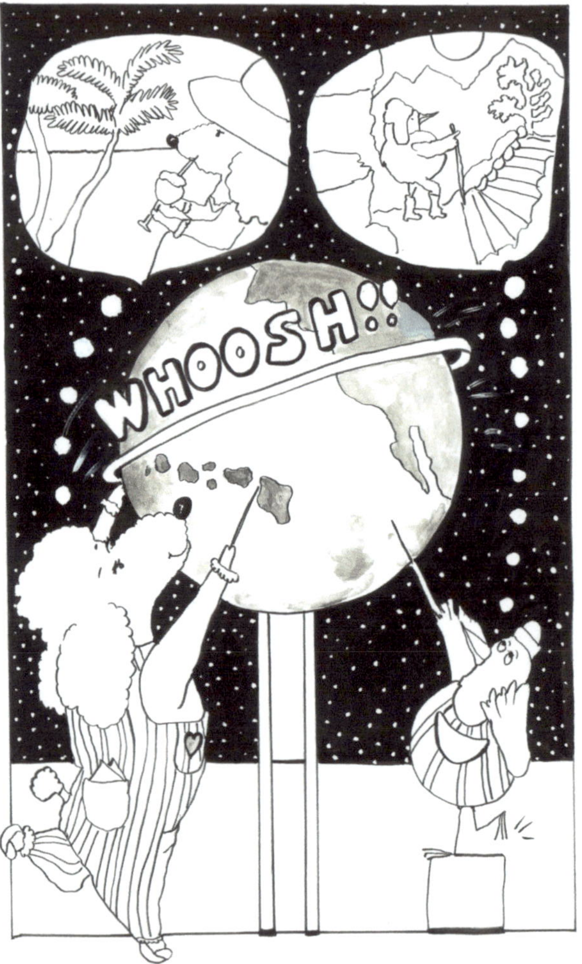

Bruno the poodle and his best friend Leroy the bird can't decide where to explore next. Bruno loved Hawai'i, yet Leroy wanted to go hiking at Mammoth Lakes, California.

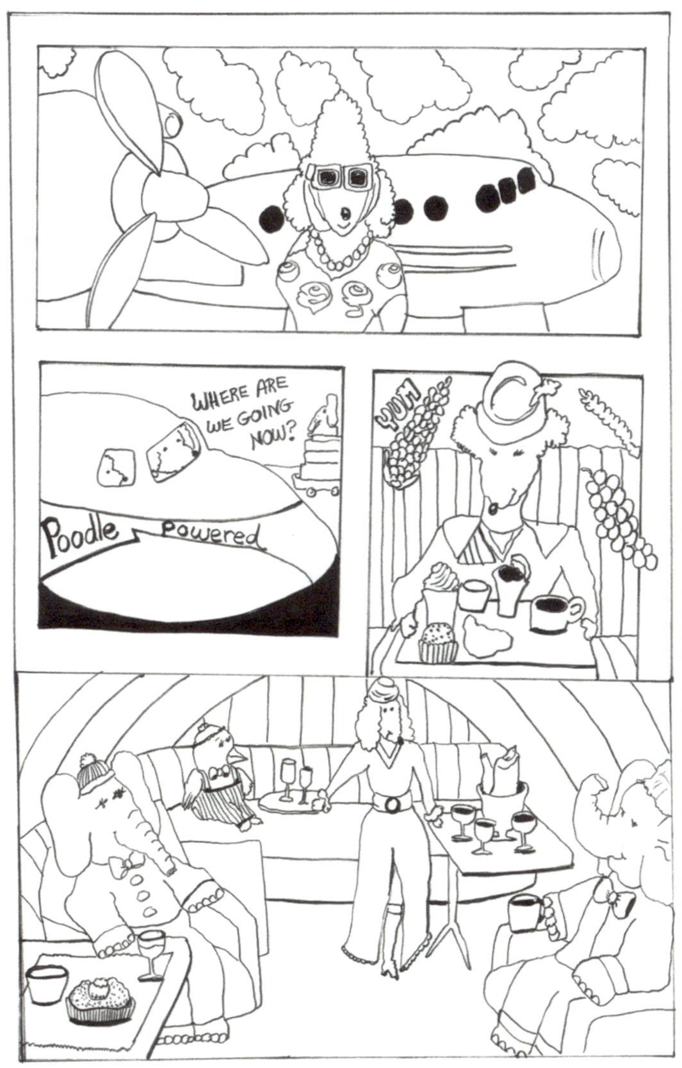

Bruno's Aunt Juanita loved being fashionably dressed for her first flight ever to Hawai'i. She is thrilled to be going with Bruno.

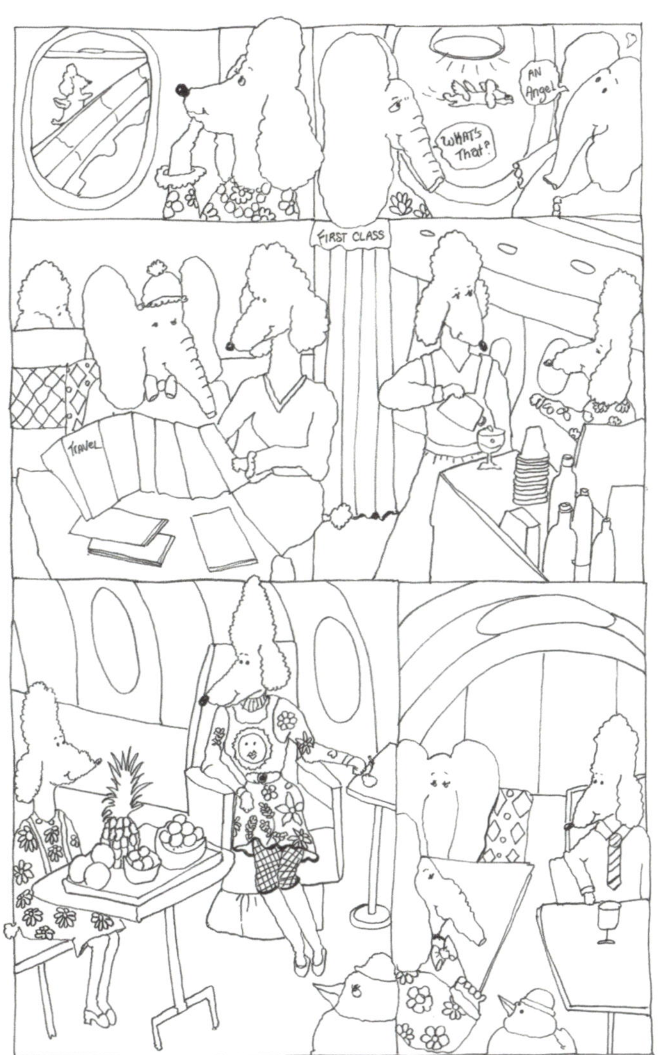

Bruno and friends flying First Class to Honolulu, Hawai'i!

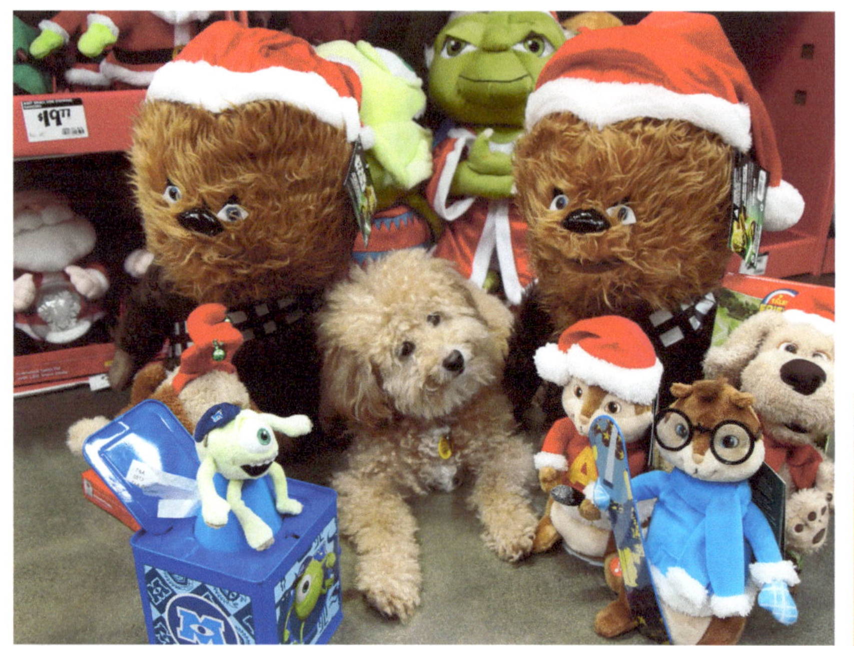

Bruno's Holiday
Celebrations

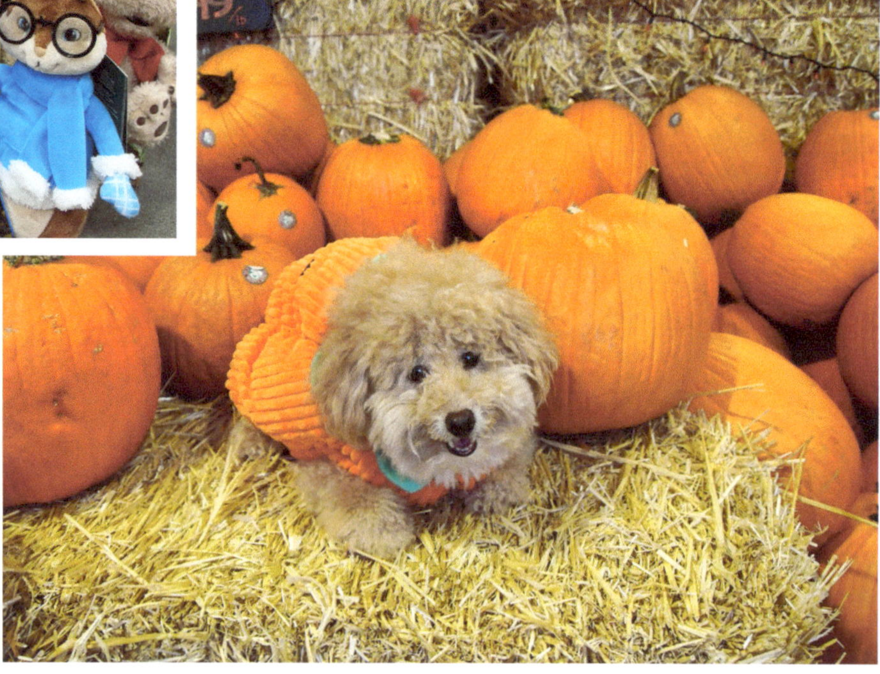

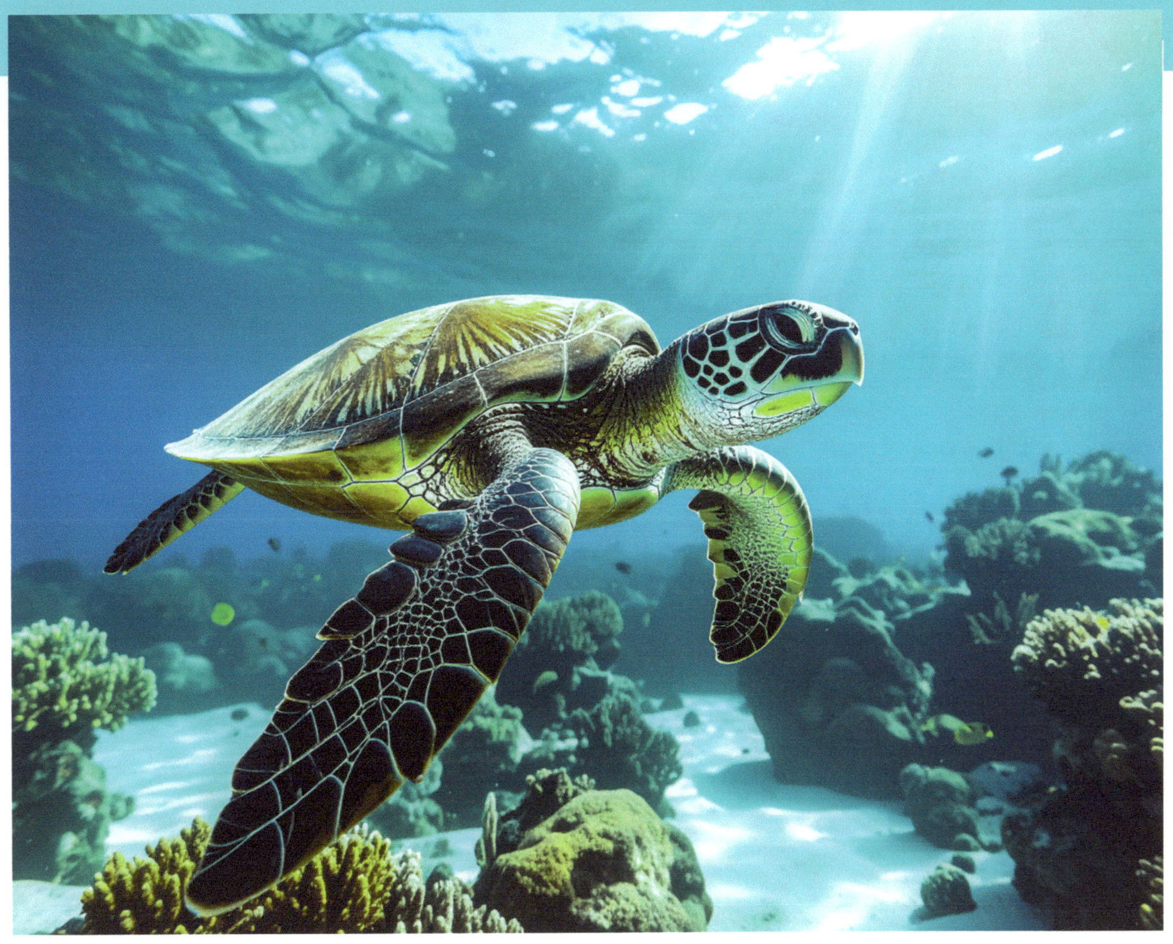

Hawaiian Green Sea Turtles (Honu) are seen in the water and on land. In the waters close to shore, you can sometimes see them swimming and feeding on algae. From land, you can typically see them sunbathing on the beach in the afternoon and evening.

They are deeply rooted in Hawaiian culture and folklore, as the green sea turtle is sacred in Hawai'i and is considered a symbol of good luck, longevity, and wisdom.

The Honu is a revered symbol of Hawaiian identity and is considered an "aumakua", or guardian spirit, by many Hawaiian families, and is believed to provide protection, guidance, and ancestral connection to families.

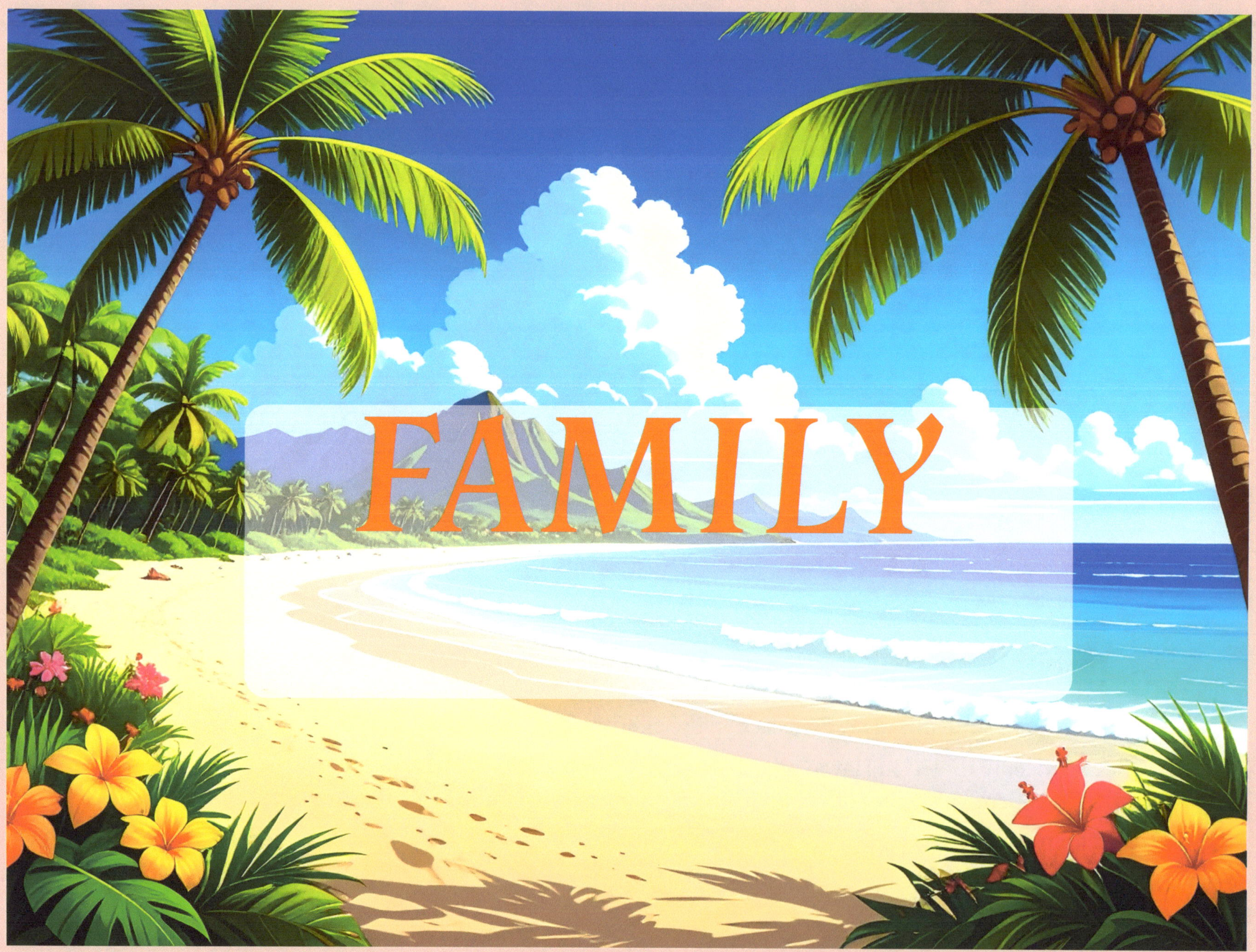

FAMILY

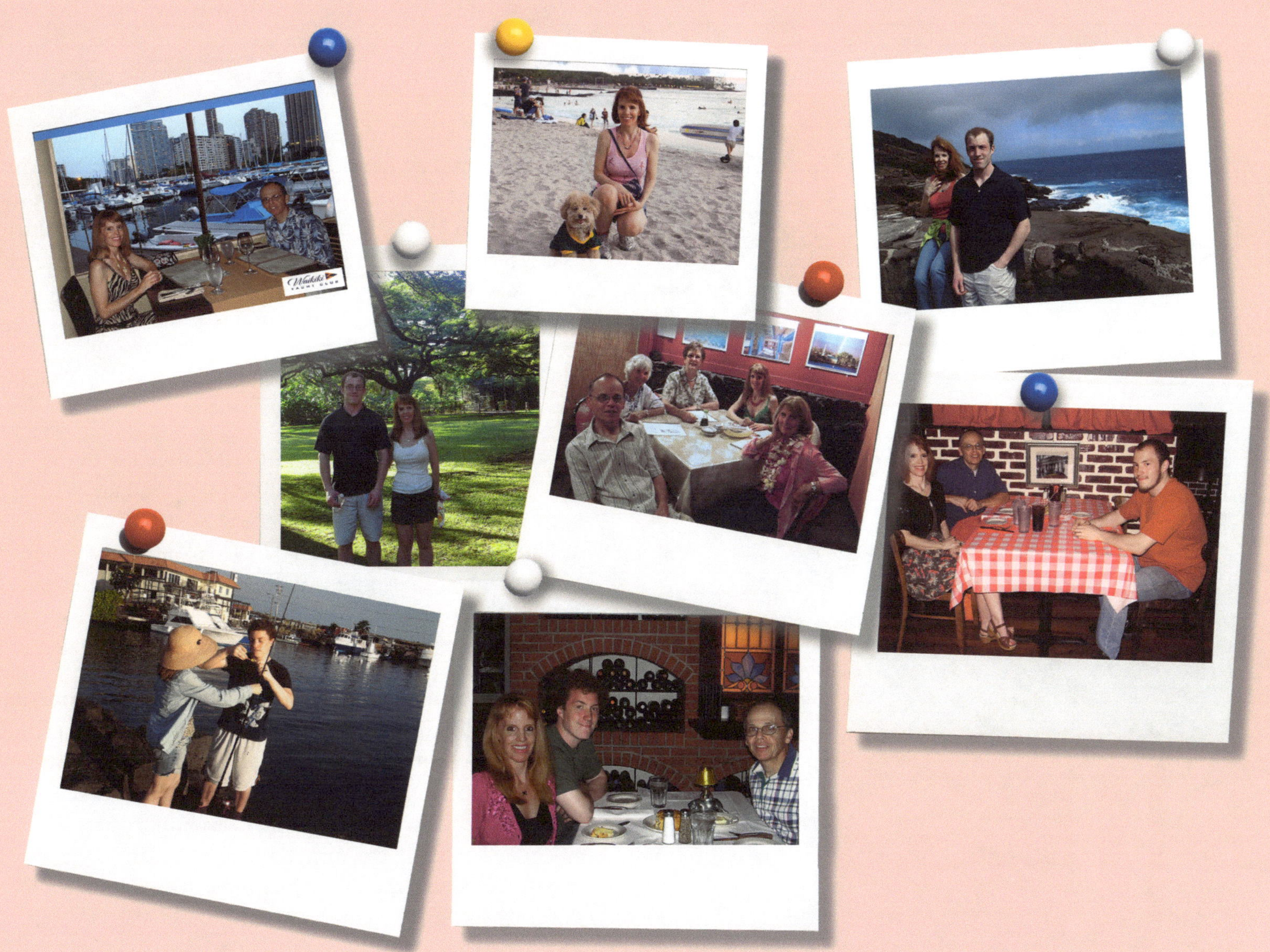

Top Row left to right: Jennifer and Chuck dining at the Waikiki Yacht Club, Jennifer and Bruno on Waikiki Beach, Jennifer and James overlooking the Pacific Ocean.
Middle Row: Jennifer and James at the Honolulu Zoo, Chuck, Jennifer, Marie Jordan and friends, Jennifer, Chuck and James.
Bottom Row: Willie and Jennifer fishing. Jennifer, James, and Chuck.

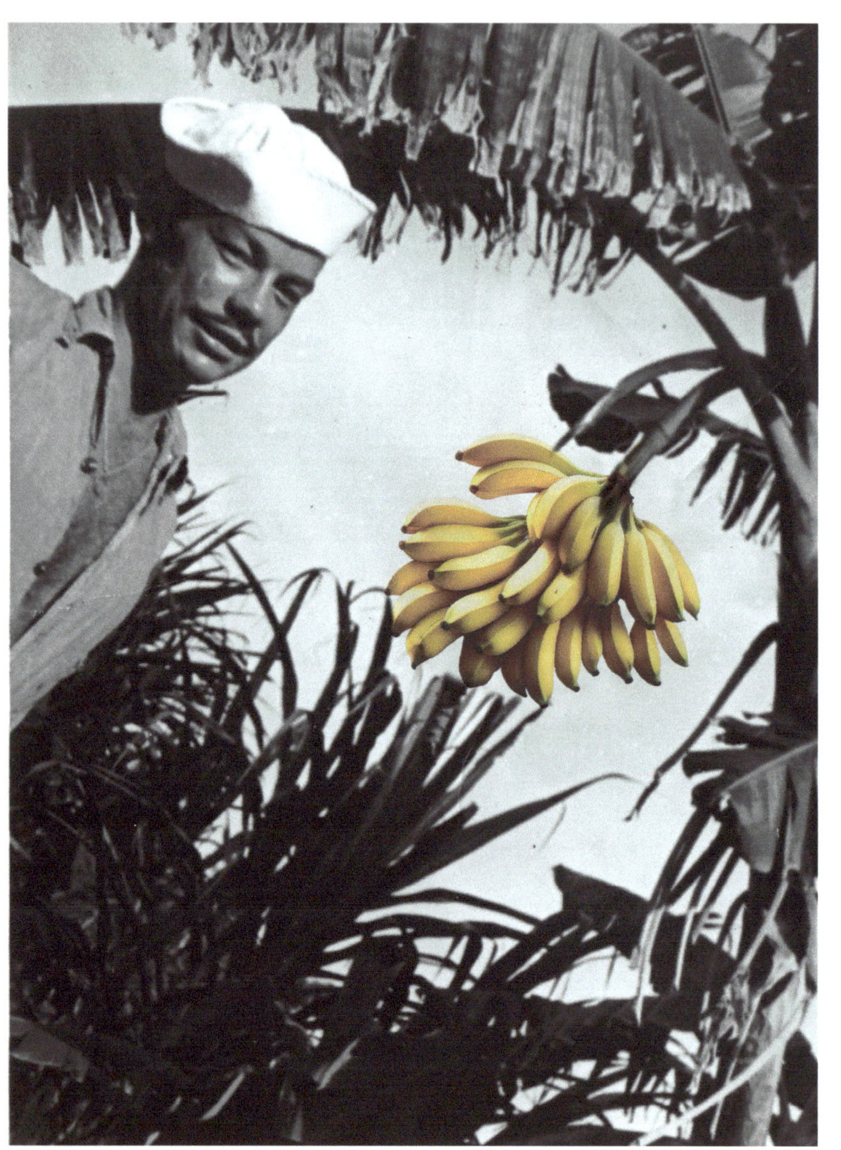

Jim Jordan, Jennifer's Dad

Born and raised in Northern California in Burlingame, Jim Jordan received an honorable discharge from the Navy in 1946, then entered Art Center as an Advertising student, graduating in 1949. He began teaching at the college during his last term. Jordan and his wife, Marie Kunz, met at Art Center College on 3rd Street in Los Angeles. They then moved to Philadelphia.

When Jordan joined the advertising agency N.W. Ayer, they worked on ads together.

 Jim and Marie returned to Southern California in the early 50s, and Jordan taught photography and advertising at Art Center throughout the decade while pursuing a freelance career in graphic Art. In 1976, he joined the Film Department as chairman, and for the next thirteen years, he devoted his energies to making the program into a successful, highly respected source for professional filmmakers.

Jordan is a member of the Director's Guild of America, and he produced many award-winning television commercials, including those for Huggies diapers, Luv's diapers, and Arco's "Kids" for the 1984 Olympics. Recipient of many awards throughout his life, Jordan was honored by the Art Director's Club of New York, the American Institute of Graphic Arts, and the Finnish Film Festival. He also won Clios, Adweek's 1985 Director of the Year / West, and a 1987 NY EFY.

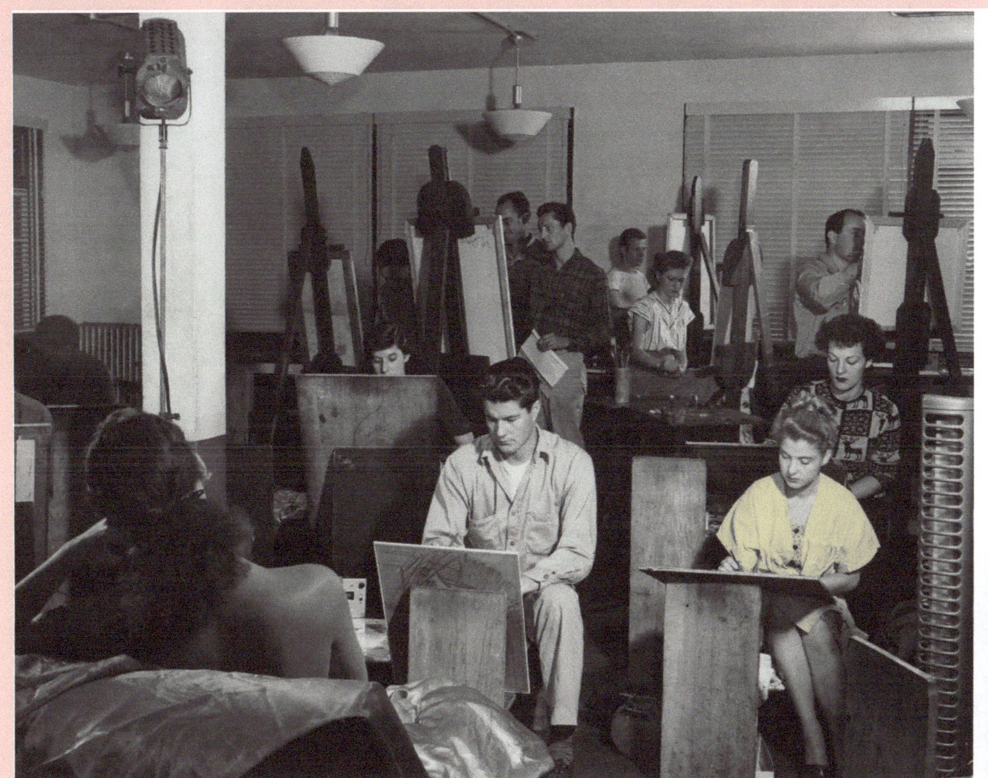

Marie Jordan drawing a life model at Art Center College of Design, Los Angeles.

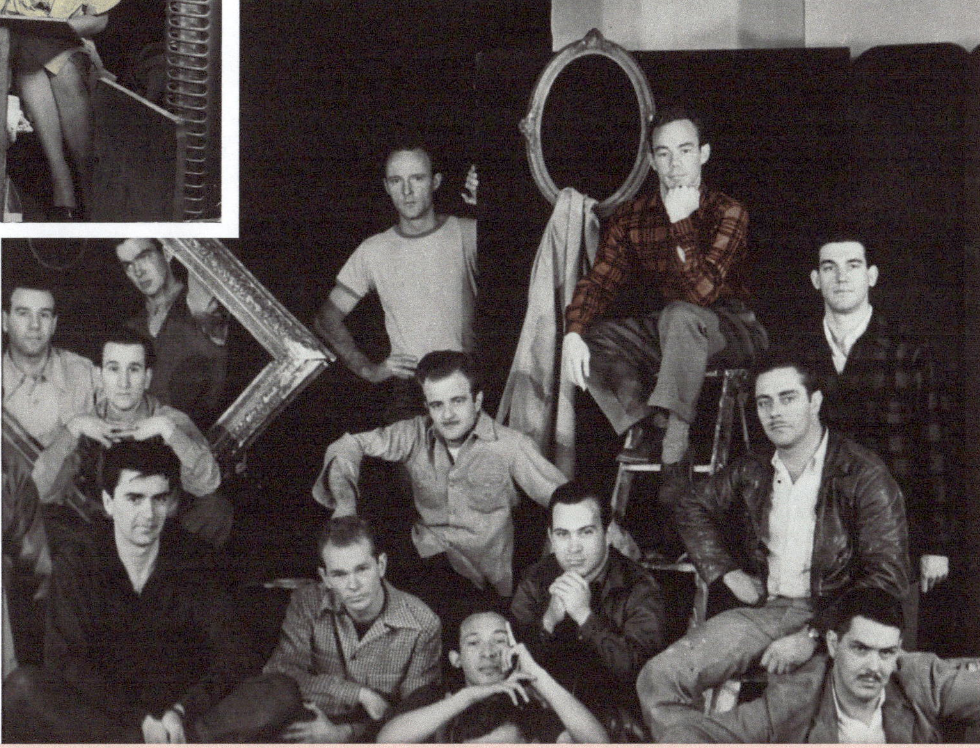

Jim Jordan with classmates at Art Center College of Design, Los Angeles.

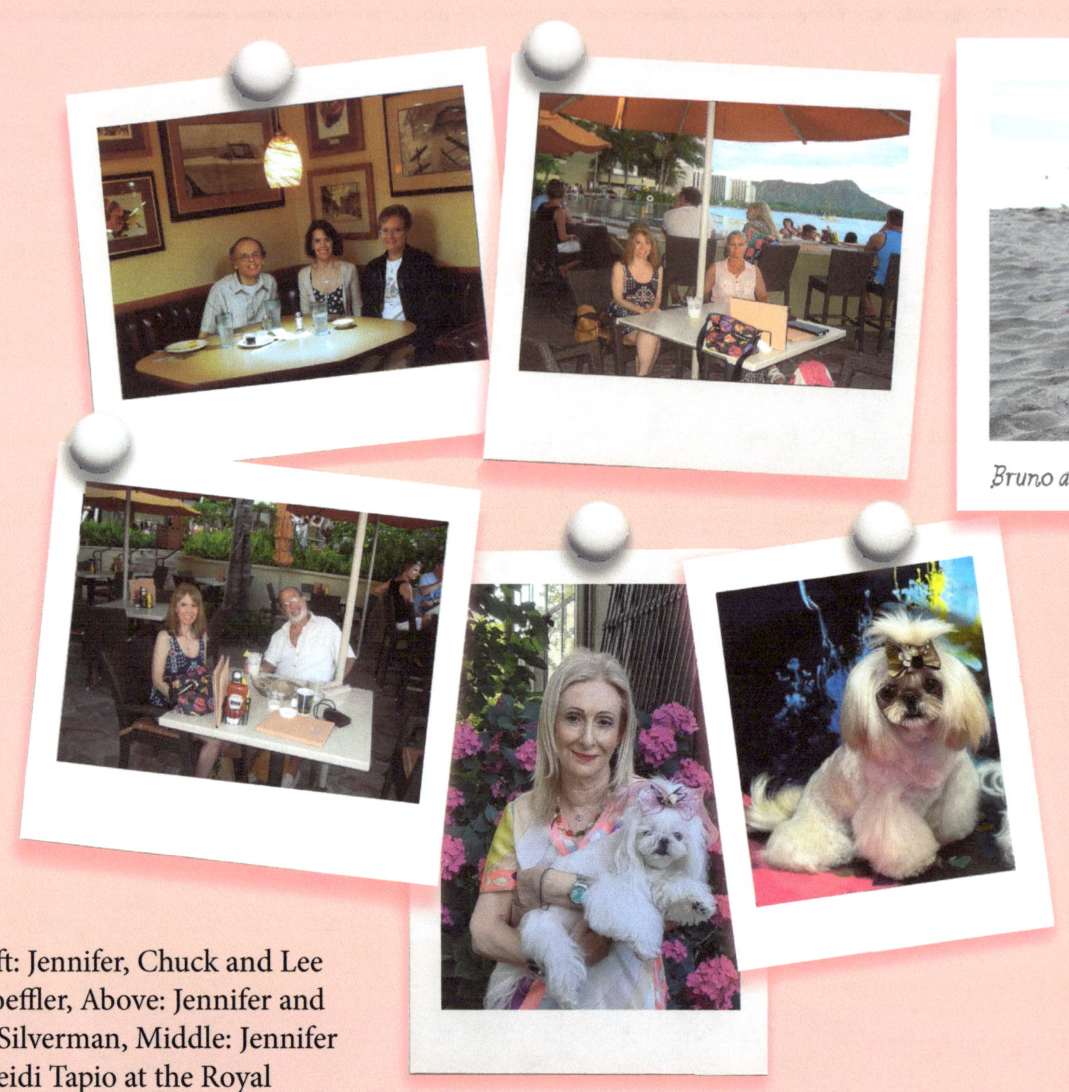

Top Left: Jennifer, Chuck and Lee Ann Loeffler, Above: Jennifer and Benny Silverman, Middle: Jennifer with Heidi Tapio at the Royal Hawaiian, Right: Marie Antonietta la Tour holding Margot, Far right: Dreamy.

One sunny afternoon, Baby met someone special—Bruno, a charming little poodle. The two crossed paths on the beach, and it was love at first sight. Despite being different species, they seemed to understand each other perfectly.

Baby is a stunning African Grey parrot who calls the beautiful island of O'ahu, Hawai'i, her home. Born and raised in the warm breezes of Ewa Beach, Baby is now 20 years old and thriving. Her breeder still lives by the shoreline in Ewa Beach, a place as rich in history as it is in beauty.

CHARITABLE ORGANIZATIONS

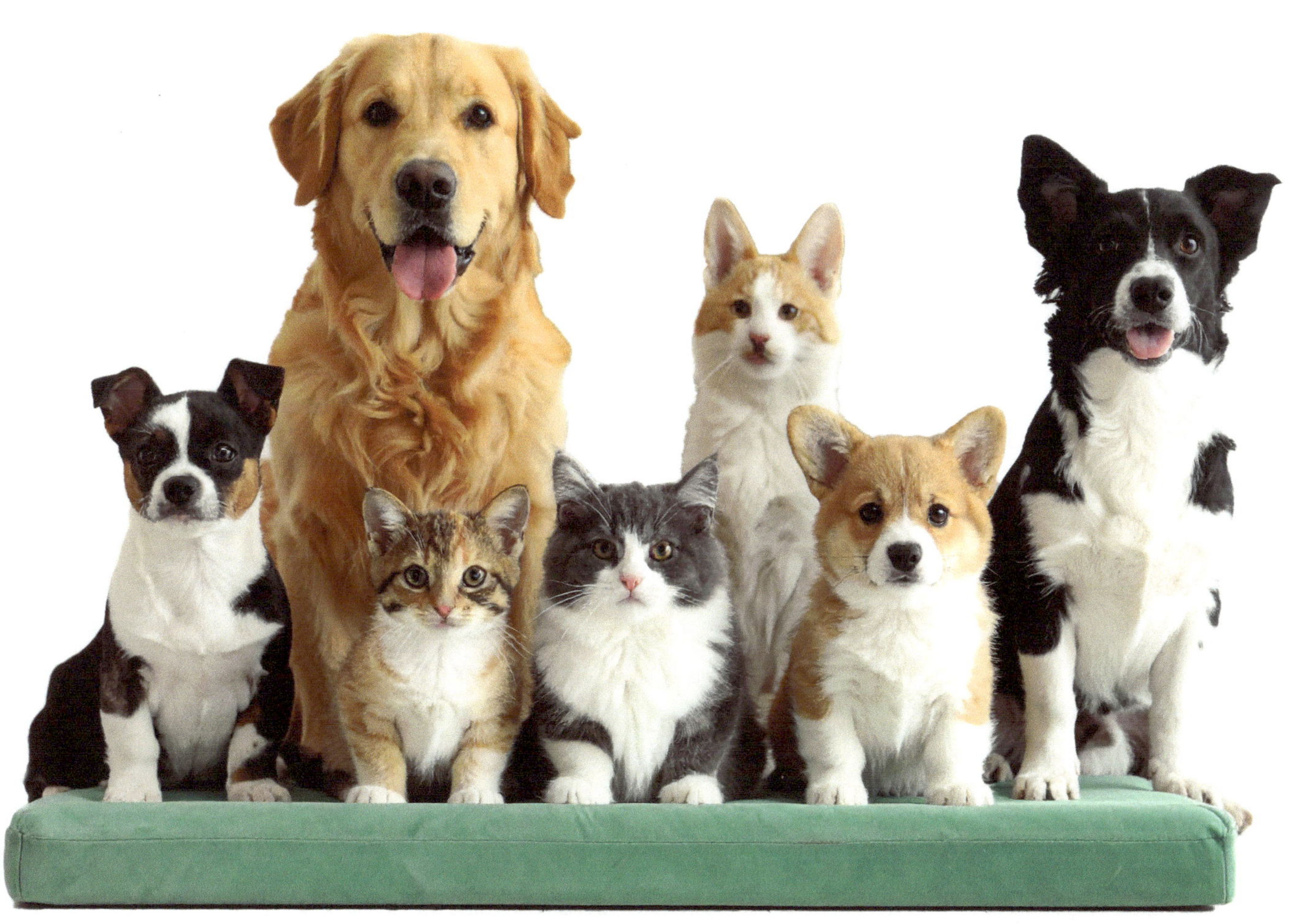

Pocket Puppies

Steven Tyler purchased his pocket puppy, *Sundance Kid*, a Morkie (a cross between a Maltese and/Yorkshire Terrier) at Pocket Puppies Boutique in Chicago, Illinois.

Sundance Kid accompanies Steven on his travels. Steven appeared on <u>Late Night with Seth Meyers</u> along with his pocket puppies.

Founded in 2006, Pocket Puppies Boutique offers true teacup, toy, and <u>small-breed puppies</u>. Rest assured that every beautiful Yorkshire Terrier, Maltese, and every small breed puppy <u>comes from a loving home.</u>

Nearly sixteen years later, our dog boutique offers the finest selection of designer dog clothes and <u>luxury dog products</u>!

View hundreds and hundreds of verified, real handwritten testimonials with photos!

Pocket Puppies is now located at:

1121 20th Ave
Pleasant Prairie, WI 53158

262-857-4365

Call 773-857-1519 for questions or directions
www.pocketpuppies.com

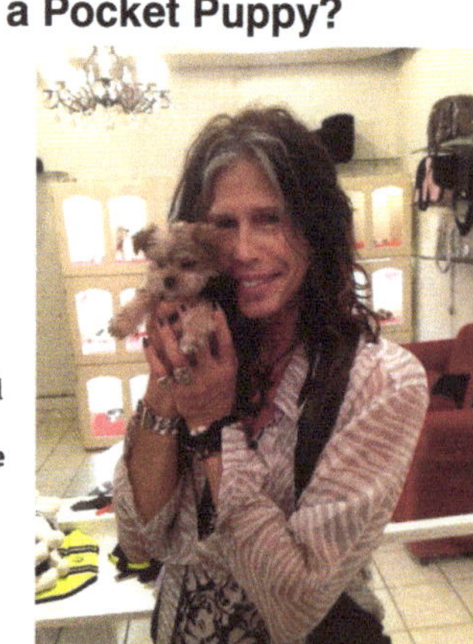

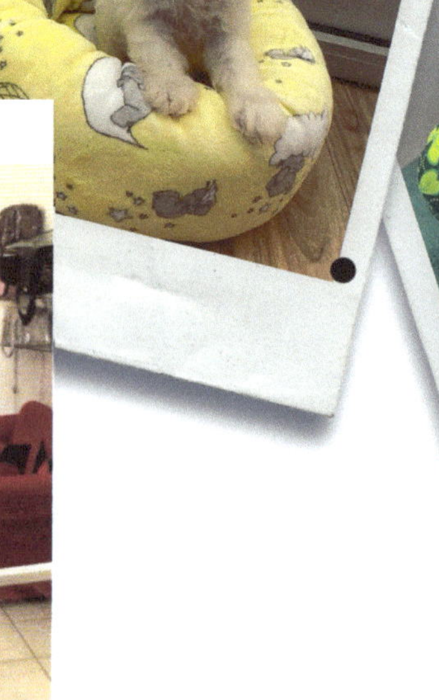

THE WISCONSIN HUMANE SOCIETY (WHS) was founded in 1879 and is the oldest and largest shelter in Wisconsin, annually serving 65,000 animals and the people who love them. WHS is an independent nonprofit and receives no general government funding and is not part of any national umbrella group. WHS operates shelters in Milwaukee, Ozaukee, Racine, Kenosha, Brown, and Door Counties, as well as the Spay/Neuter Clinic in West Allis. The Milwaukee Campus also houses one of the state's busiest wildlife rehabilitation centers. WHS offers adoption services, public veterinary services, a pet food bank, youth programs, volunteer programs, outreach programming, retail stores, wildlife rehabilitation, dog training classes, and more. WHS is ranked 4 stars by Charity Navigator, the premier independent charity watchdog group. To learn more, visit www.wihumane.org.

Wisconsin Humane Society
4500 W. Wisconsin Ave
Milwaukee, WI 53208

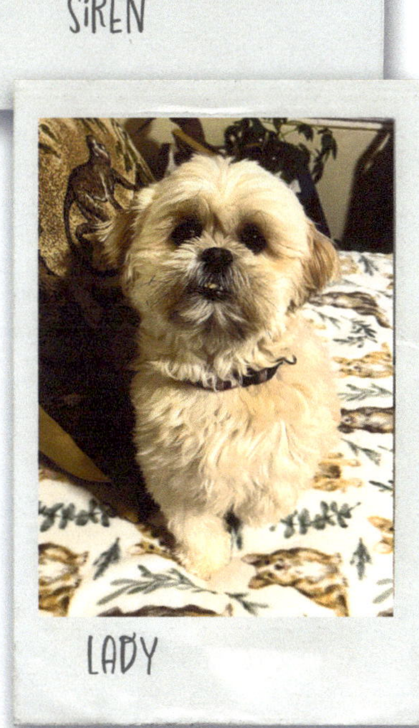

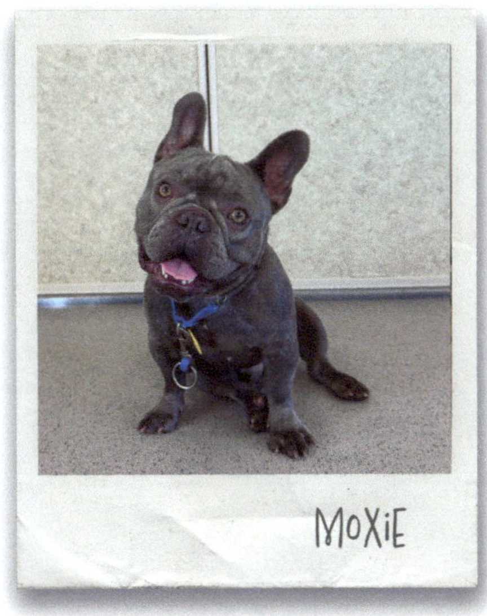

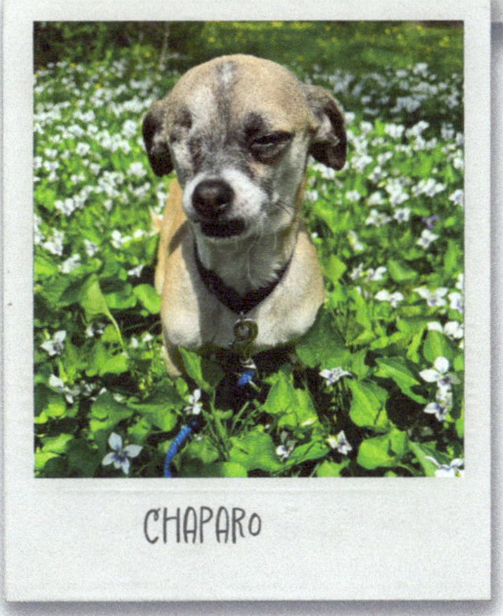

Kevin Ringstaff

Founder, Speaker, Listener

PetCloud®
(www.petcloud.pet)

Grief Education and Training for Management

Kevin's been a student of grief for many years. He spends his days listening to people from all over the world who are grieving and suffering, often alone with no one else who really understands.

He can also be found creating activities to help us move through grief and he's currently studying to be a Board Certified Chaplain.

He started PetCloud as a virtual community to support and validate people who have lost a beloved pet.

He has other fun projects that he can talk about until the cows come home. Such as:

Grieving@Work
(www.grievingatwork.com)

Teaching management and leadership how to better monitor and support their grieving employees in the workplace when they have a loss and return from bereavement leave.

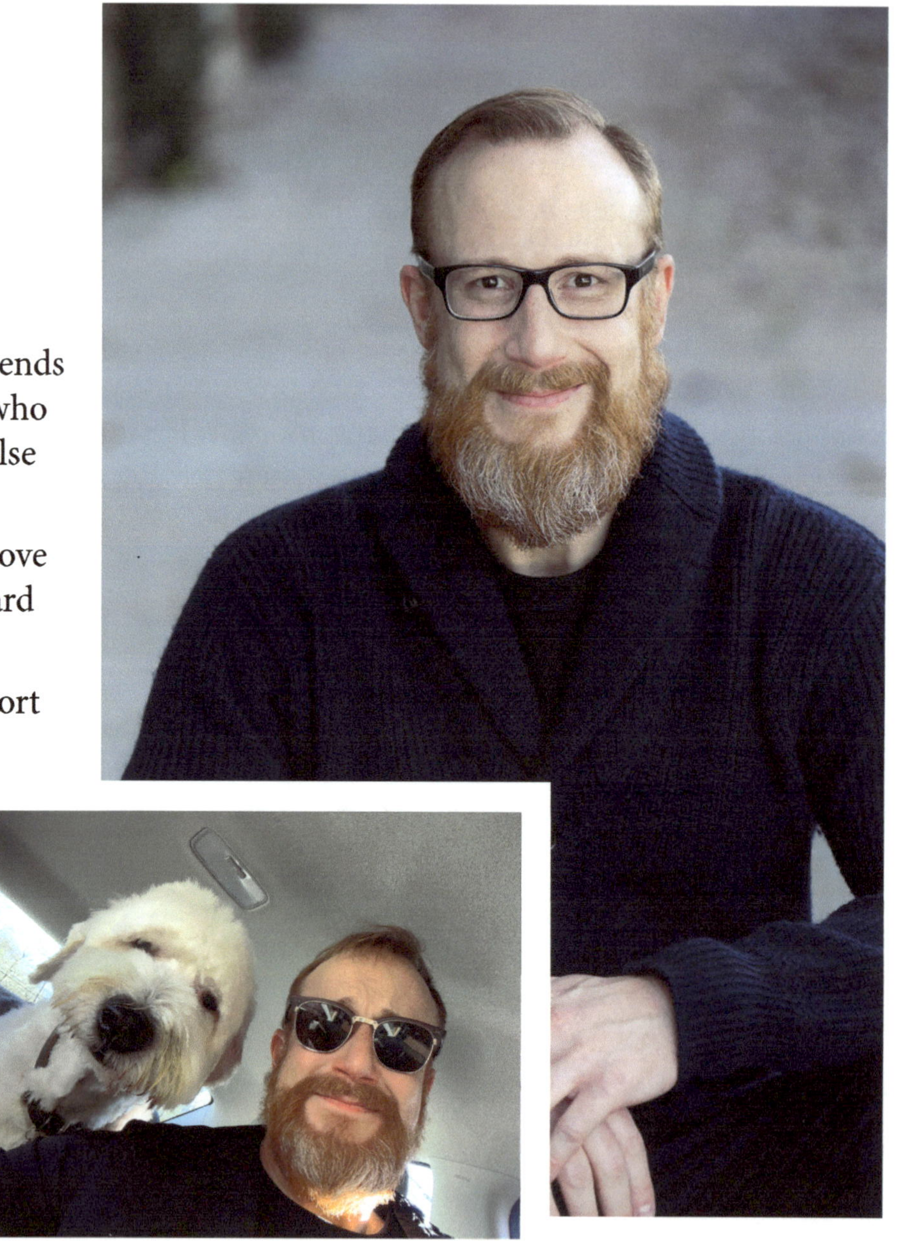

Workshops and support designed specifically, for those in the healthcare, deathcare, and veterinary professions to deal with stress, fatigue, burnout, and compassion fatigue.

His life is currently graced and occupied by three pets: his Old English Sheepdog, Sir William Broderick ("Brody"), his cat Ponce de Leon ("Ponce" and a Tarantula that he accidentally came into possession who goes by "Lucy".

Compassion Fatigue & Burnout
(www.compassionfatigueandburnout.org)

Grieving@Work (www.grievingatwork.com)

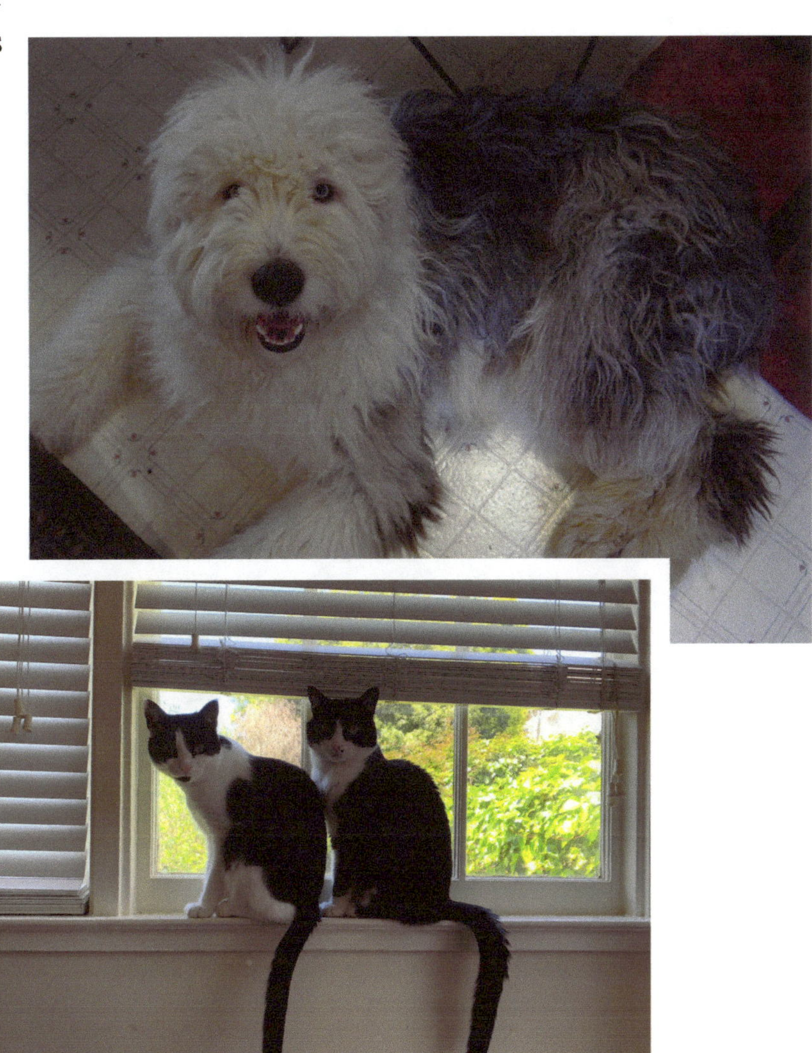

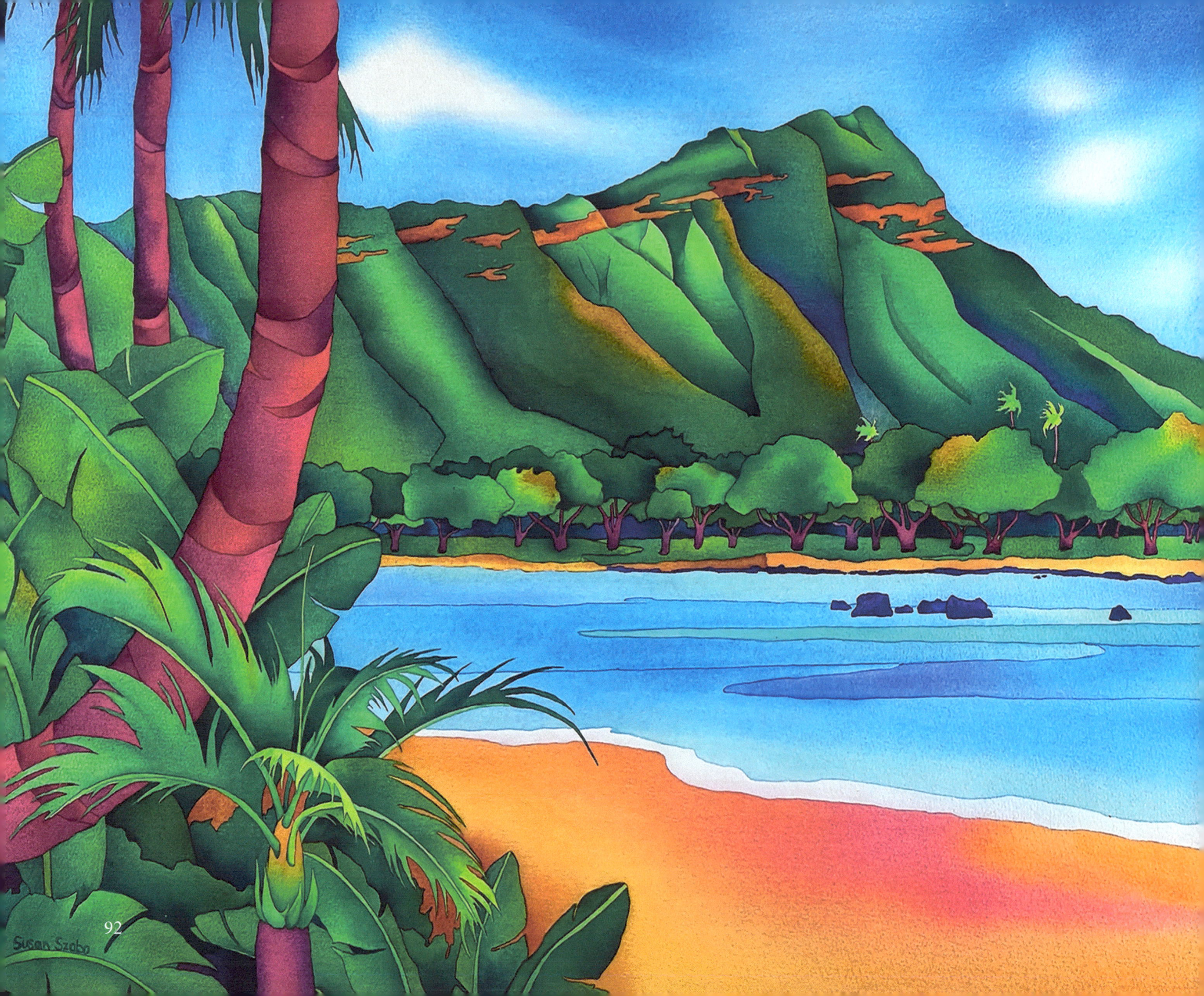

Susan Szabo
92

FAQ For Five-Day-Or-Less Program
Answers to Common Questions

It is important to understand that if all procedures are not followed in the case of Direct Airport Release (DAR) in Honolulu, the dog or cat will be denied Direct Airport Release and will undergo quarantine up to 120 days until requirements are met for release or transported out of state at the owner's expense.

Current Fees

Direct Airport Release in Honolulu $185

Do I have to submit original documents before my pet's arrival, or can I just bring the documents with me to the airport?

If you seek direct release of the pet at the airport, you must submit the required original documents so that the office receives the paperwork at least 10 days prior to your pet's arrival. Only the health certificate may arrive with the pet, due to the time constraints. If you do not submit the original documents ahead of time, it may prevent your pet from being released at the airport, and a higher fee of $244 will be assessed instead of $185.

In addition, if there is a discrepancy in the paperwork, missing documents, or external parasites are found on your pet, your pet will not be released at the airport, and your pet will be transferred to the main Animal Quarantine Station until all requirements have been met.

What do we do once our plane lands?

The airline is responsible for bringing all arriving animals to our Airport Animal Quarantine Holding Facility (AAQHF). Pets allowed to fly in the passenger cabin will be taken by airline personnel upon landing and will be transported to the AAQHF. Pets qualifying for direct release will be processed at the facility, which is located on the Ewa Service Road that runs between the Interisland Terminal and the Main Terminal. Please see the terminal map on page 101

How long does it take to process a pet for direct release at the airport?

Processing times vary, depending on how long it takes your airline to deliver the pet to our facility and the number of pets arriving for inspection at the same time. In some cases, the airline may take up to one hour or more to deliver a pet to our facility for processing. Generally, we can process pets within an hour from the time the pet is received at our facility. However, if you do not submit original documents ahead of time or problems with paperwork will significantly increase processing time. Priority is given to pet owners who properly submitted their paperwork. If you are booking connecting flights, it is recommended that you allow at least 4 to 5 hours.

What if I am not able to obtain documents verifying the first rabies vaccination?

Certification of at least two rabies vaccinations is required. If your pet has documentation for only the most recent vaccination, it will not qualify for the 5 Day Or Less quarantine program. To qualify, your pet will need to receive a booster no less than 30 days after the previous vaccination. In addition, this second vaccination must be given more than 30 days before arrival in Hawai'i. (For pets already located in Hawai'i, the second vaccine must be administered no less than 30 days after the previous vaccination and more than 14 days before departure from Hawai'i.)

Does my cat/dog need to be treated for parasites?

Dogs and cats must be treated by your veterinarian with a long-acting oral or topical product labeled to kill ticks that is equivalent to or better than Fipronil within 14 days before arrival, and the treatment must be documented on the health certificate. K-9 Advantix® is an acceptable treatment for DOGS ONLY; DO NOT USE THIS PRODUCT ON CATS. However, Revolution® IS NOT an acceptable treatment. You should always consult with your veterinarian before the application of flea/tick products to your pet.

How long is the OIE-FAVN blood test valid?

The OIE-FAVN test result is valid for 36 months from the day the blood was received at the laboratory.

Can we pay the fees at the airport?

You may pay the fees at the airport by VISA, Mastercard, travelers' check, or cash. For faster processing at the airport, payment by cashier's check or money order may be sent more than 10 days before the pet's arrival. Payment must be made in the exact amount and submitted with Form AQS-279 Dog and Cat Import Form to ensure proper credit

DETAILED STEP-BY-STEP INSTRUCTIONS ON THE FOLLOWING PAGES!

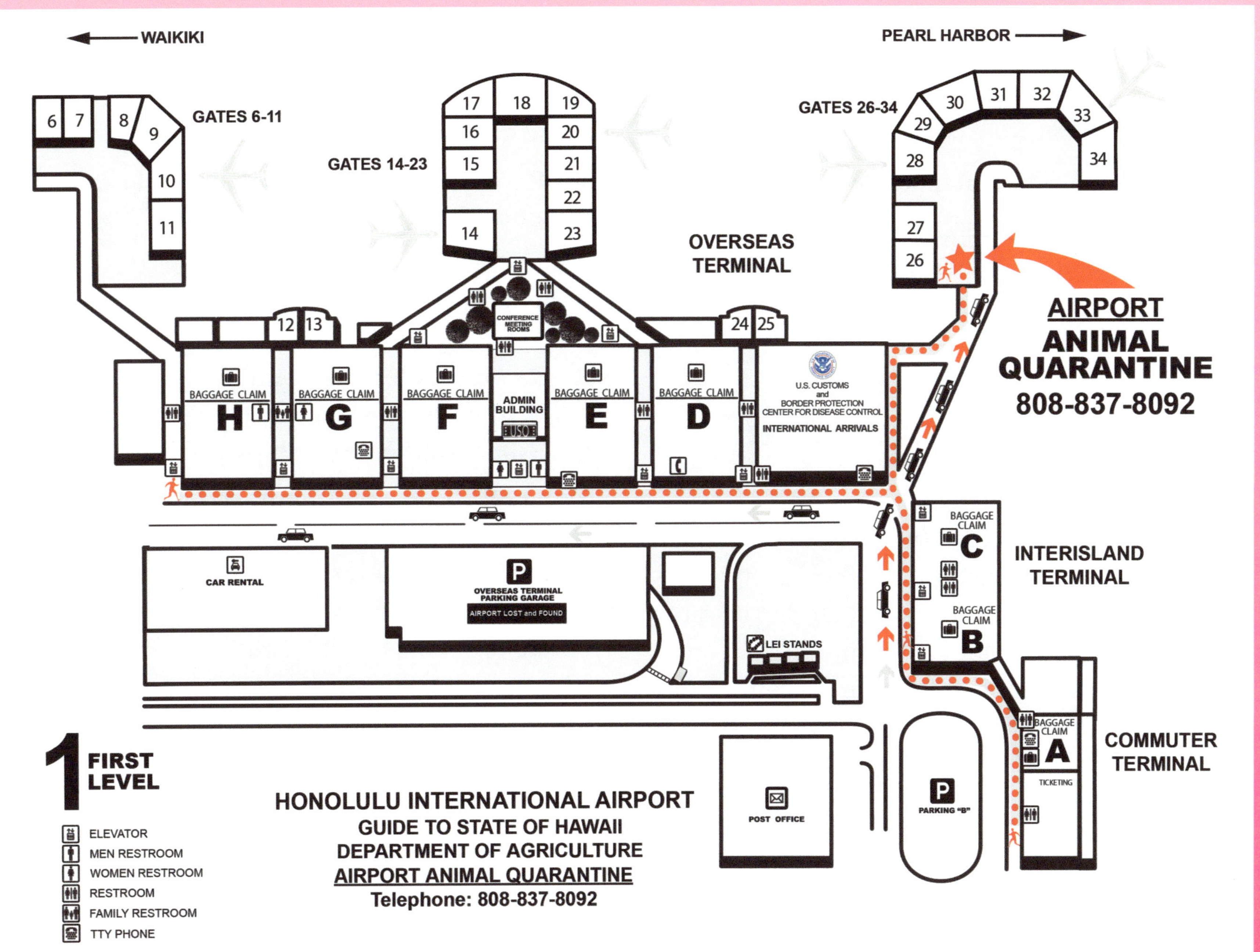

WAIKIKI
PEARL HARBOR
GATES 6-11
6 7 8 9 10 11
12 13
GATES 14-23
17 18 19
16 20
15 21
22
14 23
GATES 26-34
30 31 32 33
29
28 34
27
26
OVERSEAS TERMINAL
CONFERENCE MEETING ROOMS
BAGGAGE CLAIM H
BAGGAGE CLAIM G
BAGGAGE CLAIM F
ADMIN BUILDING
USO
BAGGAGE CLAIM E
BAGGAGE CLAIM D
U.S. CUSTOMS and BORDER PROTECTION CENTER FOR DISEASE CONTROL
INTERNATIONAL ARRIVALS
AIRPORT ANIMAL QUARANTINE
808-837-8092
CAR RENTAL
P
OVERSEAS TERMINAL PARKING GARAGE
AIRPORT LOST and FOUND
LEI STANDS
BAGGAGE CLAIM C
INTERISLAND TERMINAL
BAGGAGE CLAIM B
POST OFFICE
P
PARKING "B"
BAGGAGE CLAIM A
TICKETING
COMMUTER TERMINAL
1 FIRST LEVEL
ELEVATOR
MEN RESTROOM
WOMEN RESTROOM
RESTROOM
FAMILY RESTROOM
TTY PHONE
HONOLULU INTERNATIONAL AIRPORT
GUIDE TO STATE OF HAWAII
DEPARTMENT OF AGRICULTURE
AIRPORT ANIMAL QUARANTINE
Telephone: 808-837-8092

State of Hawai'i Animal Industry Division

https://dab.Hawaii.gov/ai/aqs/aqs-info/

Department of Agriculture and Biosecurity

https://dab.Hawaii.gov/

The checklists provided by the State of Hawai'i Department of Agriculture & Biosecurity are to assist owners in preparing their dog or cat to enter Hawai'i without quarantine. We are only supplying the checklist for animals coming from outside of Hawai'i. Other checklists may be found on the website: https://dab.Hawaii.gov.

OIE-FAVN testing laboratories are experiencing longer than usual processing times. Test results may be delayed between 1 to 2 months.

Plan accordingly to avoid arriving in Hawai'i without a passing test result.

Confirm that the Animal Quarantine Station has your pet's passing test result before arriving in Hawai'i. To see if your pet's OIE-FAVN test result was received by AQS, visit https://dab.Hawaii.gov/ai/aqs/animal-quarantine-microchip-search/.

FAVN reports that are submitted upon arrival, whether original or photocopy, must be verified with the lab first, or the Pet will not qualify for DAR and will enter quarantine until the testing laboratory confirms test results.

Neighbor Island Inspection Permits will not be issued without a confirmed passing FAVN test result.

It is strongly advised that the FAVN test be done well in advance so that a passing FAVN is obtained before requesting a Neighbor Island Inspection Permit.

Failing to do so has resulted in pet owners not obtaining a Neighbor Island Inspection Permit in time for their flight.

***Flight arrival times and COVID-19 mitigation procedures have increased the time for pet releases. Additional and extended delays are also created when pet owners do not submit their paperwork 10 days or more before arrival and have their documents reviewed at the AAQHF. It may not be possible to process these cases on arrival.**

The higher fee of $244 for each dog or cat released at the airport shall apply (instead of $185) when documents are not received by the Animal Quarantine Station 10 days or more before arrival. This includes situations where documents are submitted on arrival for review and qualification purposes.

All steps need to be completed to qualify for this program. If you are unable to meet the following requirements, your pet will undergo quarantine for up to 120 days.

STEP 1: PLANNING

Every dog or cat must meet the requirements listed on this Checklist, and all required documents must be received by the Animal Quarantine Station (AQS) 10 days or more before the intended date of arrival for Direct Airport Release (DAR) in Honolulu.

Refer to sections "Step 5 Waiting Period" and "Step 8 Other" for information on DAR.

STEP 2: MICROCHIP NOTE

Make sure the microchip is working!

Your dog or cat must have an electronic microchip implanted before the FAVN rabies antibody blood test is performed.

Have your veterinarian scan the microchip to verify that it is still working and see that the microchip number is correct.

Microchip number: _______________________

Any pet that cannot be identified by scanning the microchip will not qualify for either Direct Airport Release or the 5 Day Or Less quarantine and will be assigned to a 120-day quarantine.

STEP 3: RABIES VACCINATIONS

Your dog or cat must have been vaccinated at least twice for rabies in its lifetime.

The rabies vaccines must have been administered more than 30 days apart.

The current (most recent) rabies vaccine must have been administered:

1. More than 30 days before the pet's date of arrival in Hawai'i; and

2. Not more than the vaccine's licensed booster interval listed on the manufacturer's label.

NOTE! Two rabies vaccinations are required. The pet's most recent rabies vaccination must not have expired when your pet arrives in Hawai'i. If arrival in Hawai'i occurs before 30 days have elapsed from the most recent rabies vaccination, the animal is subject to quarantine until the 30 days are completed.

Your veterinarian will give you rabies vaccination certificates for every rabies vaccination. The date and type of vaccine must be indicated on these vaccination certificates.

STEP 4 FAVN RABIES ANTIBODY TEST

Do Not do a **RFFIT** Test

Be sure "Hawai'i" is listed as the destination on the lab submission form!

Do the FAVN Rabies Antibody Test.

Have the test done at an approved lab (Auburn University (AU), Kansas State University (KSU), University of Missouri (MU), or the DOD

Food Analysis and Diagnostic Laboratory in Texas(DOD),

The day after AU, KSU, MU, or DOD receives your pet's blood sample must not be more than 36 months and not less than 30 days before the date of arrival in Hawai'i.

NOTE! Be aware that the use of an intermediate lab (Antech, Idexx, etc.) may delay the date the approved labs, AU, KSU, MU, and DOD receive your pet's sample.

Obtain a copy of this successful blood test result from your veterinarian showing the pet's microchip number for your records.

Do not contact the laboratory directly.

STEP 5 WAITING PERIOD

NOTE! **Arriving Early = Disqualification**

Pets must have a passing FAVN rabies antibody test result and complete a 30-day waiting period from the day the laboratory received the blood sample for testing. If arrival occurs before 30 Days have elapsed; the animal is subject to quarantine until the waiting period has been completed.

Your pet must complete the 30-day waiting period before arriving in Hawai'i, or your pet will not qualify for either direct airport release or the 5 Day Or Less quarantine program when it arrives.

IMPORTANT! The waiting period begins the day after AU, KSU, or DOD received the blood sample for the OIE-FAVN test. The test must also have a result > 0.5 IU/ml.

WARNING! Arriving before the 30-day waiting period has elapsed will result in the disqualification of a pet from the 5 Day Or Less quarantine program and direct airport release.

All pets arriving before the eligible date of entry will be quarantined and assessed $14.30 each day in addition to the $244.00 program fee. There are no exceptions.

1. Completed Dog & Cat Import Form AQS-279. (Does NOT have to be notarized.)

   IMPORTANT! Authorized Handlers and Transport Companies cannot be listed as owners of an animal. Not identifying and listing the legal owner of the animal on the Dog and Cat Import Form (AQS-279) is considered fraud and will create delays in processing and disqualification.

2. Original certificates for 2 rabies vaccinations (must be signed in ink by a licensed veterinarian). The 2 rabies vaccination certificates must have the vaccine name, lot or serial number, boost interval, vaccination date, and vaccine lot expiration date listed.

3. An original health certificate in English, done within 14 days of arrival in Hawai'i, including rabies vaccine name, lot or serial number, booster interval, vaccination date, and expiration date, is required. If you do not send the original health certificate to the Animal Quarantine Station in advance of your pet's arrival with your other documents, you must provide the health certificate upon arrival to the Inspector. Failure to bring the original health certificate (photocopy not acceptable) will prevent your pet from being released. We suggest you have your veterinarian issue two original certificates.

4. A veterinarian must treat the pet for ticks with a product containing a long-acting product labeled to kill ticks (Revolution® is not acceptable) within 14 days of arrival, and the product name and date of treatment must be recorded on the pet's health certificate.

5. If you are applying for re-entry under the same FAVN blood test and rabies vaccinations used for a previous entry, you must send a copy of the Airport Release Card given to you when your pet was released at the airport on that previous arrival in Hawai'i.

1. Send documents in as a set so they are received more than 10 days before arrival in Honolulu, to:

    Animal Quarantine Station
    99-951 Halawa Valley Street
    Aiea, Hawai'i, 96701

    Send by mail with a return receipt to verify delivery, or by an overnight carrier that provides tracking of your documents.

2. Be sure to allow adequate time to ensure your documents are received by AQS more than 10 days before your pet arrives at Daniel K. Inouye International Airport (HNL) in Honolulu for DAR.

    (This includes re-entry DAR.)

3. Failure to send documents as instructed will in additional fees and can disqualify a pet from airport release. Other than the original health certificate, hand-carrying documents for review and qualification on arrival will cause a delay and result in a higher fee of $244 for DAR, and $130 for Re-Entry. Priority is given to dog and cat owners who properly submitted documents beforehand as instructed.

4. Send documents (Dog & Cat Import Form AQS-279, two rabies vaccination certificates, payment*), include a cashier's check or money order (no personal checks are accepted) for $185 for Direct Airport Release in HNL or $244 for 5 Day Or Less. Include your pet's microchip number with the payment to ensure proper credit. Payable to: Department of Agriculture.

    NOTE! <u>Faxes and photocopies are not accepted</u>!

5. If you are applying for re-entry under the same OIE-FAVN blood test and rabies vaccinations used on a previous entry, send a copy of the Airport Release card given to you when your pet was released at the airport from the previous arrival.

6. Payment must be made in full before your pet will be released. Overpayment of fees will receive refunds through the mail in approximately 8 weeks or more after a request for a refund is made.

7. Retain copies of necessary qualification documents for your files and to accompany your pet as a backup.

8. A Neighbor Island Inspection Permit (NIIP) is required to fly direct to Kona International Airport at Keahole (KOA), Kahului Airport (OGG), or Lihue Airport (LIH). Refer to the "Checklist for Requesting Direct Airport Release at Kona, Kahului, and Lihue Airports." No permit is required to fly into Honolulu at the Daniel K. Inouye International Airport (HNL), island of O'ahu.

STEP 8 OTHER

1. It is recommended that you check your pet's blood test results at the Hawai'i Department of Agriculture website: hdoa.Hawaii.gov/ai/aqs-info

2. Direct Airport Release

   Arrange for your pet to arrive at the Airport Animal Quarantine Holding Facility (AAQHF) at HNL - Daniel K. Inouye International Airport in Honolulu during normal inspection hours between 8:00 AM to 4:30 PM. It may take up to one hour for the airlines to transport a pet to AAQHF [Phone: (808) 8378092]. Animals not delivered to the facility during normal inspection hours will not be released when they arrive.

   WARNING! Inspection hours are subject to change at any time without notice.

3. Unless prior arrangements are made with the AAQHF, pets qualified for Direct Airport Release that arrive between 5:00 PM

and 8:00 AM must be picked up between 8 to 10 AM during the subsequent inspection period at the AAQHF.

If not picked up during that time, the pet will be transferred to the AQS and entered into the 5 Day Or Less program at $244. In this situation, after all necessary documents are received and verified, pets may be picked up at the Animal Quarantine Station, 99-951 Halawa Valley Street, Aiea, Hawai'i 96701, phone: (808) 483-7151, during normal office hours.

Monday through Friday: 9:00 AM to 11:00 AM &

1:00 PM to 4:30 PM
Saturday, Sunday, State Holidays:
8:00 AM to 10:00 AM & 12:00 PM to 3:30 PM Animals will not qualify for the $98 reduced re-entry fee when documents are not received by the Animal Quarantine Station 10 days or more before the re-entry. In this case, the higher fee of $130 for each dog and cat released at the airport shall apply.

4. You must contact the AAQHF and notify them at (808) 837-8092 if you cannot pick up your pet the day it is delivered to the Airport Animal Quarantine Holding Facility (AAQHF) in HNL during normal inspection hours between 8:00 AM to 5:00 PM.

    The pet may be available for pick up from between 8:00 to 10:00 AM at the AAQHF the next day, or it may be transferred to the Animal Quarantine Station (AQS) the following morning. After 10 AM or when pets are transferred to AQS, they are entered into the 5 Day Or Less program. Fee for the 5 Day Or Less program is $244 per pet.

5. Animals on international flights will need to clear U.S. Customs before they may be released from the Airport Animal Quarantine Holding Facility. Please check with your airlines regarding U.S. Customs clearance to ensure they will be open to process your pet for release.

6. Your pet will not qualify for direct airport release if ticks or other parasites are found at the time of arrival.

    NOTE! Pet owners should bring a baggage cart or other means to transport their crated pet from the Airport Animal Quarantine Holding Facility to the Inter-Island Terminal if traveling on to an outer island after release of their pet. There are no carts or porters at the Airport Animal Quarantine Holding Facility.

7. The pet owner is responsible for arranging all transportation for the pet once it is released from the Airport Animal Quarantine Holding Facility in Honolulu. An animal may only be released to:

    ☑ **The Owner listed on a Dog and Cat Import Form (AQS-279)**

    ☑ **The Consignee identified on the shipmaster's declaration, or,**

    ☑ **The Co-owner(s) or Authorized Handler listed on a Dog and Cat Import Form (AQS-279).**

If you are not traveling with your pet, you must arrange with the airlines to consign your pet to the individual who will pick up your pet.

8. Due to Federal security regulations at the Honolulu International Airport, all pets must be secured in their flight carriers when picked up from the Airport Animal Quarantine Holding Facility. Do not remove your pet from its transport carrier on airport property!

9. You must notify the Animal Quarantine Station before arrival, follow the same procedures, and meet all the requirements each time your pet enters or returns to Hawai'i.

10. You will pay a fee of $185 per pet for direct airport release or $244 per pet for the 5 Day Or Less program each time your pet enters

or returns to Hawai'i unless it qualifies for subsequent entry fees outlined in "Re-Entry Fee Requirements".

11. Any dog or cat not picked up on its scheduled date for release is considered "Overdue," and an additional $17.80 fee is added for each day a pet remains beyond its scheduled release date.

12. Due to the high volume of telephone calls, it's recommended you contact staff with questions by email to <u>rabiesfree@Hawaii.gov</u>.

Hawai'i Department of Agriculture contacts Animal Quarantine Station telephone: (808) 483-7151
Fax (808) 483-7161
email: rabiesfree@Hawai'i.gov

Jennifer raised her two sons James and William Wierzba with her husband in the beautiful, quaint town of Greendale, Wisconsin.

She currently lives in Montrose, California with her husband and two poodles.

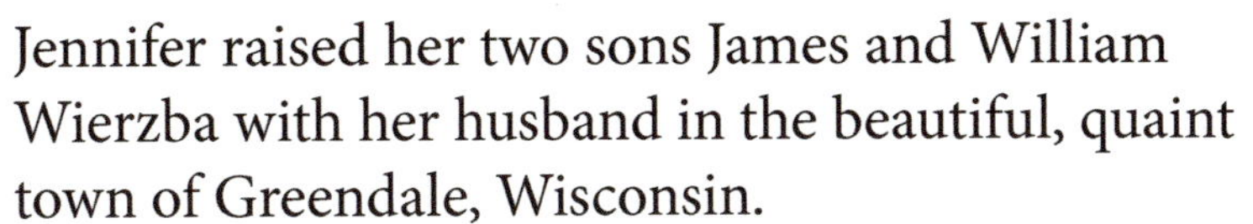

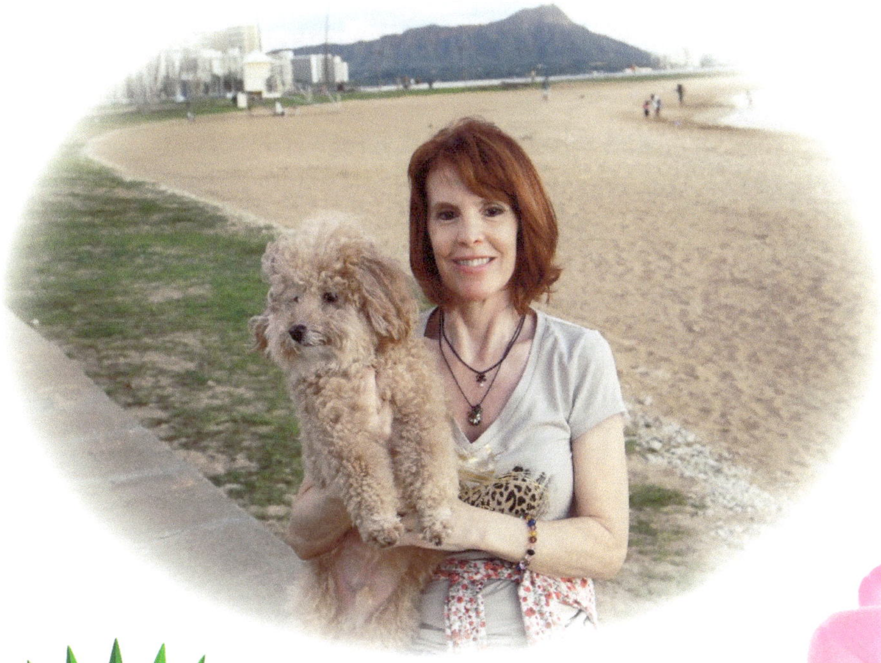

Website: jjpoodlespress.com

https://www.facebook.com/jjpoodlespress

IG: https://www.instagram.com/jj.poodles

"X": jjjpoodles

LinkedIn: https://www.linkedin.com/
in/j-j-jordan-400b7621/

Substack: J.J.Jordan @jjpoodlespress

Blog: https://www.jjpoodlespress.com/blog-1

YouTube: https://www.youtube.com/@
JJPoodlesPress

https://www.youtube.com/@JJPoodlesPress/
videos

Mailing address:

JJ Poodles Press
466 Foothill Boulevard, Suite 112
La Cañada California
91011-3518

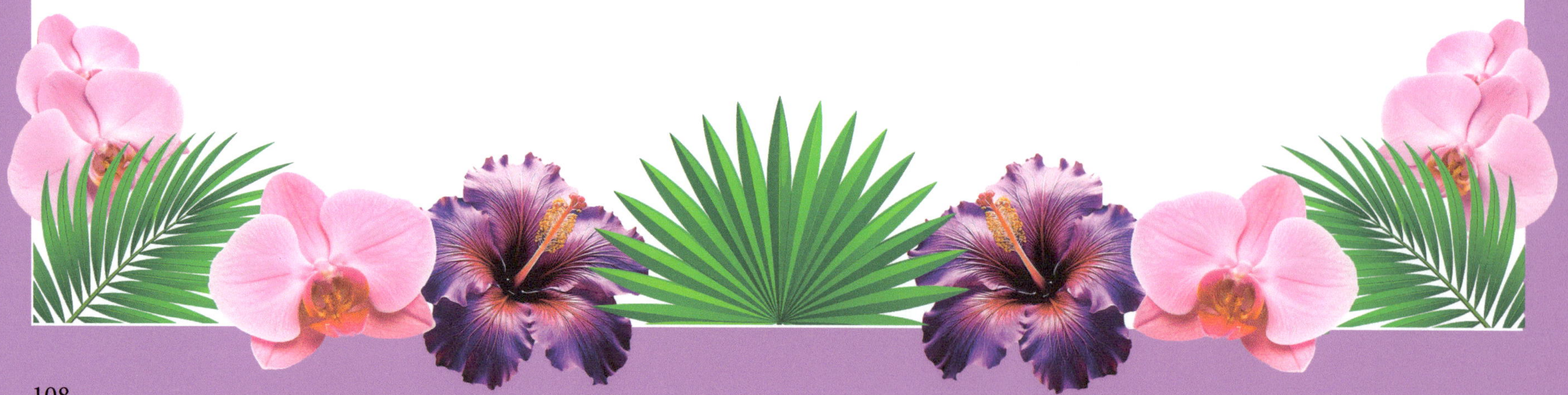

Acknowledgements

I want to thank all the talented artists and photographers, whose incredible gifts have brought this project to life—your creativity has made all the difference.

A special thank you to my inspiring professor at ArtCenter College of Design, Jeannie Winston. Your belief in my dream and your magical guidance were instrumental in making this book a reality.

A special thanks to Ginger Marks for her technical expertise and patience.

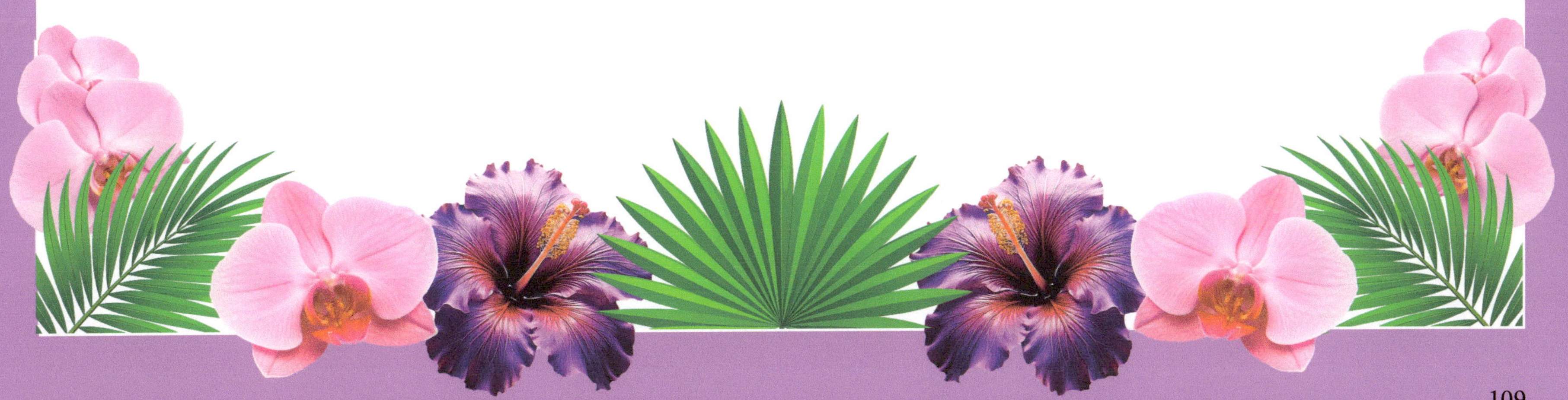

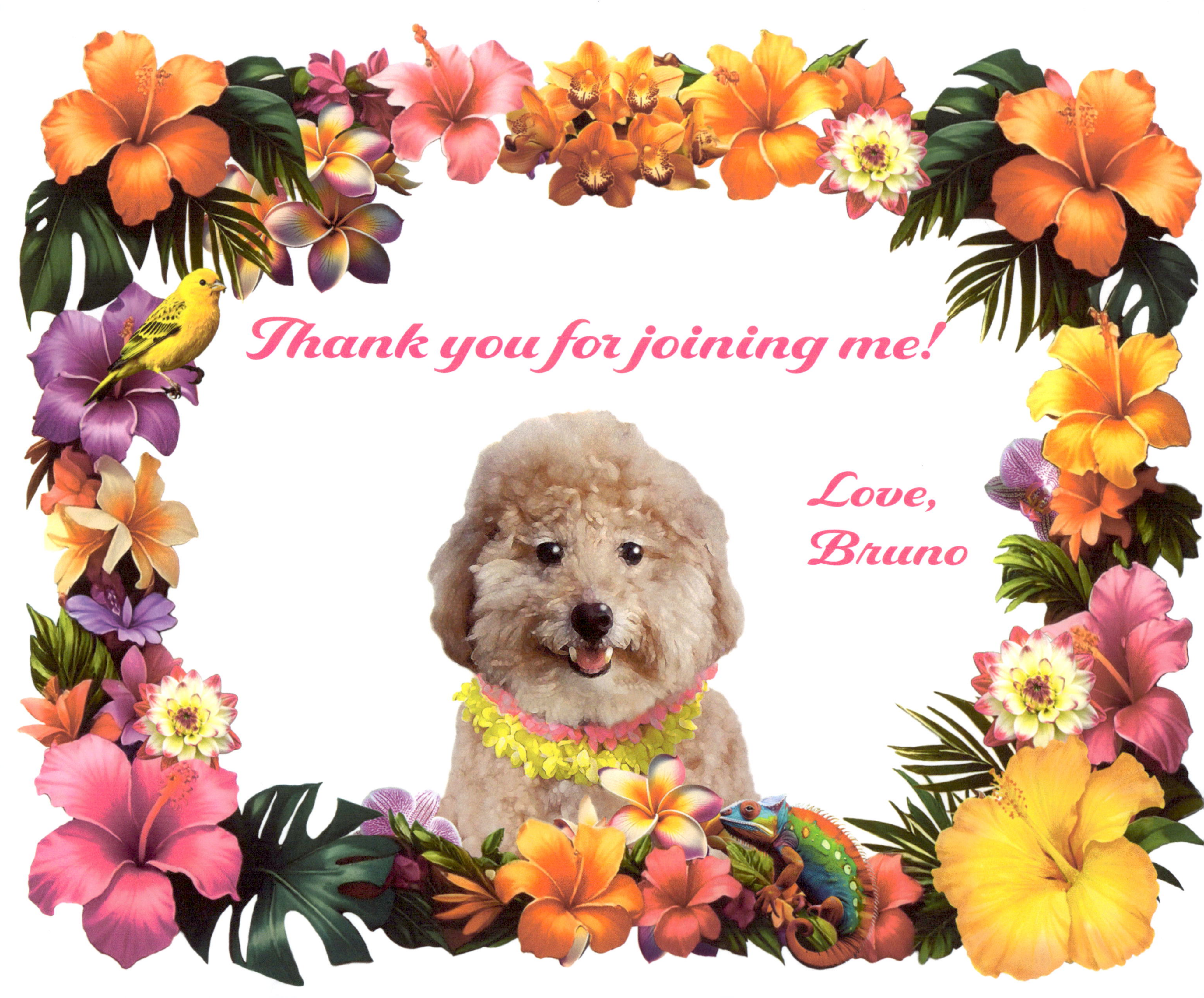Thank you for joining me!
Love,
Bruno

9 798986 531373